The Routledge Dictionary of Business Management

A fully comprehensive resource for those wanting to know about the world of business management. Students and working professionals alike can enjoy quick and accessible definitions and the extensive cross-referencing system allows readers broader access to subject areas. This dictionary covers all the topics, issues and terms in the field, including:

- Business economics
- Consumer behaviour
- Corporate strategy
- Financial management
- Human resource management
- Information technology
- Management accounting
- Marketing
- Organizational behaviour and work psychology

Dr David A. Statt was formerly Academic Director of Edinburgh Business School. He has worked as a manager, a consultant, a trainer and an academic in Britain, Canada and the United States.

The Routledge Dictionary of Business Management

Business Management

David A. Statt

Routledge
Taylor & Francis Group

LONDON AND NEW YORK

First published 1991
as *The Concise Dictionary of Management*
by Routledge

Second edition first published 1999
by Routledge

Third edition first published 2004
as *The Routledge Dictionary of Business Management*
by Routledge
11 New Fetter Lane, London EC4P 4EE

Simultaneously published in the USA and Canada
by Routledge
29 West 35th Street, New York, NY 10001

Routledge is an imprint of the Taylor & Francis Group

© 1991, 1999, 2004 David A. Statt

Typeset in Times by
Newgen Imaging Systems (P) Ltd, Chennai, India
Printed and bound in Great Britain by MPG Books, Bodmin

British Library Cataloguing in Publication Data
A catalogue record for this book is available from the British Library

Library of Congress Cataloging in Publication Data
    The Routledge dictionary of business management / David A. Statt. –
3rd ed., rev. and enl.
      p. cm. – (The Routledge dictionaries)
    Rev. ed. of: Concise dictionary of business management. 2nd ed. 1999.
1. Management – Dictionaries. 2. Business – Dictionaries. I. Statt,
David A., 1942– II. Statt, David A., 1942– Concise dictionary of
business management. III. Series.

  HD30.15.S73 2004
  658′.003–dc22   2003023572

ISBN 0–415–32819–5

For Judith

Acknowledgements

My thanks go to Rosie Waters, my editor at Routledge, for her patient and thoughtful co-operation during the commissioning and preparation of this new edition. Although I managed to do all the word processing myself this time, unlike the previous editions, I was still in great need of the unflagging support and TLC provided by my wife Judith, to whom the book is dedicated.

I would like to thank the following publishers for their kind permission to reproduce material from their publications:

Palgrave Macmillan Press Ltd. for figures taken from two of my own books, *Psychology and the World of Work* (Figure 39) and *Understanding the Consumer* (Figures 1, 10, 11, 13, 18, 31 and 32).

Figure 22 is taken from *Theories of Group Process*, C. Cooper (ed.), 1975, and reproduced by permission of John Wiley & Sons Limited.

Edinburgh
October 2003

Introduction

There are two major changes in this work from the previous edition, and both are immediately apparent to the reader. The title has changed from *Concise Dictionary of Business Management* to *Routledge Dictionary of Business Management*, and this change in turn reflects both a different approach and a considerable addition to the content of the book. This new material has taken several forms.

1 Updating

All the terms in the previous edition were considered first from a viewpoint of their relevance to the broader business orientation of this edition as well as currency of usage. Some sixty-six terms that seemed now to be outmoded, beyond the book's business management focus, or too much a part of common parlance now to require definition, have been dropped.

The remaining terms were then considered in the light of the developments in their field since the late 1990s, and modified wherever necessary to take account of these developments.

Wherever it seemed desirable terms in the dictionary were then expanded to provide more information and background while remaining within the book's spirit of being written as concisely and accessibly as possible.

2 Additional terms

About a couple of hundred new entries have been added to the previous edition in keeping with the broader business orientation of the present edition. In particular, many terms have been included from such areas (in alphabetical order of course) as business economics, consumer behaviour, corporate strategy, financial management, human resource management, information technology, management accounting, marketing, organizational behaviour and work psychology.

One other important feature of the book that has been retained from the previous edition is the *cross-referencing* to other relevant entries. These entries are printed in SMALL CAPITALS and this allows the reader quickly to identify and to follow up other terms which appear within the particular entry being consulted. With the addition of so many new terms this feature of the book has obviously been expanded considerably, and a reader interested in doing so can now follow a thread that will lead through whole areas of content such as those outlined in the preceding paragraph.

Perhaps an example might help to illustrate how this process could help the reader engaged in searching or browsing for information. Let's take the term INFORMATION, TECHNOLOGY, for instance. The entry for this term leads us through two large content areas. We will first of all find cross-references to COMPUTER, COMMUNICATION, ARTIFICIAL, INTELLIGENCE and SYSTEMS, THEORY, which in turn will give us access, if we wish to have it, to the general effects of the way electronic equipment is used in business and management.

At the same time our original entry on INFORMATION TECHNOLOGY will suggest that we consult MAN–MACHINE INTERFACE and ERGONOMICS, which in turn will lead us to such key terms as PSYCHOLOGY, and ORGANIZATION, from where we can branch out into virtually any aspect of human resource management.

Terms that use 'man', like ECONOMIC MAN or MAN–MACHINE INTERFACE, refer invariably to both men and women. However, as a dictionary has to reflect actual practice this usage has been retained.

As this revised edition so clearly shows, writing a dictionary like this is, perhaps even more than in most academic endeavours, a bit like painting the Forth Bridge. And because it *is* a continuous activity both the author and the publisher of this book would be delighted to receive suggestions from readers (whether on style, content or format) that we might be able to incorporate in the next edition.

A

ABB   See ACTIVITY-BASED BUDGETING.

ABC   See ACTIVITY-BASED COSTING.

ability   Being able to perform a particular TASK. Implicit in the use of the term
is that no further TRAINING is required in
order to do so, thus distinguishing it from
an APTITUDE. See also COMPETENCIES for
an alternative usage.

above the line advertising   This is a
form of SALES PROMOTION where an
agency is commissioned to place advertising for a client in the MASS MEDIA. It is
usually contrasted with BELOW THE LINE
ADVERTISING which has overtaken it in
popularity in recent years. The 'line' in
question was originally on a company's
balance sheet but in MARKETING this usage
has now been lost.

absenteeism   The absence from WORK
of an employee during normal working
hours, whether voluntary or involuntary.
Voluntary absence is usually considered
to be avoidable and without reasonable
cause; in effect the employee *chooses* to
be absent. Involuntary absence is usually
held to be unavoidable and outside the
employee's control, for reasons such as
unusually difficult weather conditions,
breakdown of transport, or sickness.
A high absenteeism rate is a sign of organizational ill-health in a WORK ORGANIZA-
TION. It is also likely that much of the
absenteeism through sickness is job
related, either physically in the form of
INDUSTRIAL DISEASES or emotionally in
the form of PSYCHOSOMATIC DISORDERS.
See also PRESENTEEISM.

ABT   See ACTIVITY-BASED TECHNIQUE.

access time   The amount of time taken
to retrieve information from the storage
facility of a COMPUTER and make it available for use. See also INFORMATION
RETRIEVAL.

accident prevention   The policy or
procedures followed in a workplace to
prevent accidents to employees, or at least
to reduce the occurrence of accidents. It
includes physical aspects like the proper
housing of machinery or the provision of
protective clothing, and managerial
aspects such as effective supervision and
TRAINING.

accidents   Mishaps that take place at
work and may be caused by carelessness,
by inadequate safety precautions, or by
chance. By law, in the United Kingdom,
accidents causing death or major injury
must be reported by the employers or the
appropriate authority. Employees are generally entitled to record details of any
injuries resulting from accidents in an
accident book kept at the workplace, and
this may be used as evidence for insurance purposes. Some people are thought
to be more *accident prone* than others for
psychological reasons. While people's
DEPRESSION or unhappiness may decrease
their awareness of their surroundings and
affect their reactions to a potentially dan-
gerous situation (in anyone at any time),
these factors play only a minor role in the
incidence of industrial injury.

accountability   [1] Being answerable
to others for some actions, for example, to
a SUPERVISOR for completing a task or to
a board of directors for company PER-
FORMANCE. [2] Having responsibility and

AUTHORITY for seeing that something is carried out as expected, for example, that sales targets are met or that a BUDGET has been properly spent.

accounting   The establishment, maintenance, collection and analysis of financial records. It is used to provide data on the financial position of an ORGANIZATION and any changes that have occurred or that may occur, over time. This is one fundamental aspect of the profession (or art) of accountancy. See also MANAGEMENT ACCOUNTING.

accounting period   The length of time between the financial reports produced by an ORGANIZATION. If the reports are for internal use the period is usually either a week or a month; for external information it is usually a year.

account management   The MANAGEMENT of individual client accounts in an ADVERTISING, MARKETING or PUBLIC RELATIONS agency.

acculturation   The process of learning to adapt to a new CULTURE. Of crucial importance to expatriate managers.

achievement culture   An ORGANIZATIONAL CULTURE that fosters ACHIEVEMENT and, under certain conditions, perhaps also the NEED FOR ACHIEVEMENT in its members.

ACORN   Acronym for 'A Classification of Residential Neighbourhoods'. Used in MARKETING research on GEODEMOGRAPHIC SEGMENTATION to rank neighbourhoods by SOCIO-ECONOMIC STATUS. Its most recent version lists thirty-eight types of neighbourhood by variables like household composition or age structure and uses descriptions such as 'older suburban singles'. The term is the British equivalent of the American PRIZM.

acquisitive society   A society in which people are constantly encouraged to possess things, for example our own. It has been argued by many economists and others that if we did not have this encouragement our economy would collapse.

action-centred leadership   A technique of MANAGEMENT DEVELOPMENT, first suggested in the United Kingdom in the early 1980s by John Adair, which seeks to provide TRAINING in LEADERSHIP through practical problem solving. This is an approach to leadership which emphasizes *doing* rather than being and concentrates on the particular behaviour expected of a leader. It does this by studying situations that may vary depending on the needs of the individual, the GROUP and the TASK at hand.

action learning   A technique of MANAGEMENT DEVELOPMENT produced in the United Kingdom by R.G. Revans as an antidote to formal business school methods of TRAINING. As its name implies, this technique focuses on dealing with real and immediate problems, usually within the individual's own ORGANIZATION and as part of a GROUP of MANAGERS who contribute different experiences and SKILLS. The individual is thus given the opportunity to learn about GROUP PROCESS and to gain insight into her or his own behaviour while acquiring practical knowledge and skills.

action research   First proposed by KURT LEWIN in the 1930s in his work on GROUP DYNAMICS. The objective of this kind of research is to harness an understanding of the GROUP behaviour being studied to the attempted solution of practical problems within an organizational or social setting. It therefore has both an applied and a theoretical aspect to it, and often includes monitoring and EVALUATION RESEARCH on effectiveness as well.

activities analysis One of three techniques suggested by PETER DRUCKER to help a WORK ORGANIZATION decide on its most appropriate ORGANIZATIONAL STRUCTURE. This technique is to establish what the key activities in the ORGANIZATION *actually* are as opposed to unquestioned assumptions about what they are. The other two techniques are DECISION ANALYSIS and RELATIONS ANALYSIS.

activity-based budgeting An ACCOUNTING technique which identifies the costs involved in running each aspect of a business ORGANIZATION.

activity-based costing A method for costing products, used in ACCOUNTING since the late 1980s, which links the overall cost of a product to the *total* cost of the various activities within a business ORGANIZATION that contribute to its production.

activity-based management The implementation of ACTIVITY-BASED COSTING by the MANAGEMENT of a business ORGANIZATION.

activity-based technique Any method used by the MANAGEMENT of a business ORGANIZATION to cost its activities. The most common technique is ACTIVITY-BASED COSTING.

acuity This term is used in COGNITIVE ERGONOMICS and in ERGONOMICS generally to describe someone's ability to discriminate fine detail in using one of the senses. Most often used of vision, though also used of hearing and other senses.

adaptation Originally a biological term used to describe physical or behavioural changes that increased an organism's chances of survival. Now used in PSYCHOLOGY in two ways: [1] to describe responses to change in the physical environment, for example where the eye adjusts to changes in the light, or [2] where the changed expectations of a society demand some kind of social adaptation in the behaviour of its members. For example, the greatly increased number of women at work has led in many cases to more *covert* rather than overt DISCRIMINATION against them by men.

adaptive control A form of self-regulation of an industrial process, usually by COMPUTER, where the objective is to maintain a continuous PERFORMANCE at optimum level through a changing ENVIRONMENT. See also CYBERNETICS.

added value The increase in value of goods or services that results from their PRODUCTION or DISTRIBUTION. It usually involves the transformation of materials by the actions of the workforce. It is often quantified as the difference between revenue from sales and the costs of materials and labour. The term is also used in the PUBLIC SECTOR to indicate intellectual or social gains from a particular INVESTMENT compared to other uses of the same funds; for example, the gains in understanding a social issue from the work of a single research centre as opposed to the work of isolated individuals scattered throughout the country.

adhocracy A NEOLOGISM introduced by Alvin Toffler (who also invented FUTURE SHOCK). It refers to the tendency in an ORGANIZATION to progress on the basis of temporary, *ad hoc* groups, such as a TASK FORCE brought together to deal with a particular project only.

administrative management theory An approach to the study of MANAGEMENT, based on the work of HENRI FAYOL and others in the 1930s, which emphasizes the importance of the formal structure and the HIERARCHY of an ORGANIZATION.

administrative science   The system-atic study of administration in all its aspects. It includes both the public and the private sector and attempts to formulate general principles that are applicable to all forms of ORGANIZATION.

adoption of new products   The process by which individuals adopt particular innovations in goods and services over time. Five stages in this process have been identified: *awareness, interest, evaluation, trial* and *adoption*. The individual's experience of the process may vary for reasons of both DEMOGRAPHIC and PSYCHOLOGICAL SEGMENTATION and is micro-social in nature, as compared to the macro-social process involved in the DIFFUSION OF NEW PRODUCTS. (See Figure 1.)

ADP   See AUTOMATIC DATA PROCESSING.

adrenalin   A hormone secreted by the adrenal glands (which are situated on top of the kidneys) in times of excitement or STRESS. It increases the heart rate, the blood supply, and the sugar supply from the liver into the blood stream, and alerts the muscles to impulses from the nervous system, thereby preparing the body for action. If the body is in a WORK situation and unable to take any physical action the resulting frustration can contribute to a variety of PSYCHOSOMATIC DISORDERS.

advertising   The publishing, PROMOTION and COMMUNICATION of information or opinions about a product or service, or even an ORGANIZATION, to a potential MARKET. The means used may be ABOVE THE LINE or BELOW THE LINE. Advertising is an integral part of any MARKETING MIX in the selling of CONSUMER GOODS. It is global in scope and has been so for most of its history since the advent of MASS PRODUCTION and consumption in the late nineteenth century.

affirmative action   An American term used to describe the provision of opportunities for disadvantaged groups by paying particular attention to the RECRUITMENT, TRAINING and PROMOTION of people who have been subject to DISCRIMINATION in EMPLOYMENT practices.

ageism   DISCRIMINATION against older people; for example, by ORGANIZATIONS

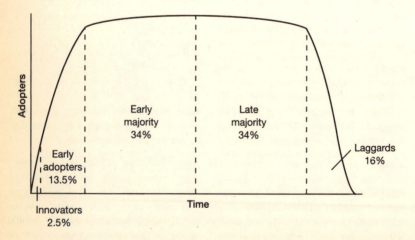

Figure 1 Adoption of new products.

reluctant to hire secretaries over forty, or models over twenty. Like RACISM and SEXISM this is based on an attribute arbitrarily determined by birth – in this case age.

AI   See ARTIFICIAL INTELLIGENCE.

ALGOL (Algorithmic Language)   A SYSTEM of words and symbols used in science and TECHNOLOGY to instruct a COMPUTER in its TASK of INFORMATION processing. See COMPUTER LANGUAGE and ALGORITHM.

algorithm   A set of rules to be used in solving a problem. It usually takes the form of a fixed procedure with a logical sequence of steps. Extensively used in COMPUTER PROGRAMS and SYSTEMS ANALYSIS. See also HEURISTIC.

alienation   A term with various shades of meaning in PSYCHOLOGY and SOCIO-LOGY, all of which refer to feelings of being estranged, separated and power-less, whether in relation to oneself, to WORK, to nature, to other people, to wealth and the means of PRODUCTION in a society, or else to society as a whole.

allocation   [1] The process of dividing resources or costs between different sections or functions of an ORGANIZATION. [2] The amount of resources in a given BUDGET.

alternative shift   A two-shift system of working in which, for example, people may work days and then nights for the same period of time, often week and week about, or perhaps alternating early and late shifts.

annualized hours   The contractual requirement by employers that their STAFF work a certain number of hours per year rather than per week thus allow-ing a company more flexibility in the

use of the working time its employees are paid for. It can thus, for example, vary the length of the working day or allow for peaks and troughs in the demand for its products over the year without having to pay overtime or hire casual workers. Compare with FLEXIBLE WORKING HOURS.

annual report   An account of an ORGANIZATION's activities over a twelve-month period, drawn up by its MANAGE-MENT. Required by law for registered companies. It may include an ACCOUNT-ING of HUMAN RESOURCES as well as finan-cial resources.

anomie   A term used by the French sociologist Emile Durkheim to describe a condition of society where SOCIAL NORMS are breaking down and people become confused both about their place in society and about their sense of IDENTITY. This may lead them to suffer a form of ALIENATION.

Ansoff Matrix   A way of classifying the four basic product strategies of MARKETING developed by Igor Ansoff: [1] market penetration, [2] market exten-sion, [3] product development and [4] diversification. (See Figure 2, p6.)

anthropology   The study of the differ-ent physical and cultural conditions of humankind, including ORGANIZATIONS and the world of WORK.

anthropometry   A branch of ANTHRO-POLOGY that is concerned with measuring human physical characteristics. It is used in a workplace ENVIRONMENT when the nature of human size, shape and move-ment is of particular concern to ERGONOMICS.

anticipatory socialization   Where people are eager to enter a new ROLE they may anticipate the situation by adopting

PRODUCT

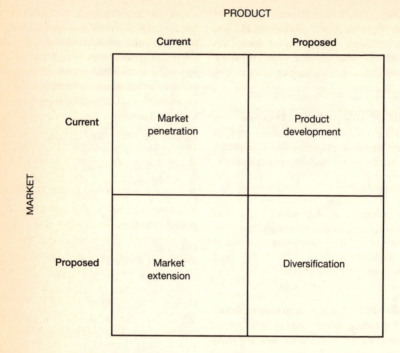

Figure 2 Ansoff Matrix.

the ATTITUDES and interests associated with it; for example, someone about to become a student, or a MANAGER, or a parent for the first time. See also SOCIALIZATION and PROFESSIONAL SOCIALIZATION.

anxiety   A term used with many shades of meaning and in many different areas of PSYCHOLOGY. It is generally held to be an unpleasant emotional state resulting from STRESS or CONFLICT, and characterized by fear and apprehension. Everyone suffers from anxiety at some time or other and some situations would make virtually everyone anxious. But if the fear and apprehension felt are vague and diffuse and not attached to a specific object, or if they seem excessive, the anxiety is considered to be a neurotic TRAIT of the individual's PERSONALITY.

applied psychology   The term normally used for those areas of PSYCHOLOGY which apply psychological theories and findings to particular issues of everyday life, such as COUNSELLING, education, MANAGEMENT or the workplace. It can also be used to describe the contributions of psychologists in a wide variety of more unusual areas such as designing instrument panels for spaceships and assisting the police in dealing with hostage takers.

appraisal interview   See PERFORMANCE APPRAISAL INTERVIEW.

apprenticeship   The period of time spent, mostly at the workplace and usually on low wages, in learning the basic SKILLS of a craft, trade or profession. This was formerly a common way for young people to enter the world of work and usually lasted several years. Outside of the more traditional professions like law or medicine, this form of entry has become relatively rare with the widespread use of fast-changing INFORMATION TECHNOLOGY.

appropriation   Money allocated to a BUDGET for a specific purpose.

aptitude   The potential for acquiring a SKILL or ABILITY after some TRAINING.

aptitude test   A technique that tries to predict a person's capacity for acquiring a certain SKILL or ABILITY. See also PSYCHOMETRICS.

arbitration   A method of settling a dispute between two parties who have failed to agree on some matter. With the agreement of both parties to abide by the arbiter's decision the dispute is put before a neutral third party, usually an independent body, for adjudication outside a court of law.

Argyris, Chris (1923–)   An American psychologist and specialist in ORGANIZATIONAL DEVELOPMENT whose work focuses on the relationship between the individual and the ORGANIZATION, and in particular the search for conditions that foster the integration of individual needs and ORGANIZATIONAL GOALS.

Army Alpha Test   The earliest example of a PAPER-AND-PENCIL TEST used by a large ORGANIZATION in the RECRUITMENT, SELECTION and PLACEMENT of very large numbers of people. This was a test of INTELLIGENCE used by the US army to screen new recruits during the First World War.

artificial intelligence   A field of study, combining PSYCHOLOGY and INFORMATION TECHNOLOGY, which uses computer systems to develop machines that exhibit characteristics of human INTELLIGENCE, like language and problem-solving. These machines are intended to reproduce human thought processes and are used especially in the development of EXPERT SYSTEMS which simulate human expertise, for example, that of bank managers making loan decisions or even doctors making diagnoses of patients. There is a certain amount of disquiet among specialists in this area about the tendency to treat this process as value-free in terms of its effects on people, which it most certainly is not.

Asch, Solomon (1907–96)   An American psychologist influenced by the GESTALT viewpoint and who has specialized in the study of CONFORMITY behaviour in small GROUPS, generally considered to be one of the most important aspects of the way an ORGANIZATION functions. His most important contribution to GROUP DYNAMICS is considered to be the finding that some people can be persuaded to doubt the evidence of their own eyes by the force of group pressure. (See Figure 3, p8.)

assembly line   A means of MASS PRODUCTION, based on the ideas of GILBRETH and TAYLOR, which was invented by HENRY FORD in 1913 for his model-T car factory. It quickly became the leading method of producing standardized goods in large volumes. The method requires workers to carry out their particular tasks on the product as it passes in front of them along a conveyor belt, each worker adding something to the product along the way. A TASK may take as little as a couple of seconds to perform, and the possible psychological effects of doing this all day long have been explored by the well-known psychologist C. Chaplin in his film *Modern Times*. See also AUTONOMOUS WORK GROUPS and DEPERSONALIZATION.

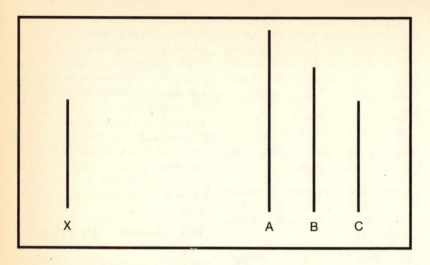

Figure 3 Asch conformity situation. Does X really = C?

assertiveness training A form of TRAINING designed to increase a person's confidence. It uses a technique of BEHAVIOUR MODIFICATION intended to help people overcome INHIBITIONS about expressing their feelings, but without becoming aggressive in the process. This technique involves a lot of ROLE PLAYING. It is quite often used in MANAGEMENT DEVELOPMENT.

assessment [1] In PSYCHOLOGY, this is a procedure to identify ABILITY, carried out on individuals as part of the processes of RECRUITMENT and SELECTION. [2] In ACCOUNTING, this is a procedure carried out on property or PROFITS to determine tax liability.

assessment centre An establishment, often set up within large ORGANIZATIONS, that specializes in identifying ABILITY as part of the processes of RECRUITMENT and SELECTION and in identifying potential for MANAGEMENT DEVELOPMENT. See also CAREER DEVELOPMENT.

assets Any resources that an ORGANIZATION owns which may be of economic benefit to it. These may be tangible (like people, machinery or property) or intangible (like GOODWILL). See also MANAGEMENT AUDIT.

asset stripping The acquisition of a business ORGANIZATION for the sole purpose of selling off its most valuable ASSETS in order to make a quick PROFIT.

association A group of people or ORGANIZATIONS sharing the same interest who wish to be affiliated with each other. This affiliation may be formal or informal, highly organized or loosely structured; worldwide in scope or restricted to a single building.

attitude A stable, long-lasting and learned predisposition to respond to certain things in a certain way. An attitude has three aspects to it: *belief, feeling* and *intention*. In PSYCHOLOGY these are often referred to as cognitive, affective and conative aspects. (See Figure 4.)

attitude scale A set of questions designed to elicit ATTITUDES from

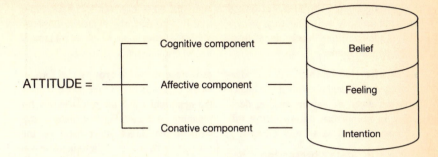

Figure 4 Attitude.

respondents on a given topic and to measure their strength.

attitude survey   The use of SURVEY RESEARCH to obtain information on ATTITUDES.

attribution theory   A way of trying to interpret and understand our own behaviour and that of other people. We seem to *attribute* certain intentions or MOTIVATIONS to the behaviour we observe. This can also be thought of as a way of describing what the study of PSYCHOLOGY is all about. In a sense it is the layperson's equivalent of what the psychologist does for a living.

audioconferencing   A TELECONFERENCE using only audio means of COMMUNICATION.

audiovisual aids   Techniques making use of hearing and (especially) vision that are used in order to improve COMMUNICATION. They range from blackboard and chalk to COMPUTER-ASSISTED INSTRUCTION in complexity – though not necessarily in effectiveness.

audit   [1] The process of verifying the ACCOUNTING records of an ORGANIZATION by an independent auditor to see whether they contain a true, fair and accurate account of the business transacted.

[2] The term may also be used in relation to HUMAN RESOURCES, as in MANAGEMENT AUDIT.

authoritarian management   A type of MANAGEMENT which emphasizes the discipline and control of people and sees little value in consulting them about the JOB. It is what you would expect from an AUTHORITARIAN PERSONALITY. It is usually contrasted with DEMOCRATIC MANAGEMENT.

authoritarian personality   A person characterized by a concern with obedience and various TRAITS of PERSONALITY that seem to be associated with it, such as low TOLERANCE FOR AMBIGUITY, high PREJUDICE, rigid adherence to conventions, superstition, servility and contempt for weakness.

authority   [1] The right, inherent in a JOB or function, to use POWER in the fulfilment of one's responsibilities. Power and authority do not always go together. People in a position of authority may be ineffective in using power because they do not command the respect or loyalty of their subordinates, and people with no official authority may exert a powerful effect on an ORGANIZATION by virtue of their personal qualities, their long experience, or the fact that they married the boss's daughter. [2] The term is also used of a public body with statutory powers and responsibilities, such as a local authority care home.

autocratic leadership   A leader-centred way of dealing with subordinates who are given no say in making decisions. In running an ORGANIZATION this becomes AUTHORITARIAN MANAGEMENT.

automatic data processing   See ELECTRONIC DATA PROCESSING.

automation   A term first used in the late 1940s by the Ford Motor Company. It is used to describe the employment of machines that reduce or dispense entirely with HUMAN COMMUNICATION, computation or CONTROL in relation to a JOB. It is particularly important in INFORMATION PROCESSING and INTELLIGENT KNOWLEDGE-BASED SYSTEMS.

autonomous work groups   A form of WORK ORGANIZATION where workers have the opportunity and the responsibility for planning and carrying out their TASKS without the direct supervision of the MANAGEMENT. It is thought to increase JOB SATISFACTION and product QUALITY, and possibly also PRODUCTIVITY. It is in direct opposition to the model of the ASSEMBLY LINE, though it has been almost as widely adopted in the car industry, which produced them both. In fact neither of them is now in general use in that industry.

B

balanced scorecard A MANAGEMENT tool aimed at increasing organizational effectiveness. It employs a range of both quantitative measures (like PROFIT and PRODUCTIVITY) and qualitative measures (like CUSTOMER SERVICE and STAFF TRAINING) to balance money-oriented and people-oriented factors in setting ORGANIZATIONAL GOALS and assessing their performance.

banding A way of organizing a SALARY STRUCTURE where a series of different levels is first established into which jobs are then classified by level, or band, rather than fixing a different rate of PAY for each job individually.

bandwidth [1] A term used in the FLEXIBLE WORKING HOURS system to describe the total working day of an ORGANIZATION from the earliest permitted starting time to the latest permitted finishing time. [2] A term used in TELECOMMUNICATIONS for the frequency limits to a given communications band.

bar chart A graphical method of illustrating statistical information (as in Figure 5). It takes the form of a diagram in which quantities or frequencies are expressed as columns of different height. See also GANTT CHART and HISTOGRAM.

bar code A computer code which appears as a series of parallel lines and spaces marked on retail products. This code is then read by a laser scanner at the ELECTRONIC POINT OF SALE and converted

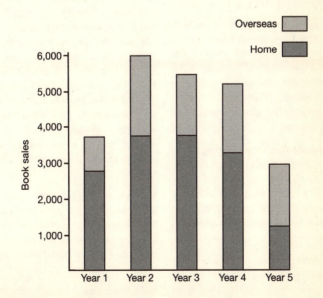

Figure 5 Bar chart.

into information about price and stock supply.

bargaining   [1] A term used in INDUSTRIAL RELATIONS to describe negotiations between two parties, usually employers and employees or their representatives, to achieve a settlement regarding wages and conditions of EMPLOYMENT. [2] The kind of behaviour studied in various areas of SOCIAL PSYCHOLOGY, especially GAME THEORY, where people with different interests try to influence each other in order to improve their position. [3] Transacting business, whether on the stock exchange or in a street market.

bargaining zone   An area of overlap in the interests of two parties within which BARGAINING can occur.

BARS   See Behaviourally Anchored Rating Scale.

BASIC   An introductory COMPUTER LANGUAGE that combines ALGOL, COBOL and FORTRAN.

batch production   A type of PRODUCTION different from MASS PRODUCTION or CONTINUOUS PROCESS PRODUCTION in that it is used where identical items are to be manufactured and processed in groups, or batches, rather than individually. Examples might be gloves, toolkits or matching lingerie.

Behaviourally Anchored Rating Scale An ASSESSMENT instrument that often uses the CRITICAL INCIDENT TECHNIQUE, thereby 'anchoring' it in employees' actual behaviour. It may then be used to assess a given person in a PERFORMANCE APPRAISAL INTERVIEW.

behavioural science   The study of the behaviour of people and animals by use of experiment and observation. It is centred on PSYCHOLOGY but branches out towards biology and physiology in one direction and ANTHROPOLOGY and SOCIOLOGY in the other. (See Figure 6.)

behavioural theory of the firm A concept proposed in the early 1960s by two American psychologists, Richard Cyert and James March, which argues that a business ORGANIZATION consists of a coalition of different interest groups with different goals representing a variety of views and which are continuously BARGAINING for POWER. This means that decision-making is an inherently uncertain business – contrary to the assumptions of rational behaviour made by proponents of CLASSICAL ORGANIZATION THEORY or ECONOMIC MAN. See also CHAOS THEORY.

Behaviourism   A school of PSYCHOLOGY founded by an American psychologist, J.B. WATSON, in 1913. Watson believed that the work of PAVLOV on CONDITIONING represented the future of psychology, which should deal solely with the objective study of human and animal behaviour and eschew 'woolly' concepts like mind and consciousness. Watson is now generally regarded as much too extreme and simpleminded, having been superseded by B.F. SKINNER and other theorists of Behaviourism. For cultural and historical reasons Behaviourism has continued to flourish more in the United States than elsewhere. Watson himself left academia to pursue a successful career in ADVERTISING with the J. Walter Thompson Company.

behaviour modification   The deliberate changing of a particular pattern of behaviour (e.g. the attempt to reduce smoking or drinking in times of STRESS) by using methods based on the theory of BEHAVIOURISM.

Belbin groups   Named after Meredith Belbin, the British MANAGEMENT

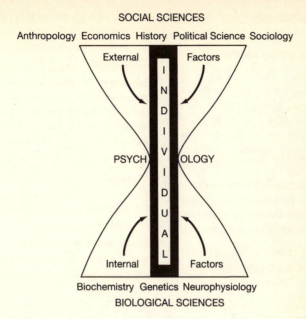

SOCIAL SCIENCES

Anthropology Economics History Political Science Sociology

External   Factors

PSYCH   OLOGY

Internal   Factors

Biochemistry Genetics Neurophysiology
BIOLOGICAL SCIENCES

Figure 6 Behavioural science.

CONSULTANT who was concerned with the effects of different TEAM ROLES on group performance.

bell-shaped curve   This describes the shape of the curve obtained by plotting the kind of FREQUENCY DISTRIBUTION known as a NORMAL DISTRIBUTION on a graph.

below the line advertising   This is an ever-increasing form of SALES PROMOTION which uses outlets such as direct mail, the internet, special discounts and point-of-sale offers, on which no agency commission is paid, as opposed to the MASS MEDIA used in ABOVE THE LINE ADVERTISING. The 'line' in question was originally on a company's balance sheet but this usage has now been lost in MARKETING.

benchmarking   Currently fashionable JARGON for setting standards.

benefit in kind   Any payment for work performed, other than money. The most common example is the company car. See also BLACK ECONOMY, FRINGE BENEFIT and PERK.

benefit segmentation   A form of MARKET SEGMENTATION which is based on a knowledge of the benefits that consumers seek from a particular product. To use it a marketer needs to include the appropriate characteristics – or at least an impression of them – within a given product. In a sense this form of segmentation is right at the heart of the MARKETING CONCEPT; find out what people want (or might want, or think they want) and give it to them. For instance, if the customer wants 'sleek and stylish' from her or his electronic equipment, matt black is usually considered a more appropriate colour than mauve.

bimodal distribution   A FREQUENCY DISTRIBUTION that has two MODES.

bio-data   See BIOGRAPHIC DATA.

biofeedback   The FEEDBACK of information to individuals about their biological functions. Using biofeedback it is possible for people to gain a certain amount of CONTROL of such functions as heart rate, blood pressure and brain waves through a form of CONDITIONING process.

biographic data   The kind of personal information recorded in a CURRICULUM VITAE. It is used in the RECRUITMENT and SELECTION of applicants for jobs.

biological clock   Not a physical structure but a term used to describe the biochemical process that controls our BIORHYTHMS.

biorhythms   Biological systems that have regularly recurring cycles. The best known of these are the menstrual cycle and the CIRCADIAN RHYTHMS, the latter of which are of particular interest to psychologists.

biotechnology   The use of biologically based processes in existing manufacturing and service industries.

black economy   The widely used name for the set of informal economic activities engaged in outside the official systems of EMPLOYMENT and TAXATION, on which no documents are kept and no tax paid. PAYMENT IN KIND, or cash, is the usual procedure. Contrary to popular mythology the people involved in this activity may well be regularly employed rather than unemployed and actively MOONLIGHTING on the side.

blacking   A type of INDUSTRIAL ACTION adopted by employees of an ORGANIZATION in support of employees in another organization who have an INDUSTRIAL DISPUTE with their employers. It involves a refusal to handle the movement of goods and services to or from the other organization.

blackleg   A derogatory term (origin unknown) used to describe someone who does not support the INDUSTRIAL ACTION of his or her fellow workers and, for example, continues to work during a STRIKE or replaces a striking worker.

blacklist   A list of people or ORGANIZATIONS against whom some kind of DISCRIMINATION will be practised, usually for political reasons.

black market   An illegal trade in goods or services, the demand for which has outstripped the officially available supply. It is caused by the imposition of official measures which are designed to cope with the shortfall, like rationing or price controls.

Blau typology   A technique used by the American sociologist Peter Blau which classified FORMAL ORGANIZATIONS according to the criterion 'who benefits?' Four classes of ORGANIZATION are thereby distinguished: [1] *mutual-benefit associations*, like clubs and political parties; [2] *business concerns*, like banks and shops; [3] *service organizations*, like hospitals and schools; [4] *commonweal organizations*, like the fire and police services.

blind test   A technique used in MARKET RESEARCH for obtaining the opinions of consumers on a product where all of the product's identifying marks are removed. Several products are sometimes compared at the same time in this fashion.

blue chip   [1] The term used to describe the ordinary shares of long-established, large and reputable companies. Such shares are generally regarded as being a good long-term INVESTMENT. [2] More generally, the term may be used of anything that is highly regarded for its reliability and PERFORMANCE.

blue-collar worker Popular term for a MANUAL WORKER in a factory or other industrial workplace. The name derives from the typical shirts or overalls worn. Usually contrasted with a WHITE-COLLAR WORKER.

body language NON-VERBAL COMMUNICATION with other people by means of physical postures, movement or gestures that may be conscious or UNCONSCIOUS on the part of the communicator.

body-shopping A term sometimes used of the practice whereby a CONSULTANCY supplies people to work on a temporary contract basis in place of regular STAFF in the PUBLIC SECTOR.

BOGOF Abbreviation used in MARKETING for 'buy one get one free'. Apparently, it sounds like a better deal than 'two for the price of one'.

bookkeeping The method of recording an ORGANIZATION's financial transactions that allows a clear picture of its

financial situation to be obtained at any time, such as by reference to its 'books'. See also DOUBLE ENTRY BOOKKEEPING.

boomerang effect A term used in SOCIAL PSYCHOLOGY, in the study of ATTITUDE change. It refers to people who change their attitudes in the opposite direction from that being advocated to them.

Boston Matrix Developed by the Boston Consulting Group and used in MARKETING as a way of classifying products by business growth and relative competitive position. [1] *star* – high growth, market leader/high market share, should invest; [2] *cash cow* – low growth, high market share, mature, should generate cash for investment; [3] *question mark* – high growth, low market share, should become star or divested; [4] *dog* – low growth, low market share, should divest. (See Figure 7.)

bottom line An ACCOUNTING term denoting the last line of a balance sheet which calculates the PROFIT and loss of a business. It is now used more widely in MANAGEMENT to mean something like 'in the final analysis' or 'the most important thing'. A nice example of the way

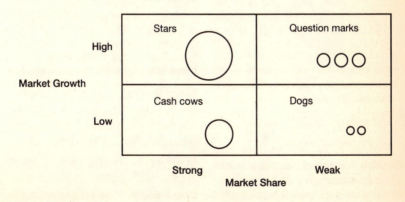

Figure 7 Boston Matrix.

accountants have taken over the language of discourse in the ORGANIZATION.

boundaryless organization   The idea that creativity and innovation can be fostered in an ORGANIZATION that tries to break down traditional barriers not only between departments within the organization but between the organization itself and the significant others in its environment, like its customers and suppliers, who are re-conceptualized as partners in the same enterprise.

BPR   Acronym for BUSINESS PROCESS RE-ENGINEERING.

brainstorming   In SOCIAL PSYCHOLOGY this term refers to the free generation of ideas by the members of a GROUP for the purpose of solving a specific problem. See also DELPHI METHOD and SCENARIO WRITING.

brainwashing   An attempt to coerce someone into radically changing his or her beliefs or behaviour by using psychological manipulation; for example, in ADVERTISING. Despite much hysterical pronouncement on the subject there is no good evidence that it can actually be done.

brand   A mark, name, LOGO or TRADE-MARK that identifies a product or service or ORGANIZATION and distinguishes it from its competitors.

brand awareness   The extent to which potential customers are aware of a given BRAND and its attributes.

brand equity   BRANDS started out as intangible repositories of values like customer LOYALTY and GOODWILL but since the 1980s have become such an important aspect of MARKETING that they may even be listed on a company's balance sheet along with its other ASSETS. They can

thus have a *tangible* value calculated in billions of dollars when a large company with several successful brands is subject to a TAKE-OVER bid.

brand extension   A way of using a well-known existing BRAND NAME to introduce a new product. The extension may be just a variation on a successful product (e.g. Heinz' 57 varieties) or a switch into a whole new MARKET (e.g. from Caterpillar tractors to Caterpillar boots). The BRAND LOYALTY of existing customers is an important factor in the success of the extension.

brand identity   The meaning of a BRAND to the company that owns it, as expressed through its ADVERTISING. Compare with BRAND IMAGE.

brand image   The meaning of a BRAND to potential consumers based on their perceptions of its ADVERTISING. Compare with BRAND IDENTITY.

branding   The use of a BRAND to describe a product, service or ORGANIZATION. At its most successful it becomes a generic term for its whole field; for example, the use of 'Xerox' for photocopier.

brand leader   A term used in MARKETING to describe a BRAND or a product that appears to be the most prominent one in its field to consumers, and is marketed accordingly – and differently from a follower in the MARKET or a new product.

brand loyalty   A situation where consumers remain loyal over time to a particular BRAND of goods or services, even if it costs more than its competitors.

brand mark   A symbol or LOGO unique to a particular BRAND.

brand name   The name by which a BRAND is identified. If it is sufficiently important to the BRAND IDENTITY and BRAND IMAGE of a product it can become a registered TRADEMARK.

brand personality A way of characterizing the image of a BRAND by giving it personal associations as though it were an individual. Using descriptions like 'masculine', 'feminine', 'traditional', 'safe' or 'assertive' is the most common way of trying to distinguish a brand from its competitors. More ambitious marketers may try to provide the brand with a whole, rounded and consistent personality of its own that the customer can hang a proper name on, like Dr Pepper or Mr Coffee in the United States and Messrs Bradford and Bingley in the United Kingdom.

brand value Both the tangible (financial) and the intangible (psychological) value of a given BRAND EQUITY.

break-even point The point in an ORGANIZATION's financial life where its INCOME equals its costs.

brightness A term used in ERGONOMICS to describe both the objective intensity of the physical stimulus from a source of light and the subjective sensation of the person who experiences it.

brownfield site A location for a new industrial or commercial development on the cleared site of a former development. Compare with GREENFIELD SITE.

brown goods Consumer products which are presented within a wood or imitation wood case, like television sets or kitchen cabinets. Compare with WHITE GOODS.

browser A COMPUTER PROGRAM that allows a user to browse through the web pages on the WORLD WIDE WEB and then to read and download pages as desired.

BS 5750 A standard of QUALITY set by the British Standards Institution. Its successful achievement by an ORGANIZATION is attested by a certificate.

buddy system The American equivalent of SITTING NEXT TO NELLIE.

budget [1] The financial statement of an ORGANIZATION's planned INCOME and expenditure for a given length of time. [2] The proposed income and expenditure of the British government over the coming year as presented to Parliament by the Chancellor of the Exchequer. [3] Sometimes used in place of APPROPRIATION.

budget-based institution An ORGANIZATION that is required to prepare, and work to, a BUDGET.

buffering A form of CONFLICT MANAGEMENT that attempts to use the outputs of one work group as the inputs of another to reduce potential conflict between them. Most often used in arranging stock INVENTORIES between two groups. However, it runs counter to the fashionable approach of JUST-IN-TIME PRODUCTION.

bug An error or fault in the SOFTWARE which causes a COMPUTER PROGRAM to malfunction.

Buggin's turn 'Joe Buggin' is the classic organizational time server who gets rewarded or promoted (has his 'turn') simply by being there long enough. In a time of MACHO MANAGEMENT, with lots of DELAYERING and RIGHT-SIZING, this is not supposed to happen.

built-in obsolescence The deliberate design and manufacture of a product so that it needs replacing after a certain length of time.

bureaucracy [1] A term coined by the German sociologist Max Weber in the early twentieth century to describe an ORGANIZATION that has (a) a clearly defined HIERARCHY with top-down AUTHORITARIAN MANAGEMENT, (b) highly specialized responsibilities, ROLES and TASKS for its members and (c) a heavy emphasis on rules and procedures. Though these characteristics are mainly associated with large organizations they are found to some extent in all organizations. [2] 'The bureaucracy' is a term sometimes used in the PUBLIC SECTOR to describe the Civil Service.

burnout　A term used to describe people at work who have suffered from the effects of STRESS to the point where they are overloaded and no longer able to function productively. People in this situation may become cynical and just go through the motions if the source of stress is not dealt with. See also PRESENTEEISM and RETIREMENT ON THE JOB.

business cycle　Regular patterns of fluctuation over time in the business activity of an economy. Four distinct phases are usually identified; *boom*, RECESSION, DEPRESSION and *recovery*. The causes of the cycle are partly economic and partly political. For example governments will try to engineer a boom shortly before an election by use of fiscal or monetary policy.

business ethics　The application of ethical concerns to the world of business usually takes one of three forms: [1] *codes of ethics*, where industries, PROFESSIONS or individual companies have explicit guidelines for their members about what constitutes acceptable behaviour to STAKEHOLDERS like staff or consumers; [2] *changes in the board of directors* to include people from outside the business world who reflect broader interests; [3] *social responsibility* by a company in the MARKETING of its goods and services.

business game　A form of TRAINING for MANAGEMENT where the elements of a business situation are presented to the trainees, who then have to make decisions about how best to manage the situation. It involves ROLE PLAYING, is usually done in a group, sometimes competitively, and increasingly with the aid of COMPUTER SIMULATION.

business model　The practical day-to-day guidelines for running a business that can be drawn from a CORPORATE PLAN.

business plan　See CORPORATE PLAN.

business process re-engineering　See RE-ENGINEERING.

business re-engineering　See RE-ENGINEERING.

business transformation　See RE-ENGINEERING.

busy-work　The American version of MAKE-WORK.

buyer's market　A MARKET situation in which buyers have more POWER to influence prices and conditions of sale than sellers, usually because supply exceeds demand. Always contrasted with SELLER'S MARKET.

buying-in　The practice of hiring expert help as required by an ORGANIZATION rather than employing such experts on its STAFF.

buzzword　A term that describes a current MANAGEMENT fad or fashion, for example, TQM, RIGHTSIZING or the LEARNING ORGANIZATION.

C

CAD See COMPUTER-AIDED DESIGN.

CAD/CAM system An integrated SYSTEM used in INDUSTRIAL ENGINEERING that employs both COMPUTER-AIDED DESIGN and COMPUTER-AIDED MANUFACTURING.

CAE See COMPUTER-AIDED ENGINEERING.

cafeteria benefits A form of REWARD where employees are given some choice from a range of FRINGE BENEFITS.

CAI See COMPUTER-ASSISTED INSTRUCTION.

call centre A location where telephone calls to and from customers are handled. The location is often remote from – indeed sometimes on a different continent from – both the caller and the business he or she is trying to deal with. Operators are generally expected to keep calls (often to a fixed script) as brief as possible and process as many as possible during their shift. Their PERFORMANCE is monitored by a SUPERVISOR for the purpose of REWARD or DISCIPLINE. It is an ASSEMBLY LINE for the twenty-first century.

CAM See COMPUTER-AIDED MANUFACTURING.

capital [1] In ACCOUNTING, capital is the term for the total financial ASSETS of an ORGANIZATION whether in the form of money, property, goods or equipment. It represents the organization's stock of wealth as opposed to its INCOME. The organization's HUMAN RESOURCES may be represented in the form of HUMAN ASSET ACCOUNTING. [2] In ECONOMICS, capital is traditionally one of the three major factors necessary for PRODUCTION along with labour and land.

capital-intensive The term used of an ORGANIZATION with a relatively high degree of CAPITAL invested in AUTOMATION as opposed to people; for example, a car manufacturer. It is therefore the opposite of LABOUR-INTENSIVE.

capitalism An economic SYSTEM characterized by the private ownership of a society's resources; by COMPETITION in the pursuit of financial gain; and by support for the ideal (if not the practice) of a FREE MARKET in goods and services.

captive product A relatively insignificant product that must be purchased regularly to service a more important product. For example, ink cartridges for a printer or top-up cards for a mobile phone.

career A line of work that a person expects to pursue for his or her foreseeable working life, though it might include changes in job or employer. In fact, it is now generally accepted that both job and career changes are an inevitable, and probably desirable, aspect of a career and that these changes will often be associated with periods of education and TRAINING.

career anchors A concept developed by the American theorist of ORGANIZATIONAL PSYCHOLOGY, Edgar Schein, to study the guidelines and priorities in the working life of a MANAGER. It deals with the way in which a person's SELF-IMAGE focuses on the needs, motives, talents and values and the clarification of what is most important to her or him, such as the use of technical SKILLS or finding stability or security within an ORGANIZATION.

career break   A period of time when someone's CAREER is interrupted for personal reasons (like childcare) or professional reasons (like studying for a qualification) before the career is resumed at the same level.

career development   The planning of a person's future CAREER within an ORGANIZATION in order to maximize his or her contribution to the organization and the fulfilment of his or her own potential. This is a primary function of PERSONNEL MANAGEMENT. See also ROLE and TRAINING.

career ladders   Recognized routes of PROMOTION and advancement within an ORGANIZATION.

career patterns   The identification of regularities or typical paths through an ORGANIZATION that show up in people's CAREERS.

cartel   A combination of two or more independent ORGANIZATIONS which produce the same product, for the purposes of eliminating or restricting COMPETITION between them and preventing new competitors from entering the MARKET. This is accomplished by fixing prices, level of PRODUCTION or MARKET SEGMENTATION. It is illustrated, for example, by the Organization of Petroleum Exporting Countries (OPEC) and is a common development in mature industries.

cascade briefing   A technique for communicating information down through an organizational HIERARCHY. It begins with the most senior level of MANAGEMENT briefing the next level down, and so on.

case studies   A form of TRAINING for MANAGEMENT used extensively to develop the intellectual SKILLS of analysis, reasoning and judgement. It is based mainly on past real-life situations. Case studies are associated particularly with the teaching methods of the Harvard Business School. Unlike BUSINESS GAMES, case studies have no action component to them. One important criticism of the method is that it encourages students to believe that every 'problem' has a 'solution' if only they are clever enough to find it, and that this does not prepare them to deal with situations which neither they nor anyone else have ever encountered before – which is much more like the real world. See also CHAOS THEORY.

cash cow   One of the MARKETING situations in the BOSTON MATRIX. It is characterized by low growth and a strong MARKET position. A cash cow is a product with a steady INCOME stream and may be used to generate cash for investment.

cash flow   [1] The amount of cash flowing into and out of an ORGANIZATION as INCOME and expenditure. [2] The amount of cash required to finance operating expenses or further PRODUCTION over a given period of time.

casualization   A process, much used by the FLEXIBLE FIRM, of reducing the number of permanent employees in favour of temporary staff who are only paid as and when they are required to work. An increasingly popular form of casualization with employers is the ZERO-HOURS CONTRACT.

cautious shift   A form of GROUP POLARIZATION where people make more cautious decisions under the influence of a group than they do when they are by themselves. The opposite of RISKY SHIFT.

caveat emptor   Latin for 'let the buyer beware'. It is used to illustrate the widely held legal principle that the onus is on the buyer, rather than the seller, to check that he or she is getting the goods and services paid for.

CBA   See COST–BENEFIT ANALYSIS.

CBP   See COMPUTER-BASED PRACTICE.

CBT   See COMPUTER-BASED TRAINING.

CD ROM   An acronym for COMPACT DISK READ ONLY MEMORY.

cell organization   A form of WORK ORGANIZATION that groups together workers concerned with the various activities of one part of a manufacturing process into a 'cell' or unit. It is often used in BATCH PRODUCTION.

CEO   See CHIEF EXECUTIVE OFFICER.

CEO disease   A behaviour pattern that has been observed among CHIEF EXECUTIVE OFFICERS who become intoxicated with the POWER and PERKS of office. Symptoms include believing in their own omnipotence, surrounding themselves with yes-men and responding brutally to any opposition.

central bank   Usually a national government's own bank, like the Bank of England (which performs that function for the United Kingdom) or the Federal Reserve Bank in the United States, which carries out the government's financial policy. It also oversees the operation of a country's financial SYSTEM, acting as a banker to the other banks.

centralization   The policy and process of trying to run everything in an ORGANIZATION from one central point.

central route to persuasion   It is widely accepted in CONSUMER PSYCHOLOGY that there are two different 'routes to persuasion' for a COMMUNICATION aimed at prospective purchasers. The central route, which requires rational thought by the consumer, is followed when the consumer's involvement and MOTIVATION in assessing the product are high. Compare with PERIPHERAL ROUTE TO PERSUASION.

certification   The process of obtaining an official document to satisfy some institutional requirement. Most often used in the field of education or TRAINING or the provision of professional services.

chain of command   The arrangement by which instructions and information are passed down through the HIERARCHY of LINE MANAGEMENT in an ORGANIZATION.

chairman's brief   A document usually written by the Secretary of an ORGANIZATION or COMMITTEE to prepare the Chairman of the organization or committee for a forthcoming meeting.

change agent   A person who acts as a catalyst within an ORGANIZATION to assist the introduction, implementation or facilitation of changes as a result of an ORGANIZATIONAL DEVELOPMENT programme (or perhaps the whim of the CHIEF EXECUTIVE OFFICER).

chaos theory   A theory developed by natural scientists and mathematicians beginning in the early 1970s. It is the opposite of the scientific model of direct links between cause and effect, leading to prediction and CONTROL, that has traditionally been the model not only for natural science but for BEHAVIOURAL and SOCIAL SCIENCE as well. Chaos theory argues that behaviour is essentially random and unpredictable when looked at in detail but that there is an underlying pattern or rhythm to it when considered at a deeper level. Attempts at planning and control in businesses, as in any other ORGANIZATION, are therefore doomed to failure. So managers need to be aware of the fluid, dynamic and ever-changing nature of events as they impinge on the business. In line with recent thinking in MANAGEMENT research and consultancy, this will require them to be facilitators and coaches rather than SUPERVISORS in dealing with their STAFF. It will also require them to be flexible and adaptable in their dealings with customers, suppliers and all the other interest groups they deal with.

chargehand   The leading member of a WORK GROUP under the supervision of a FOREMAN.

charisma   An elusive quality of PERSONALITY, often described as 'personal magnetism' (whatever that may be), which is widely considered to be an important element in LEADERSHIP, especially TRANSFORMATIONAL LEADERSHIP.

charm price   An alternative term for PSYCHOLOGICAL PRICE.

chart   A diagrammatic way of expressing information; for example, BAR CHART, HISTOGRAM, PICTOGRAM and PIE CHART.

chief executive officer   The most senior EXECUTIVE officer of an ORGANIZATION; for example, the permanent secretary of a British government department or the managing director of a company.

Chinese walls   Imaginary barriers to COMMUNICATION which are set up voluntarily between two departments or sets of activities within the same company. The point of the exercise is to protect their clients' rights to receive impartial advice, which might be compromised by privileged information being passed freely throughout the company. This applies, for example, to the MARKET-making and brokerage functions of a stockbroking firm,

where market-makers might be keen to sell a stock because they expected its value to fall, and the brokers then recommended the stock to clients. Numerous financial scandals in the 1980s and 1990s have shown that the walls are a lot more porous in practice than theory. Why the Chinese have been accorded such a dubious attribution is unclear.

chip   A shortened, colloquial form of MICROCHIP.

chi square   In STATISTICS this is a simple TEST, represented by the Greek letter chi (χ), which is widely used in research in PSYCHOLOGY and the BEHAVIOURAL SCIENCES to see whether observed results differ from those expected by chance alone.

chronobiology   The study of BIORHYTHMS.

chunking   The process of grouping items of information into units, or 'chunks', as an aid to memorizing them.

CIM   See COMPUTER-INTEGRATED MANUFACTURING.

circadian rhythm   The term 'circadian', from the Latin meaning 'about a day', refers to those BIORHYTHMS which function on roughly a 24-hour cycle, like sleeping and changes in blood pressure and body temperature.

CIT   See CRITICAL INCIDENT TECHNIQUE.

classical organizational theory   The attempt, in the early years of the twentieth century, to formulate a set of general principles of ADMINISTRATION that would serve as a guide to the effective MANAGEMENT of any ORGANIZATION. It is associated with the work of FAYOL and TAYLOR, among others.

clique   An INFORMAL GROUP whose members associate with each other at work (as in society generally) on the basis of mutual interests, or even just physical proximity. In SOCIOLOGY, where it was first used, the term does not have quite the pejorative connotation of in-group exclusiveness and hostility to out-groups that it has in popular usage.

clock time The process of ordering our lives and synchronizing our work activities via the external clock (as opposed to our internal BIOLOGICAL CLOCK, for example). It is the way we experience LINEAR TIME.

closed shop A situation in which all the members of an ORGANIZATION must belong to the appropriate TRADE UNION. After legislation passed in the 1980s this is no longer formally possible in the United Kingdom.

closure [1] A GESTALT principle, generally accepted in PSYCHOLOGY, that the brain has a built-in tendency to perceive meaning, completion and coherence where the objective sensory facts may have no meaning or be incomplete or incoherent. Thus, a figure with a part missing will be perceived as though it were whole. (See Figure 8.) [2] The term is also used in PSYCHOTHERAPY (and even in general parlance) to denote a line of investigation that is being brought to completion. [3] A related usage is that of 'closing' a deal.

cluster sampling A term used in MARKET RESEARCH for the practice of drawing a sample of informants from a geographically localized area (like a single street) – a much cheaper procedure than RANDOM SAMPLING or even QUOTA SAMPLING.

CNC machines Machines that are under COMPUTER NUMERICAL CONTROL.

coacting group A sociological term for people who share the same GOAL but work towards it without communicating or interacting. In doing so they may be exhibiting PLURALISTIC IGNORANCE.

COBOL An acronym for Common Business Oriented Language. This is a SYSTEM of words and symbols used in business to instruct a COMPUTER in its TASK of INFORMATION PROCESSING. See COMPUTER LANGUAGE.

code of practice A set of guidelines outlining expected standards of behaviour by people working in an industry or a profession. Such a code is not legally binding and may, indeed, be adopted to forestall governmental regulation that would be so.

coefficient See CORRELATION COEFFICIENT.

coercion The use of POWER to get people to do something they would not otherwise do. Typical of AUTHORITARIAN MANAGEMENT.

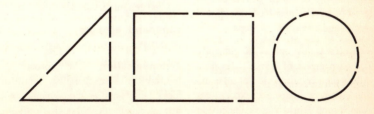

Figure 8 Closure.

coercive power   A form of POWER which denotes the ability of someone in an ORGANIZATION to punish others, for example, by demotion or the withholding of a salary increase. It is a kind of negative REWARD POWER and these two kinds of power are usually held by the same person.

cognition   A general term which includes all the psychological processes by which people become aware of, and gain knowledge about, the world.

cognitive dissonance   A theory developed in SOCIAL PSYCHOLOGY by the American psychologist LEON FESTINGER. The theory states that because we have a powerful DRIVE towards consistency (or consonance), if we hold two *psychologically* inconsistent COGNITIONS (beliefs, ATTITUDES, values or ideas) at the same time, or if our behaviour clashes with those cognitions, we will be in an unpleasant state of tension which we are strongly motivated to reduce. As the theory deals with psychological rather than logical inconsistency, it proposes that we are not so much concerned with actually *being* consistent as with *feeling that we are* consistent.

cognitive ergonomics   A form of ERGONOMICS in which factors of COGNITION are more important than physical factors.

cognitive map   A mental representation of the way in which a GOAL can be achieved or a problem solved, as opposed to a technique or a series of steps.

cohort effect   A cohort is generally defined as a group of people who have lived through a certain period of time and shared common historical experiences like the Second World War or the advent of personal computers. It is used in particular of people born in the same year. It is thought that cohorts born several decades apart, for instance, may be affected in systematically different ways by the different ZEITGEIST and social/environmental conditions of their times.

cold calling   A form of selling where the salesperson approaches a prospective customer – by telephone, post, e-mail or in person – with no prior contact being made.

collective bargaining   An INDUSTRIAL RELATIONS process in which employers or their representatives negotiate with employees or their (TRADE UNION) representatives on the level of wages and the conditions of EMPLOYMENT for a GROUP of employees as a whole, rather than for individuals.

colour blindness   A total or partial inability to distinguish colours. Total colour blindness is very rare but partial colour blindness (particularly the inability to distinguish red and green from each other or from grey) is surprisingly common. It has been estimated that about 8–10 per cent of males are born with this defect, though it is uncommon in females. This finding is of some relevance to ERGONOMICS.

command and control organization   An ORGANIZATION run on traditional lines by a relatively rigid and multi-layered HIERARCHY, with an emphasis on top-down COMMUNICATION of instructions to employees and centralized decision-making.

command economy   See PLANNED ECONOMY.

communication   The process of transmitting or exchanging information, ideas, beliefs and opinions, mainly by the use of language – though NON-VERBAL COMMUNICATION can also be important in certain situations. Transmission of information may be by FORMAL COMMUNICATION or INFORMAL COMMUNICATION. See also CHAIN OF COMMAND, COMMUNICATION NETWORK, INFORMATION TECHNOLOGY, INFORMATION THEORY and SOCIAL DISTANCE.

communication network A method, form or pattern of COMMUNICATION. The two most frequently studied types of networks are wheel-shaped and circle-shaped. (See Figure 9.) The wheel network facilitates quick and accurate communication but is less equipped to handle complexity and change. The circle network adapts well to complexity and change in COMMUNICATION and seems to involve and satisfy its members better. These networks are often discussed when a comparison is being made between a MECHANISTIC ORGANIZATION and an ORGANIC ORGANIZATION.

communication theory See INFORMATION THEORY.

communicator credibility In SOCIAL PSYCHOLOGY, this term describes the extent to which the communicator of a message is believable. It is thought to be related to whether the communicator is perceived as expert and trustworthy or not.

commuter marriage A marriage where the partners spend considerable time living apart because the work needs

of both cannot be fulfilled by living together all the time. It usually involves people sharing a family home, and perhaps being together at weekends, but working in different towns (or even countries).

Compact Disk Read Only Memory A CD ROM is a computer disk which contains data that can only be read, but not altered, by the user. It is either sold to the customer or leased to subscribers.

company town A town dominated by a single employer. Such towns are usually small, but there are exceptions. Washington DC is sometimes described as a company town, the 'company' in this case being the US government.

company union An employer's version of a TRADE UNION within a single ORGANIZATION. It does not have the independent STATUS or POWER to represent the employees in any INDUSTRIAL RELATIONS matters.

compatibility [1] People being able to work together. [2] Machines and units of TECHNOLOGY being able to work together.

compensation [1] Payment for injury, damage or loss. [2] The term is also used, particularly in the United States, for the remuneration of staff, including salary and FRINGE BENEFITS.

compensatory consumption A form of buying behaviour in which people of

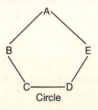

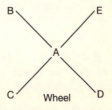

Figure 9 Communication network.

low SOCIO-ECONOMIC STATUS (SES), and having relatively little disposable income, may spend a much greater proportion of that income than people of high SES on luxury goods such as jewellery, clothing and electronic equipment in an attempt to compensate themselves *psychologically* for their material poverty.

competencies   A competence is the ABILITY required to do a given job. In MANAGEMENT, the term 'competencies' is often used to describe the set of disparate SKILLS that MANAGERS require, which are identified and fostered in TRAINING courses.

competition   The attempt to do better than others supplying goods and services in the same MARKET. Fostering competition is one of the basic principles of CAPITALISM, which was first formulated in the eighteenth century by ADAM SMITH.

competitive advantge   Anything that gives an ORGANIZATION an edge over the COMPETITION in its MARKET.

compliance   [1] In SOCIAL PSYCHOLOGY, this is a form of yielding to group pressure, where a change of behaviour is exhibited by someone but without any underlying change of ATTITUDE. [2] Obeying a statutory requirement or a legal obligation.

compressed hours   A way of organizing the working week into fewer working days, for example, a 40-hour week consisting of four 10-hour days rather than five 8-hour days. See also ANNUALIZED HOURS and FLEXIBLE WORKING HOURS.

comptroller   Traditional form of the term CONTROLLER, from the French verb *comptroller*, meaning 'to check off'.

compulsion   [1] An overwhelming UNCONSCIOUS need to engage in some

behaviour that is usually contrary to one's conscious wishes. [2] Being made to obey a statutory requirement or a legal obligation.

computer   An electronic machine for processing information automatically and very quickly. According to SOD'S LAW it is always 'down' when needed most.

computer-aided design   A process in which a designer interacts with a computer system to produce a design, from the original idea to the finished product, by electronic manipulation and the use of a VISUAL DISPLAY UNIT rather than pencil and paper. Closely associated with COMPUTER-AIDED MANUFACTURING.

computer-aided engineering   The process that links COMPUTER-AIDED DESIGN with COMPUTER-AIDED MANUFACTURING; for example, in the manufacture of tools or machines under COMPUTER NUMERICAL CONTROL.

computer-aided   manufacturing   COMPUTERIZATION of all the steps in the manufacture of a product.

computer-assisted instruction   A method of PROGRAMMED LEARNING in which a COMPUTER is used as a TEACHING MACHINE.

computer-based practice   A method of LEARNING in which the medium of instruction is the COMPUTER or COMPUTER TERMINAL.

computer-based training   A method of TRAINING in which the medium of instruction, with which the individual interacts, is the COMPUTER or COMPUTER TERMINAL rather than a human teacher.

computer-integrated manufacturing   The ultimate form of industrial AUTOMATION, in which every aspect of manufacturing, from the initial design to the delivery of the finished product, is both controlled and co-ordinated by COMPUTER.

computerization   The installation of COMPUTERS as part of a process of AUTOMATION.

computer language   A SYSTEM of words and symbols used to instruct a COMPUTER in its TASK of INFORMATION PROCESSING. The most popular computer language in business is COBOL; in science and TECHNOLOGY ALGOL and FORTRAN are commonly used. An introductory computer language that combines aspects of all three is called BASIC.

computer literacy   'The ABILITY to use COMPUTER LANGUAGE' is how this term used to be defined, but it is now commonly applied to people who simply know which buttons to press.

computer numerical control   The control of machines by COMPUTER using numerical information.

computer package   This refers to the SOFTWARE required for a particular application.

computer program   A set of instructions to a COMPUTER, written in a COMPUTER LANGUAGE, that tells it to perform a particular task. The spelling of 'program' is usually American, in recognition of the American MARKETING predominance in this field.

computer simulation   A SIMULATION exercise conducted by COMPUTER; for example, to produce the realistic experience of flying in the TRAINING of airline pilots.

computer terminal   A machine linked to a COMPUTER, however remote, and having access to all its data.

concept testing   A MARKETING research technique used in the early stages of NEW PRODUCT DEVELOPMENT. The idea or 'concept' of the product being considered is presented to samples of potential consumers for their reactions before a serious financial commitment is made to its development.

conditioning   A process of LEARNING in humans or animals, via an experimental procedure using REINFORCEMENT, where a given stimulus produces a response other than its normal, natural or automatic one. In the classical form developed by PAVLOV, a dog learned to salivate at the sound of a bell and not just when food was presented. B.F. SKINNER developed a procedure called *operant conditioning*, in which an animal's simple response could be used as the basis of TRAINING it to engage in very complex behaviour, like circus tricks. Humans can be trained to control bodily processes like blood pressure or brain waves in coping with STRESS, for example, by using similar techniques.

conflict   A situation in which there are mutually antagonistic interests, needs or motives involving individuals or groups. The most easily recognized indicator of conflict in a WORK ORGANIZATION is a STRIKE but a lot of conflict may be unspoken, or even UNCONSCIOUS, and is very difficult for organizations to handle.

conflict management   The conscious attempt to identify CONFLICT within an ORGANIZATION and deal with it in such a way that its potential for disruption is minimized.

conflict resolution   The conscious attempt to identify CONFLICT within an ORGANIZATION and to deal with it in such a way that it disappears. Much more ambitious, and much rarer, than CONFLICT MANAGEMENT.

conformity   The tendency to allow one's ATTITUDES, opinions, perceptions and behaviour to be influenced by others. This may be due to a deep-rooted TRAIT of someone's PERSONALITY or to the kind of group pressures that would lead most people to conform. This area is an important part of SOCIAL PSYCHOLOGY, to which leading contributions have been made by ASCH and MILGRAM, among others.

confrontation meeting   A meeting where employees are invited to be completely frank with the MANAGEMENT about their concerns. Used in assessing JOB SATISFACTION, but not too often.

Confucian Ethic   The basis for a SOCIAL SYSTEM, suggested by the fifth-century BC Chinese moral philosopher Confucius, which emphasizes the harmony of mutual loyalties and reciprocal duties among members of a society. Relationships between people should be governed by formal differences in STATUS. It is sometimes claimed that the Confucian Ethic has had as powerful an effect on the Asian world of work and MANAGEMENT as the PROTESTANT WORK ETHIC has had in the West.

conglomerate   A business ORGANIZATION, usually comprising a group of companies, with diverse and often unrelated financial interests but sometimes trading under the one name.

consensual validation   Checking one's perceptions of something with other people as a way of knowing whether what is being perceived is real or illusory. This is the psychological basis of the ASCH experiments on CONFORMITY.

conspicuous consumption   A form of buying behaviour in which a consumer lays claim to membership of the highest SOCIO-ECONOMIC STATUS group by displaying products commonly associated with that group, like driving a Rolls-Royce or ordering vintage champagne, regardless of her or his *actual* social and financial status. People who are particularly concerned to impress by using such STATUS SYMBOLS might even drive a *white* Rolls or order *Dom Perignon* by name.

constructive dismissal   The legal term for a situation in which an employee leaves an ORGANIZATION, apparently (or technically) of her or his own free will, but where in reality she or he has been forced out by the actions of the employer. See also UNFAIR DISMISSAL.

construct validity   The extent to which each item of a PSYCHOLOGICAL TEST measures or predicts what it is supposed to.

consultative committee   A committee in which representatives of employees in an ORGANIZATION meet regularly with the SENIOR MANAGEMENT, usually to discuss the welfare of the STAFF and the impact of policy decisions on them.

consumer awareness   The term used to describe the way in which people think of themselves in the role of consumers as opposed to other roles they might occupy, like those of voters or parents. This is the basis for the social phenomenon of CONSUMERISM.

consumer decision-making   The process by which people decide what goods and services to buy. A typical model of the stages in this process is illustrated in Figure 10.

consumer disposables   Another term for non-durable products which are FAST MOVING CONSUMER GOODS. Compare with CONSUMER DURABLES.

consumer durables   Relatively expensive and infrequently purchased products,

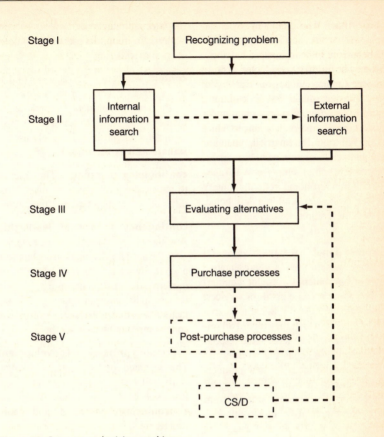

Stage I	Recognizing problem

Figure 10 Consumer decision-making.

like cars, furniture and laptop computers, which are expected to last for a
period of years. Compare with CONSUMER
DISPOSABLES.

consumer goods Goods for direct
consumption, like food, clothing and cars,
as opposed to things like machinery
and tools which are used to make other
goods. Traditionally, a distinction has
been made between CONSUMER DISPOS-
ABLES (like food) and CONSUMER DURABLES
(like cars), but this distinction is somewhat blurred by the effects of BUILT-IN
OBSOLESCENCE.

consumerism A movement that is
concerned with the interests of the consumer in the marketplace by trying to have
the safety, QUALITY and informational content of CONSUMER GOODS and services
improved. In its modern form it can be
traced back to the efforts of RALPH NADER
in the early 1960s to publicize serious
safety hazards in the manufacture of
American cars.

consumer life cycle effects The part
played in consumer behaviour by the
stage of life a person is at. For most people in a given society these effects will be

based on their age group, lifestyle and disposable income. The stages most commonly defined by marketers and advertisers are as follows: childhood; youth; bachelor (unmarried person under 35); newly married (under 35, no children); full nest I (married, youngest child under 6); full nest II (married, youngest child 6–12); full nest III (married, youngest child in teens); empty nest I (married, children left home); empty nest II (married, children left home, retired); solitary survivor (widow/er, children left home, still working); retired solitary survivor (as above, but retired).

consumer panel   A MARKET RESEARCH technique which uses a representative group of consumers to provide continuous data about specific goods or services. Respondents are usually asked to keep a weekly diary in which they record all relevant purchases. The views of the respondents about these goods and services and their response to ideas for new products are then discussed with them at regular intervals. This technique differs from SURVEY RESEARCH in being a continuous rather than a one-off source of data.

consumer psychology   The PSYCHOLOGY of an individual when acting as a consumer.

consumer satisfaction/dissatisfaction Since the 1970s, the study of what makes consumers satisfied or dissatisfied with the products they have bought has become a major focus of research. The key seems to lie in the comparison we make between what we *expected* the product to be like and the way we *actually* experienced it. The final stage in the process of CONSUMER DECISION-MAKING. (See Figure 11.)

consumer socialization   The specific aspect of SOCIALIZATION concerned with the way children learn how to be consumers. An important part of this process is CO-SHOPPING.

content analysis   The analysis of data to see what categories or themes emerge, or the analysis of data by prearranged theme or categories to test a HYPOTHESIS or make a diagnosis. It is widely used in MARKET RESEARCH.

contingency planning   The attempt to anticipate emergencies or unexpected difficulties that might arise in the future.

contingency theory of leadership Any theory of LEADERSHIP which emphasizes the need for flexibility in dealing with a given situation. The complexity of the modern ORGANIZATION means that effective leadership is contingent upon a great many factors: what may be successful in one context may not be so in another.

continuing professional development The repeated updating of knowledge, skills and techniques throughout a professional career. It is now becoming a requirement in more and more PROFESSIONS.

continuous improvement   See KAIZEN.

continuous process production   A manufacturing technique in which raw materials are fed in at one end of a process and finished products emerge at the other in one continuous uninterrupted flow – hence the alternative name FLOW PRODUCTION. The petrochemical and electricity industries are important users of this type of production. See also for comparison BATCH PRODUCTION and MASS PRODUCTION.

contracting out   [1] Hiring another person or ORGANIZATION to do part of the WORK. (Similar to SUBCONTRACTING.) [2] Refusing to join a TRADE UNION or pay

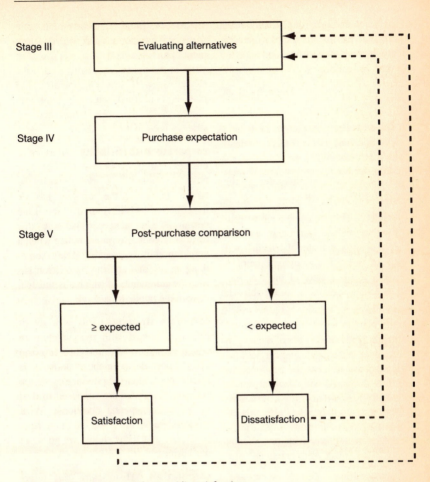

Figure 11 Consumer satisfaction/dissatisfaction.

a political contribution. [3] Leaving an employer's pension scheme for a private one.

control [1] In terms of ACCOUNTING, control refers to the process of checking actual financial PERFORMANCE against planned performance. [2] In general, the POWER to direct an ORGANIZATION.

controller The senior manager responsible for the finances of an ORGANIZATION.

convergent thinking Thinking along conventional lines in an attempt to find the best *single* answer to a problem, unlike DIVERGENT THINKING. See also LATERAL THINKING.

co-operative A group of producers or purchasers who set up a trading ORGANIZATION, the PROFIT from which is shared out among the members of the group.

co-opting Inviting someone to join an already established group because of some particular quality or SKILL, the need for which may not have been foreseen when the group was set up.

co-ordination   The process of integrating all the parts and functions of an ORGANIZATION.

coping strategy   A pattern of behaviour that someone uses repeatedly in dealing with perceived STRESS.

copy   In ADVERTISING this refers to the text of an advertisement.

copyright   The exclusive right to produce or reproduce particular written, musical or artistic material over a fixed period of time. The copyright belongs originally to the creator of the material, who normally assigns it to a publisher in exchange for a ROYALTY on each item sold.

core business   The key products and MARKETS at the heart of a company's operations.

core time   Under FLEXIBLE WORKING HOURS core time refers to those periods during which all employees must be present at the workplace. The rest of the working day is made up of FLEXIBLE TIME.

corporate culture   See ORGANIZATIONAL CULTURE.

corporate governance   The SYSTEM of accountability that a business ORGANIZATION has in dealing with the various sets of people that affect it, such as STAFF, customers, shareholders, suppliers and so on. The way this system is supposed to work is contained within the FORMAL ORGANIZATION; the way it actually works will be found in the INFORMAL ORGANIZATION.

corporate image   The impression of itself that an ORGANIZATION presents to the outside world.

corporate plan   A document that maps out the future work and development of an ORGANIZATION over a period of years in the light of its resources and the ENVIRONMENT in which it operates. The plan is concerned with the long-term objectives of the organization and the strategy used to achieve them.

corporate responsibility   Part of a business ORGANIZATION'S SYSTEM of CORPORATE GOVERNANCE deals with the responsibility that the company has for the effects of its behaviour on others. Like corporate governance in general, this invariably comes to public notice when a corporation is accused of doing something wrong and abusing its relationship with the community in which it is situated, or with the public in general.

corporate strategy   This is a set of issues concerned with the direction in which a business ORGANIZATION is going and its positioning in the MARKET. It is usually considered the province OF SENIOR MANAGEMENT, who are supposed to deal with the fundamental questions: 'What business are we in?', 'Are we in the right business?' and 'How should we go about our business?'

corporatism   Historically, this refers to the replacement of owners by professional managers in the running of companies. But the term is also widely used to describe collective action by employers' trade and industrial ORGANIZATIONS.

correlation   In STATISTICS, this refers to the relationship, or dependence, between two variables. It is measured by a statistic called a CORRELATION COEFFICIENT.

correlation coefficient   In STATISTICS, this is a measure (denoted by the letter r) of the extent to which two variables are correlated. It can range from zero

CORRELATION to perfect *positive* correlation ($r = 1.00$), where the variables are always associated in the same way, or perfect *negative* correlation ($r = -1.00$), where the variables are always associated but in different ways.

co-shopping When parents take their children shopping with them they act as ROLE MODELS for them in their earliest CONSUMER SOCIALIZATION. Co-shopping usually begins with mother and child, and with the ever-increasing participation of women in the world of paid employment this is a way in which mothers and children are spending an ever-increasing proportion of their time together.

cost–benefit analysis A technique for comparing all the costs (both tangible and intangible) of a particular course of action with the resulting benefits expected. It normally, therefore, includes social or environmental costs as well as financial ones.

cost centre A unit whose direct costs can be ascertained, and to which fixed costs can be allocated, in the pursuit of effective financial CONTROL. This unit may be a department, a place, a person or even a machine. Contrast with PROFIT CENTRE.

cost effectiveness A measure of the extent to which money has been effectively spent on something. It is found by seeing whether the benefits that have resulted could have been obtained with a lower expenditure. See also VALUE FOR MONEY.

cost leadership A low-cost strategy for acquiring COMPETITIVE ADVANTAGE in a product MARKET.

cost plus This is probably the most common form of PRICING policy, where a company would take as the basis for its price the cost (or an estimate of the cost) of producing the product or service in question before deciding on the PROFIT margin or the fee to add on.

counselling The act of listening to people with personal problems and giving them practical advice. It may happen informally at any level of an ORGANIZATION and, for example, is often done by a FOREMAN for his or her workers. In a more formal sense it is usually seen as a PERSONNEL function, where systematic counselling may be given by people, on either a STAFF or CONSULTANCY basis, with appropriate TRAINING in PSYCHOLOGY. This training would probably be based on one of the major theories of psychology, like BEHAVIOURISM or PSYCHOANALYSIS, or on the NON-DIRECTIVE THERAPY of HUMANISTIC PSYCHOLOGY.

country club management style Description of people on the MANAGERIAL GRID who score high for concern with people but low for PRODUCTION.

Coverdale training A form of SENSITIVITY TRAINING based on GROUP DYNAMICS developed in the United Kingdom by Ralph Coverdale. It emphasizes the performance of real group TASKS – as opposed to ROLE PLAYING – and is used in MANAGEMENT DEVELOPMENT to improve SOCIAL SKILLS and sharpen COGNITION. See also ACTION LEARNING.

CPA See CRITICAL PATH ANALYSIS.

CPD See CONTINUING PROFESSIONAL DEVELOPMENT.

creative accounting A form of ACCOUNTING in which the presentation of financial data is manipulated to the advantage of an ORGANIZATION in any way possible within the law (or not, as the case may be).

creative conflict   A form of CONFLICT RESOLUTION suggested by the American social worker Mary Parker Follett in the early years of the twentieth century. It advocates that opposing views should not be fudged, compromised or avoided, but that a bold attempt be made to examine them with a view to integrating them and moving forward in a way that is in everyone's interest. A very modern view in many ways.

creativity   The ABILITY to produce new ideas; for example, by using DIVERGENT THINKING or INSIGHT LEARNING.

credit squeeze   The governmental control of credit, aimed at making it more difficult and expensive to obtain, by imposing high interest rates, restrictions on hire purchase and bank lending, and similar measures. The GOAL is to damp down demand in order to reduce the risk of INFLATION.

crisis management   The form of MANAGEMENT adopted in an emergency or an exceptional situation which focuses all the resources of the ORGANIZATION on getting through a temporary period of difficulty, leaving more fundamental or longer-term issues aside. There is a great temptation for senior managers to allow this state of affairs to degenerate into MANAGEMENT BY CRISIS.

critical incident technique   A technique which analyses the impact of key incidents in past PERFORMANCE in order to improve future performance. It is used, for example, to study the safety of equipment in the workplace and in various aspects of MANAGEMENT EDUCATION and TRAINING. It can be used as the basis for an INTERVIEW during a SELECTION procedure, where inferences may be drawn from a candidate's behaviour during critical incidents in a previous job to his or her likely behaviour in a future job.

critical path analysis   A form of OPERATIONAL RESEARCH in which a project is represented by a diagram containing a time schedule for each of the different parts of the project. The 'critical path' through the diagram is then the arrangement of jobs on the project which will result in the project taking the shortest amount of time, and therefore incurring the least cost. This is a particularly important technique in the PLANNING of large construction projects such as roads and bridges.

critical success factors   The ADDED VALUE provided by a company's human and material resources which give it a COMPETITIVE ADVANTAGE in its field.

CRM   See CUSTOMER RELATIONSHIP MANAGEMENT.

cross-sectional research   The study of a relatively large and diverse set of people at a single point in time. Compare with LONGITUDINAL RESEARCH and see also COHORT EFFECT.

CS/D   See CONSUMER SATISFACTION/ DISSATISFACTION.

culture   In ANTHROPOLOGY, culture is usually defined as the shared beliefs, values, ATTITUDES and expectations about appropriate ways to behave that are held by the members of a social group. This term is also important in PSYCHOLOGY, where the *unquestioned* assumptions people share about the world, about the human condition, and about what is right, wrong or NORMAL are perhaps even more important. Both of these uses apply to an understanding of ORGANIZATIONAL CULTURE.

culture lag   The continued use of outmoded ways of doing things even after the introduction of more effective means of attaining the particular goals of a society, or of an ORGANIZATION. A social version of DECENTRING. See also PRODUCT LIFE CYCLE.

culture shock The feelings of dislocation and bewilderment that people may experience when they come into contact with a different society or CULTURE. This can even apply to a move from one ORGANIZATION to another, where the job in question may be similar but the way of doing it very different; for example, in a move from the PUBLIC SECTOR to the PRIVATE SECTOR, or vice versa.

curriculum vitae From the Latin meaning 'course of life'. A summary of a person's previous CAREER including work experience, qualifications, achievements and usually some basic BIOGRAPHIC DATA. It is used by employers in the RECRUITMENT and SELECTION of applicants for JOBS.

curve of forgetting A graphic representation of the rate at which the forgetting of learned material occurs. (See Figure 12.)

curvilinear relationship A relationship between two variables depicted graphically by a curve rather than a straight line. (See Figure 13.)

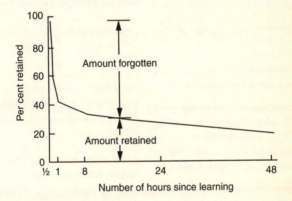

Figure 12 Curve of forgetting.

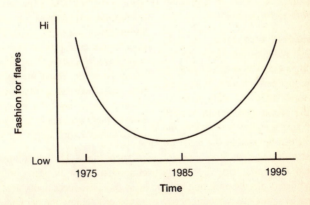

Figure 13 Curvilinear relationship (for changing fashions in flared trousers).

customer consciousness Awareness of a customer's needs with regard to a product or service.

customer–contractor principle A term used in the PUBLIC SECTOR to describe research commissioned or sponsored by a government department from a publicly funded research council. The research council is the contractor, or MIDDLEMAN, for the funds which it awards to professional researchers, and the government department is the end-user or customer for the research findings.

customer focus The idea that all ORGANIZATIONS, and particularly those in the ever-growing SERVICE SECTOR should be aware of their customers' identity and needs, whatever other strategy they might adopt.

customer intimacy What may result if companies adopt a CONSUMER FOCUS.

customer relationship management An attempt by an ORGANIZATION to retain its customers by fostering their PERCEPTION that they each have a relationship with it beyond the mere buying and selling of products.

customer service The development of specific policies and procedures to care for customers. This can range from empathizing with a customer's needs (see EMPATHY) to exhorting her or him to 'have a nice day'.

c.v. See CURRICULUM VITAE.

cybernetics From a Greek term meaning something like 'steersman', introduced in 1948 by Norbert Wiener, an American computer engineer. It is usually defined briefly as the study of regulatory mechanisms (like thermostats). Out of this field came the analogy of the brain as a COMPUTER and the MODEL of psychological processes as SYSTEMS of messages with their own built-in FEEDBACK.

cyberphobia An irrational fear of computers. A specialized form of TECHNOPHOBIA.

cycle time The time normally taken by a worker to perform a TASK. Usually the longer the cycle time the more responsible the task.

cyclical time Experiencing repeated events that occur at regular and predictable intervals; for example, in the work of a farmer or an ASSEMBLY LINE operator. Compare with LINEAR TIME.

D

DAT See DIFFERENTIAL APTITUDE TEST.

database A store of information, usually held in a COMPUTER, which is logically arranged for a certain use; for example, a list of people on a company's payroll or a list of its regular customers.

database marketing A form of MARKETING which makes use of a company's customer DATABASE to encourage further purchases. It would make use of information like name, address, telephone number, e-mail address, previous purchases, etc. in sending a personalized COMMUNICATION to each customer.

data processing There are manual, mechanical or ELECTRONIC DATA PROCESSING systems. By any of these means raw information, or data, may be *processed*; that is, collected, recorded, organized, analysed, and converted into a form where it may conveniently be used or stored.

Data Protection Act Legislation passed by the parliament of the United Kingdom in 1984 to regulate the information held by ORGANIZATIONS on individuals and to ensure its confidentiality.

day release An arrangement whereby an employee is given time off WORK (usually one day a week) without loss of pay, to further his or her education or TRAINING with formal study.

dead time A term used in PAYMENT-BY-RESULTS schemes and very similar to DOWNTIME. It refers to the time people spend waiting around during working hours before they can actually start a piece of work because, to take a common example, the COMPUTER is down.

decentralization The opposite process to CENTRALIZATION. One or other of these is invariably suggested as a cure for ORGANIZATIONAL PATHOLOGY.

decentring The process of continuing to perceive a situation in a way that changing circumstances have rendered ineffective. A psychological version of CULTURE LAG.

decision analysis One of three techniques suggested by PETER DRUCKER to help a WORK ORGANIZATION decide on its most appropriate ORGANIZATIONAL STRUCTURE. This technique is to establish what the key decisions to be made in the ORGANIZATION actually are as opposed to unquestioned *assumptions* about what they are. The other two techniques are ACTIVITIES ANALYSIS and RELATIONS ANALYSIS.

decision-maker Anyone charged with the formal responsibility for making decisions in an ORGANIZATION. The term is usually applied mainly to SENIOR MANAGEMENT people.

decision tree A kind of FLOW CHART used to summarize a possible sequence of decisions in which alternative choices are open at each stage and where each alternative is dependent on choices already made.

decoding In INFORMATION PROCESSING, this is the attempt, by the recipient, to make sense of a COMMUNICATION. Compare with ENCODING.

decoupling Reducing the friction between two conflicting groups by removing or reducing the amount of contact between them. In ORGANIZATIONS this may, however, result in duplicated effort.

deferred compensation Payment intended by an ORGANIZATION for its employees at some future date; for example, as pensions upon their RETIREMENT.

deindividuation Feelings of anonymity and being part of a crowd. A blurring of individual IDENTITY and a loosening of INHIBITIONS often follows. This is the psychological basis for any kind of mob behaviour.

delayed gratification In SOCIOLOGY, this term is used to describe the act of foregoing present satisfaction for the sake of greater satisfaction in the future; for example, saving money rather than spending it. It is supposed to be most typical of the middle classes in our type of society, who can afford to be more future-oriented.

delayering This euphemism for firing people is used specifically for removing entire levels or layers of MANAGEMENT (usually middle, sometimes junior, never senior) from an organizational HIERARCHY.

Delphi method A technique of FORECASTING, using a panel of experts in science and TECHNOLOGY to predict the likely future of a particular issue. Each member of the panel makes his or her own forecast and the different forecasts are assembled in a composite report, which is then sent round the panel for comment. This process is then usually repeated until a workable consensus on the likely future emerges. See also BRAINSTORMING and SCENARIO WRITING.

demand curve A graphic measure which is used in ECONOMICS to show how much of a certain product is likely to be bought at certain prices. A fall in price, for example, usually leads to a rise in demand. (See Figure 14.)

demarcation dispute In INDUSTRIAL RELATIONS this is a disagreement between TRADE UNIONS about the way in which work should be divided between different groups of workers, where each union claims the right to do certain types of work exclusively for its own members. With the decline in trade union

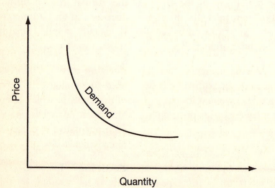

Figure 14 Demand curve.

membership since 1980 these disputes are now relatively rare.

Deming, W. Edwards (1900–93) An American engineer and statistician regarded as the founder of the 'QUALITY' movement. He worked for a time at the Hawthorne works, where ELTON MAYO conducted his famous studies. When he was invited to Japan in 1950, his lectures on QUALITY CONTROL had an enormous influence on Japanese industry. Japanese success in Western markets then awakened American interest in this kind of work.

democratic leadership A form of LEADERSHIP which tries to replace the usual focus on the leader in favour of a focus on the contributions of followers. In an ORGANIZATION this takes the form of DEMOCRATIC MANAGEMENT.

democratic management A type of MANAGEMENT which emphasizes the importance of consulting people about the work of the ORGANIZATION and involving STAFF at all levels in the process of making decisions. Usually contrasted with AUTHORITARIAN MANAGEMENT.

demographics A set of figures describing a POPULATION, both in general terms (like births, deaths and marriages) and in specific terms like the consumption of particular goods and services. DEMOGRAPHIC SEGMENTATION is widely used in MARKETING.

demographic segmentation A form of MARKET SEGMENTATION that deals with the ways of categorizing statistically all the inhabitants in a national population. The most important forms of segmentation for marketers are usually thought to be by age, sex and SOCIO-ECONOMIC STATUS.

denationalization The opposite of NATIONALIZATION. It involves the transfer of state-owned industries or services from the PUBLIC SECTOR to the PRIVATE SECTOR. This is also called PRIVATIZATION.

denial The EGO DEFENCE in which people simply refuse to accept either that a painful experience has occurred to them or the existence within themselves of an ANXIETY-provoking impulse.

depersonalization The loss of one's IDENTITY or SELF-IMAGE. In a business ORGANIZATION this occurs when people are treated like machines. It is often associated with the ASSEMBLY LINE, but is more a matter of MANAGEMENT philosophy than PRODUCTION technique as such.

depreciation In ACCOUNTING, this is a financial measure of the reduction in value of fixed capital ASSETS over time; for example, the wear and tear of equipment.

depression [1] In PSYCHOLOGY, this is one of the most common forms of emotional disturbance, which can vary in intensity from an everyday attack of the 'blues' to a seriously disturbed condition of paralysing hopelessness. It is characterized by ANXIETY, dejection and a general lowering of activity. There is a difference of opinion as to whether (or to what extent) the causes of depression are to be found in unconscious CONFLICT or in biochemical malfunctioning of the brain. [2] In ECONOMICS, depression also denotes a serious lowering of activity – in business – usually accompanied by high UNEMPLOYMENT and low industrial PRODUCTIVITY.

deprivation The lack of something considered essential to well-being, either psychological, social or material. See also SOCIAL DEPRIVATION.

depth interview An INTERVIEW in which an interviewer tries to get beyond the conscious responses of the interviewee to probe his or her UNCONSCIOUS feelings.

depth psychology The area of PSYCHOLOGY that studies the part the UNCONSCIOUS plays in human behaviour. See also DYNAMIC PSYCHOLOGY and FREUD.

descriptive statistics STATISTICS that summarize or describe a set of measurements; for example, MEASURES OF CENTRAL TENDENCY. Compare with INFERENTIAL STATISTICS.

deskilling Any process that reduces the amount of SKILL required for the PERFORMANCE of a job.

desk research A term used in MARKET RESEARCH to describe the gathering, collation and analysis of available data, as opposed to fieldwork, which generates fresh data. It is often used as the preliminary stage of a new project. It is the opposite of FIELD RESEARCH.

desktop publishing A feature of the ELECTRONIC OFFICE. A way of preparing documents that involves a MICROCOMPUTER with word processing, COMPUTER GRAPHICS and SOFTWARE which allows a combination of text and pictures to be assembled and displayed on a screen. The final HARD COPY is produced by a laser printer.

devaluation The reduction of the official rate at which the currency of a country is exchanged for other currencies, thereby lowering its value. It has the effect of making imported goods dearer and the country's own exports cheaper in overseas MARKETS.

deviance Behaviour that is different from the expected NORM of a society.

deviation Generally speaking, a departure from the NORM, whether social,

psychological or statistical. In STATISTICS, it refers to the difference of a given score from the MEAN.

Differential Aptitude Test This is actually a battery involving eight different tests of APTITUDES, like verbal reasoning and spatial relations. The test is used to assess educational and vocational PERFORMANCE.

differentials In INDUSTRIAL RELATIONS, this refers to the differences in levels of PAY between different categories of workers.

differentiation In ORGANIZATION THEORY, this term describes the tendency an ORGANIZATION has to set up specialized functions as a way of dealing with increasing complexity in its operations.

diffusion of new products The process by which innovations in goods and services spread throughout a society over time. Many such innovations appear but very few are commercially successful. This is a *macro-social* process, as compared to the *micro-social* process involved in the ADOPTION OF NEW PRODUCTS.

diffusion of responsibility In SOCIAL PSYCHOLOGY, this is the idea that taking responsibility for initiating action or offering help in an emergency is spread among the people present in the situation. Sometimes the responsibility is so diffuse that no action is taken by anybody. The term can also be used more generally about the diffusion of decision-making responsibility in the presence of other people in a given situation.

Dilbert Principle This was suggested by the American cartoonist Scott Adams and states that the most ineffective workers in a business ORGANIZATION are systematically moved to the place where they can do the least damage – MANAGEMENT.

Adams regards his idea as the natural successor to the PETER PRINCIPLE.

diminishing returns [1] In ECONOMICS, this is the point beyond which any additional input of resources will result in a less than proportionate increase in output. [2] This idea has been borrowed by PSYCHOLOGY, where it describes an improvement that gets progressively smaller with each succeeding increment. For example, it is used in the study of LEARNING and MEMORY, where, after a large gain at the beginning, extra practice begins to provide less and less gain.

directed interview See STRUCTURED INTERVIEW.

direct labour costs The costs associated with those members of the workforce directly involved in the PRODUCTION of goods and services. Compare with INDIRECT LABOUR COSTS.

direct mail advertising A form of BELOW THE LINE ADVERTISING where COMMUNICATIONS are sent directly to customers or potential customers by mail.

direct marketing A form of MARKETING where producers of goods and services deal directly with potential consumers rather than going through retail outlets. The media used for such marketing include the traditional MAIL ORDER and door-to-door selling and the more recent additions of local radio and television, telephone and online COMPUTERS.

direct taxation The TAXATION of individuals or ORGANIZATIONS on their INCOME or PROFITS; for example, income tax or capital gains tax. Tax due is paid directly to the government, unlike INDIRECT TAXATION.

discipline In PERSONNEL MANAGEMENT terms, this refers to the CONTROL necessary to do a particular job, whether externally imposed or self-imposed, and therefore the basic requirement of all members of a functioning WORK GROUP.

discontinuous innovation A situation in which a new product is introduced to the MARKET whose use requires some new form of behaviour by the consumer, behaviour that is 'discontinuous' from existing behaviour. This is the rarest form of innovation – usually the result of great technological discoveries – but the one with the greatest social and psychological impact. Examples include the telephone, car, radio, television, personal computer and microwave oven.

discrimination In PSYCHOLOGY, this is simply the ABILITY to perceive differences. In a social or political context 'difference' often comes to signify something to be feared or rejected; for example, something to discriminate *against*, like sex or colour. This kind of discrimination is usually illegal.

diseconomies of scale The disadvantages resulting for a large, as opposed to a small, scale of operation in an ORGANIZATION. They include difficulties of CO-ORDINATION, COMMUNICATION and adaptability to changing circumstances. Compare with ECONOMIES OF SCALE.

dispersion In STATISTICS, this term describes the concentration or the spread of scores in a FREQUENCY DISTRIBUTION. The most commonly used measure of dispersion is the STANDARD DEVIATION.

displacement In PSYCHOANALYSIS, this is an EGO DEFENCE which involves the UNCONSCIOUS shifting of feeling from its real object to another where it is less threatening to the EGO; for example, shouting at the television set rather than arguing with the boss.

distress   An unpleasant feeling of being weighed down, oppressed and constricted, which usually accompanies the experience of being under STRESS. It is often contrasted with EUSTRESS.

distributed practice   A technique of LEARNING in which the lessons or periods of PRACTICE are spread out as widely as the available time permits. This is a much more effective method of learning in most cases than MASSED PRACTICE, with which it is usually contrasted.

distribution   [1] In STATISTICS, this is the term for the arrangement of data in categories and their display in the form of a graph or table. [2] In ECONOMICS, it is the study of how wealth is spread through a POPULATION.

distributive bargaining   A form of COLLECTIVE BARGAINING in which the resources to be distributed are regarded as fixed and one side's gain is therefore the other side's loss, as in a ZERO-SUM GAME.

distributive justice   A situation in which everyone receives her or his just REWARD. Even though this situation frequently does not occur in real life, it has been suggested in PSYCHOLOGY that people need to operate on the basis that it does; that is, on the basis of a JUST-WORLD HYPOTHESIS.

divergent thinking   Creative and original thinking that deviates from the obvious and the conventional to produce several possible solutions to a particular problem. Usually contrasted with CONVERGENT THINKING. See also LATERAL THINKING.

diversification   The extension of an ORGANIZATION's activities or products beyond its existing range into new areas.

divisional organization   This is literally the division of an ORGANIZATION into sub-units. These may take the form of a FUNCTIONAL ORGANIZATION (finance, MARKETING, PRODUCTION and so on) or separate business units co-ordinated by SENIOR MANAGEMENT at the centre of the organization.

division of labour   In ECONOMICS, this is a concept introduced by ADAM SMITH in the eighteenth century. It involves breaking down the work of a business ORGANIZATION into a series of TASKS or operations which allows SPECIALIZATION by workers in one area of activity. See also ASSEMBLY LINE and BUREAUCRACY.

dog   One of the MARKETING situations in the BOSTON MATRIX. It is characterized by both low growth and low market share. A dog is a product which a company needs to divest itself of as soon as possible.

domestic labour   Unpaid labour that is performed in the home, the vast majority of it by women (even those in full-time paid EMPLOYMENT outside the home).

dominance   The term used of a strong need to CONTROL, or to be more important than, other people.

double-entry bookkeeping   The normal method of BOOKKEEPING or ACCOUNTING in an ORGANIZATION, where total credits equal total debits because every transaction is recorded twice, as a credit to one account and a debit to another.

double-loop learning   Central to the concept of ORGANIZATIONAL LEARNING as pioneered, notably, by CHRIS ARGYRIS. It involves not only learning from previous behaviour (i.e. SINGLE-LOOP LEARNING) but also a critical examination of the assumptions underlying that behaviour. This is often described as 'learning how to learn' and is regarded as crucial in situations of rapid change, with the high levels of uncertainty and unpredictability which accompany them. See also TOLERANCE FOR AMBIGUITY.

double time A form of OVERTIME working in which time worked is paid at twice the normal rate. See also TIME-AND-A-HALF.

downsizing A euphemism for REDUNDANCY. See also RIGHTSIZING.

downstream integration See VERTICAL INTEGRATION.

downtime Any period of time during which no work can be done for reasons beyond the CONTROL of the workforce; for example, machine failure or bad weather. The term overlaps with DEAD TIME.

downward communication Any COMMUNICATION from SENIOR MANAGEMENT to lower levels of employees within an ORGANIZATION. Compare with HORIZONTAL COMMUNICATION and UPWARD COMMUNICATION.

drive A general term for a strong urge in an animal or a person, including those urges that are sometimes referred to as instinctive. See also MOTIVATION.

drive reduction The weakening of a DRIVE in an animal or human, usually as a result of the appropriate needs being satisfied.

Drucker, Peter (1909–) An American expert on MANAGEMENT who popularized the concept of MANAGEMENT BY OBJECTIVES and introduced the techniques OF ACTIVITIES ANALYSIS, DECISION ANALYSIS and RELATIONS ANALYSIS to the study of ORGANIZATIONAL BEHAVIOUR. Widely regarded as the original management guru.

duopoly A MARKET in which only two firms compete or which is dominated by two firms. See also MONOPOLY and OLIGOPOLY.

dyad In SOCIOLOGY, this is a way of referring to a two-person group.

dynamic psychology The term applied to those aspects of PSYCHOLOGY that are concerned with MOTIVATION and with understanding the causes of behaviour in all its ramifications. PSYCHOANALYSIS and psychoanalytically influenced areas of psychology are the prime, but not the only, examples of dynamic psychology. GESTALT psychology would also qualify, for instance.

dynamic strategic planning This is a recent American development of SYSTEMS ANALYSIS: *Dynamic* refers to the uncertainty of the world and therefore the need for flexibility. Strategic refers to the need for a long-term outlook. *Planning* refers to the MANAGER's continued need for coherent guidelines.

dysfunctional Anything that disturbs the normal FUNCTIONAL operations of an ORGANIZATION. It is also used more widely to mean a way of doing things that does not work.

E

EAP See EMPLOYEE ASSISTANCE PROGRAMME.

early adopters Consumers who follow the earliest innovators in the ADOPTION OF NEW PRODUCTS.

early retirement The procedure whereby an employee opts for RETIREMENT before the usual retiral age, usually with an enhanced pension. If it happens as a result of DELAYERING or DOWNSIZING or any other form of REDUNDANCY, the element of choice for the employee may be more apparent than real.

e-business Any business linking suppliers and consumers which is conducted electronically, that is, by computer using the INTERNET. It is a form of DIRECT MARKETING.

echo chamber effect The insulating effect of hearing only one's own ideas coming back from other people. Can afflict SENIOR MANAGEMENT without their being aware of it. One symptom of CEO DISEASE.

e-commerce See E-BUSINESS.

econometrics The branch of ECONOMICS that deals with the mathematical or statistical relationships between economic variables.

economic determinism The concept that one's place in the economy, or even what one does for a living, determines one's views of society and politics. This concept is usually traced back to KARL MARX.

economic man An invention of economists to support the belief that the MOTIVATION of workers depends solely on rational, financial REWARD and punishment. The beauty of the invention is that it saves them from thinking about the effects of complicated things like GROUP NORMS or UNCONSCIOUS MOTIVATION.

economics A SOCIAL SCIENCE that concentrates on the PRODUCTION, DISTRIBUTION and consumption of wealth, and of goods and services, as well as the individual and social behaviour involved in these processes. It is therefore concerned with issues like the working of the MARKET, PRICING, business confidence, economic growth, INFLATION and UNEMPLOYMENT.

economies of scale The advantages resulting from a large, as opposed to a small, scale of operation in an ORGANIZATION. They include lower unit costs, greater purchasing power by buying in bulk, opportunities for TRAINING and so on. Compare with DISECONOMIES OF SCALE.

EDP See ELECTRONIC DATA PROCESSING.

efficacy A term sometimes used in PSYCHOLOGY to describe how effective a person feels in influencing matters of importance to him or her.

ego Latin for the 'I', the conscious awareness of oneself (of one's SELF). According to FREUD the ego is that part of the PERSONALITY closest to external reality, which holds the ring between the UNCONSCIOUS drives of the pleasure seeking ID on the one hand and the internalized restrictions of the SUPEREGO on the other. Neurosis, in Freud's view, is thus the result of the ego being unable to maintain harmonious relations with the id and superego because the POWER of their unconscious drives is too much for it to cope with.

ego defence   In PSYCHOANALYSIS, this is a term for the ways in which the EGO protects itself from the threatening UNCONSCIOUS ideas of the ID or the SUPER-EGO, or from external dangers in the ENVIRONMENT. See also DENIAL, PROJECTION, RATIONALIZATION, REGRESSION, REPRESSION, SELF-KNOWLEDGE and SUBLIMATION.

80 : 20 rule   See PARETO ANALYSIS.

e-learning   A form of E-BUSINESS where the supplier is an educational institution and the consumer is a student. Has increased greatly in popularity, since the 1990s, among students of business.

electronic brainstorming   BRAINSTORMING by electronic COMMUNICATION rather than sitting round the same table.

electronic data processing   Any kind of collection, manipulation or analysis of data that makes use of a COMPUTER.

electronic mail   The SYSTEM of transmitting COMMUNICATIONS electronically between individual COMPUTER TERMINALS or within networks of such terminals. It includes the FACSIMILE TRANSMISSION of HARD COPY.

electronic office   A term used to describe an (ideal) office which has taken maximum advantage of COMPUTERIZATION and the latest developments in office AUTOMATION and INFORMATION TECHNOLOGY. Such an office would exhibit the following features, among others: DESKTOP PUBLISHING, ELECTRONIC MAIL, FACSIMILE TRANSMISSION, MICROCOMPUTERS, PERSONAL COMPUTERS, TELECONFERENCING, TELEWORKING and WORDPROCESSORS.

electronic point of sale   The modern form of the cash register. A piece of electronic technology which records a great deal of information automatically when a sale is registered, such as the product, price, time, operative, method of payment, etc.

e-mail   See ELECTRONIC MAIL.

emergent change   A recent approach to ORGANIZATIONAL CHANGE which is sceptical about the effectiveness of *planned* change. In particular, evaluations of the 'one-size-fits-all' or 'recipe' approach of planned change seem to suggest it is inadequate for extremely complex organizations which have to operate in volatile, unstable and uncertain environments. The conceptual core of the emergent approach are the two popular and interlinked ideas of institutionalizing *continuous improvement* in their work by all staff (known to the Japanese for many years as KAIZEN) and the development of a *learning culture* in the organization.

emotional intelligence   The ability to identify and monitor one's own and others' feelings and emotions, to discriminate among them, and to use this information to guide one's thinking and actions. It is meant to be contrasted with the COGNITION which makes up the traditional content of INTELLIGENCE and INTELLIGENCE TESTS.

emotional labour   Managing one's emotions so as to present a particular face to the customer on behalf of the organization, as salesmen or air stewardesses do. Of increasing prevalence with the growth of the SERVICE SECTOR, especially in jobs done by women.

empire-building   Seeking the aggrandizement of oneself or of one's ROLE in an ORGANIZATION by the pursuit of greater CONTROL or POWER, without regard to the needs of other people or of the organization as a whole. Can end in CEO DISEASE.

employee assistance programme A form of confidential help for people suffering from STRESS at WORK, or particular symptoms of it like alcohol or drug abuse.

employee ownership A situation in which the people who work for an ORGANIZATION own some, or even all, of its shares. Figures vary from country to country, but most employees own no shares at all in the organization for which they work. See also EMPLOYEE SHARE OWNERSHIP PLAN.

employee profile Following a JOB ANALYSIS, this is a descriptive list of the background, experience and ABILITY considered necessary for the PERFORMANCE of the job.

employee share ownership plan A loan scheme to help employees buy some or all of the shares in their company. See also EMPLOYEE OWNERSHIP.

employers' association An ORGANIZATION of employers within an industry or an economy. It is the organization which engages with TRADE UNIONS by representing its members in COLLECTIVE BARGAINING and matters of EMPLOYMENT, as well as lobbying on behalf of its members' interests with government and regulatory bodies.

employment Working for someone else in a job which is usually paid and part of an ORGANIZATION. See also SELF-EMPLOYMENT and UNEMPLOYMENT.

empowerment Being given the POWER to do something. This is a term used especially of TRANSFORMATIONAL LEADERSHIP. It denotes the kind of DELEGATION in which subordinates 'own' the task they have been entrusted with and accept full responsibility for it, being inspired to extend themselves by the force of the vision and commitment they are shown rather than by any kind of COERCION. This is particularly important if a company wants to become a LEARNING ORGANIZATION.

encoding In INFORMATION PROCESSING, this is the attempt, by the sender, to convert information into a form which can be stored, processed and then DECODED.

encounter group A form of PSYCHOTHERAPY which is conducted in a GROUP rather than with an individual. It has been adapted for use in MANAGEMENT TRAINING generally, where people are encouraged to express their emotions and to hear how other people perceive them. The technique may also be used more specifically in ASSERTIVENESS TRAINING.

endogenous variables Factors (usually of change) that occur within an ORGANIZATION and therefore, at least in theory, within the CONTROL of MANAGEMENT. The term may also be used with reference to a given national economy. Contrast with EXOGENOUS VARIABLES.

engineering psychology An American term for ERGONOMICS.

enterprise [1] The willingness to try new initiatives and to accept responsibility and risks. [2] A synonym for a business.

enterprise culture A social or company climate that celebrates ENTERPRISE and the ENTREPRENEUR.

entrepreneur A person who risks his or her judgement – and often CAPITAL – in a search for PROFIT from new business opportunities. Such a person is considered to have a high NEED FOR ACHIEVEMENT. Having a critical mass of such people is considered essential to the successful working of CAPITALISM.

entropy In INFORMATION THEORY, this is technically an indication of the lack of

ORGANIZATION in a SYSTEM, or the degree of openness in the message being conveyed. For example, if a message begins 'the cat . . .' there is a vast number of possible ways in which it can be completed, and entropy is therefore high. But if the message reads 'the cat sat on the mat in front of a warm . . .' it is already highly organized or structured and there is very little choice about the next word. Entropy is therefore low.

entry barrier Any impediment that prevents or hinders a new competitor from entering a MARKET. This can be anything from lack of trained employees to government tariffs or the existence of a price-fixing CARTEL.

environment All the external surroundings of an individual or an ORGANIZATION that affects him or her in some way. See also ERGONOMICS.

environmental audit A survey of all the ways in which the activities of an ORGANIZATION affect its environment, often as part of a COST–BENEFIT ANALYSIS. It is particularly concerned with identifying (and possibly correcting) negative factors like pollution, wastage of energy and resources, etc.

EPOS See ELECTRONIC POINT OF SALE.

EQ Stands for 'Emotional Quotient'. A measure of EMOTIONAL INTELLIGENCE.

equal opportunities A situation in which access to EMPLOYMENT, PROMOTION, TRAINING and other aspects of work is available to individuals regardless of non-work-related personal factors like age, colour or sex.

equity [1] Receiving the same pay as other people doing the same job (a crucial aspect of MOTIVATION). [2] The ordinary shares in a company.

equity theory A theory of MOTIVATION that is concerned with our sense of fairness and justice about the way we and others are treated at work in terms of the ratio of *inputs* (like experience, qualifications and effort) to *outcomes* (like pay, promotion and status).

ergonomics The study of the interaction between people and the ENVIRONMENT in which they work, and in particular their relationship to machines and equipment. It draws most heavily on PSYCHOLOGY as well as on engineering, anatomy, physiology and other sciences. The field owes a great deal to the early twentieth-century pioneers like FRANK GILBRETH and F.W. TAYLOR.

ESOP See EMPLOYEE SHARE OWNERSHIP PLAN.

ethical investment The policy of investing money in companies whose activities one approves of on ethical grounds. In practice, this usually means *avoiding* companies one *disapproves* of. For most ethical investors these are companies involved in alcohol, animal abuse, environmental degradation, pollution, pornography and tobacco, and those that have poor INDUSTRIAL RELATIONS with their employees.

ethnocentrism The tendency to regard the groups one identifies with, and especially one's *ethnic* group, as superior to any other. It involves the inability to step outside the perceptual framework of one's own group and see life from the viewpoint of a different group of people.

Etzioni Model A contribution to ORGANIZATIONAL THEORY by the American sociologist Arnitai Etzioni, who classified organizations in terms of the kind of POWER or AUTHORITY they used. The typology includes *coercive* (e.g. prisons), *utilitarian* (e.g. business), *normative* (e.g. colleges) and a *mixed* category.

euro   The common European currency, and successor to the ECU, which came into general circulation in the year 2002 among those countries which had signed up for economic and monetary union.

European Union   An alliance of European countries based on the Treaty of Rome (1958) which established a Common MARKET with an integrated economic policy and the aspiration for greater social and political integration. Originally six countries, there are now fifteen and many more countries from Central and Eastern Europe (and beyond) are due to join in the next few years.

eustress   A term sometimes given to the only positive aspect of stress, a feeling of stimulation and excitement that can sometimes result in enhanced performance, at least in the short term. The prefix 'eu' is from the Greek for 'good', which gives the term a bit of class. It is usually contrasted with DISTRESS.

evaluation research   The systematic study of the effects and effectiveness of a research, TRAINING or intervention programme.

exchange economy   A simple economy where goods and services are bartered directly rather than through the medium of cash or credit. This may take place in either a pre-cash economy or in the BLACK or GREY segments of our own INFORMAL ECONOMY, where it may use an alternative trading medium like LETS.

exchange rate   The rate at which one country's currency can be exchanged for another's.

executive   [1] An individual with the AUTHORITY to take decisions in an ORGANIZATION. [2] The people responsible for implementing the decisions of a legislature.

executive search   The process of looking systematically for supposedly talented EXECUTIVES and offering them an INCENTIVE to move to another ORGANIZATION. See also HEAD-HUNTING.

executive washroom   An American term for the lavatory used exclusively by SENIOR MANAGEMENT. The term is used metaphorically to distinguish the people with high status in an ORGANIZATION from the rest. Having the key to the executive washroom is a STATUS SYMBOL.

exercise   [1] The use of an attribute like AUTHORITY or POWER. [2] An activity used in TRAINING to analyse or develop a particular SKILL.

ex gratia payment   Payment made as a gift or favour and not in fulfilment of a contract or legal obligation. From the Latin for 'out of grace'.

exit interview   An INTERVIEW with an employee who is leaving an ORGANIZATION to find out that person's reason for leaving and his or her perception of the ORGANIZATION.

exogenous variables   Factors (usually of change) that occur outside an ORGANIZATION, and therefore beyond the direct control of MANAGEMENT. The term may also be used with reference to a given national economy. Contrast with ENDOGENOUS VARIABLES.

expectancy theory of motivation   A way of looking at the relationship between MOTIVATION and the PERFORMANCE of a JOB. It suggests that people behave in accordance with the expected outcome of their performance and the value they place on that outcome. Thus people would be motivated to produce more only if they expected that their increased performance would lead to greater satisfaction for them.

expert power   This form of POWER in an ORGANIZATION depends on the possession of knowledge and SKILLS that other people, particularly at the top of the organization value highly, for example, in areas like accounting, finance, law, science and technology.

expert systems   The COMPUTERIZATION of human knowledge, experience and SKILL in a particular field; for example, banking or medicine. This is a central concern of research in ARTIFICIAL INTELLIGENCE.

external validity   The extent to which a psychological test or research finding is valid when applied to everyday life.

extranet   An information site derived from the INTERNET which belongs to a given ORGANIZATION and can be accessed externally by a password. Now widely used in DIRECT MARKETING. Compare with INTRANET.

extraversion   According to the Swiss psychoanalyst Carl Gustav Jung this is a basic PERSONALITY dimension of openness and outward-looking sociability. It is usually contrasted with INTROVERSION.

extrinsic motivation   Doing something for reasons of REWARD or punishment external to the activity itself; for example, staying in a boring job because you need the money to pay the mortgage. Usually contrasted with INTRINSIC MOTIVATION.

extroversion   More properly EXTRAVERSION.

eye–hand span   In ERGONOMICS, this is a measure of how far the eye is ahead of the hands in the PERFORMANCE of some manual TASK. It is tested experimentally by suddenly darkening the room and recording how much of the task the subject continues to perform. It is used, for example, in designing keyboards and equipment for sorting letters in the post office.

eye–voice span   In ERGONOMICS, this is a measure of how far the eye is ahead of the voice in reading out loud. This is tested experimentally by suddenly darkening the room and recording how many words the subject continues to say. It is used in measuring reading SKILLS and in the ASSESSMENT of reading problems.

F

face saving   See FACEWORK.

face-to-face group   A term used in SOCIAL PSYCHOLOGY, particularly in GROUP DYNAMICS. It describes a small group of people in close enough physical proximity for each person in the group to interact directly with each of the others. Such a group will usually contain no more than six to eight people.

face validity   The extent to which a PSYCHOLOGICAL TEST or other procedure appears relevant to the variable it is dealing with. It is also used more loosely in PSYCHOLOGY in the sense of 'having credibility'.

facework   In SOCIAL PSYCHOLOGY, this term is sometimes used to describe social rituals that save 'face' or enhance a public image at the expense of honest emotion.

facsimile transmission   The process of transferring material electronically from one location to another by use of a TELECOMMUNICATIONS network. The image is converted into electronic data, which when received is converted back into the original image on paper. Any form of document may be sent or received in this fashion.

factor analysis   A technique used in STATISTICS for analysing complex CORRELATIONS of scores and tracing the factors underlying these correlations.

fad surfing   Riding the crest of each new MANAGEMENT wave the tide brings in, preferably without getting your feet wet and having to change.

family life cycle   A series of stages used in MARKETING to categorize the different situations an individual consumer may go through in the course of a lifetime. The most commonly used such series is as follows.

- *Bachelor*: unmarried person under 35
- *Newly married*: under 35, no children
- *Full nest I*: married, youngest child under 6
- *Full nest II*: married, youngest child 6–12
- *Full nest III*: married, youngest child in teens
- *Empty nest I*: married, children left home
- *Empty nest II*: married, children left home, retired
- *Solitary survivor*: widow(er), children left home, still working
- *Retired solitary survivor*: as above, but retired.

fast-moving consumer goods   A term used in MARKETING and MARKET RESEARCH to describe relatively small products that have a quick turnover in a retail outlet. Supermarkets and chemists are among the most common examples of such outlets.

fatigue   In ERGONOMICS, this is a term that includes both the subjective feeling of tiredness that a worker may report and the objectively observed decrease in his or her level of PERFORMANCE of a TASK. The issue of finding the most efficient and effective SYSTEM of work and rest periods is of particular importance in matters of safety; for example, with airline pilots or junior hospital doctors.

FAX   See FACSIMILE TRANSMISSION.

Fayol, Henri (1841–1925) A French pioneer of ORGANIZATIONAL THEORY and MANAGEMENT, who set out the structural principles of FORMAL ORGANIZATION. The CHIEF EXECUTIVE OFFICER of a mining company himself, he was mainly interested in SENIOR MANAGEMENT. He believed that general principles of management could be found that were relevant to all kinds of ORGANIZATION and which could be used in MANAGEMENT TRAINING. Fayol is responsible for introducing the concepts of CHAIN OF COMMAND, JOB DESCRIPTION, MANAGEMENT AUDIT, ORGANIZATION CHART and SPAN OF CONTROL.

fear of failure A fear that is aroused when someone feels pressured to achieve something. It is particularly prevalent in people with a high NEED FOR ACHIEVEMENT.

fear of success Mainly used to describe the MOTIVATION in some women to avoid doing well and achieving success (especially in competition with men) because their SOCIALIZATION has led them to perceive such behaviour as unfeminine.

featherbedding [1] A restrictive labour practice where more STAFF are employed than is necessary for the work to be done. [2] An economic ENVIRONMENT which provides companies with easy PROFITS; for example, because of the way tax is regulated. [3] The subsidizing of an unprofitable industry by government.

feedback A term borrowed from CYBERNETICS, where it refers to the direct relationship of the input of a SYSTEM to its output. The concept of a return flow of output information which can be used to regulate future input is now widely used in PROGRAMMED LEARNING and the development of TEACHING MACHINES.

Festinger, Leon (1919–89) A leading American contributor to SOCIAL PSYCHOLOGY, best known for his theory of COGNITIVE DISSONANCE.

field research An important part of MARKET RESEARCH. It involves the collection of data about products or ADVERTISING from actual or potential customers, usually by means of INTERVIEW or QUESTIONNAIRE. The opposite of DESK RESEARCH.

field theory In its best-known form, the GESTALT school of PSYCHOLOGY argued that, in the functioning of the brain and in the behaviour of humankind and the higher animals, the whole is greater than the sum of all its parts; that the brain could be understood better as a total *field* than as a collection of nerve cells; and that the cause of a particular piece of behaviour lies in the totality of a field of interacting elements rather than in the most obvious stimulus. In its social applications, field theory is closely associated with the work of KURT LEWIN.

FIFO See FIRST IN, FIRST OUT.

Fifth Discipline An idea introduced by the American MANAGEMENT specialist Peter Senge in 1990. In Senge's words 'it is the cornerstone of the LEARNING ORGANIZATION' and it requires the use of five basic disciplines or 'component technologies'. These are: [1] systems thinking, [2] personal mastery, [3] mental models, [4] building shared vision and [5] team learning.

fifth generation computer The new generation COMPUTER, which uses STATE-OF-THE-ART technology in design and applications. It is expected to have a more sophisticated MAN–MACHINE INTERFACE – thus making computers more USER FRIENDLY – and new SOFTWARE, incorporating principles of ARTIFICIAL INTELLIGENCE intended to help computers approximate more closely in their operations to human COGNITION.

filtering   The process of screening out certain stimuli from the ENVIRONMENT, such as dust or heat or glaring light. The term is used in PSYCHOLOGY as a metaphor for the way we filter out those sensory stimuli not needed for us to make sense out of our PERCEPTION of the environment.

financial management   Any action taken by an ORGANIZATION to manage the funds it has at its disposal. Deals particularly with the generation of capital and revenue and the control of costs. See also BUDGET and COST–BENEFIT ANALYSIS.

financial year   The twelve months chosen by an ORGANIZATION as its ACCOUNTING PERIOD.

first in, first out   [1] A method of valuing stock or taking INVENTORY in a business ORGANIZATION, where the prices of the oldest items purchased are applied to the entire stock. Items received first are the first to be sold. [2] A method of choosing people for REDUNDANCY in an organization where the first to be hired are also the first to be made redundant.

first-in strategy   A business strategy which seeks COMPETITIVE ADVANTAGE by being first into a new MARKET. See FIRST-MOVER ADVANTAGE.

first-line supervisor   The supervisor responsible for the MANAGEMENT of PRODUCTION workers on the SHOP FLOOR. The term refers to anyone at the level above CHARGEHAND and is most often synonymous with the term FOREMAN. The first step in the management HIERARCHY of a business ORGANIZATION.

first-mover advantage   The supposed competitive advantage of being the first company to enter a new MARKET because of the unique link made in the minds of consumers between the company and the goods or services it offers. In some markets, first-mover may really be an advantage and in others it may not, with later-movers learning from the mistakes made by their predecessors and acquiring a LATE-MOVER ADVANTAGE. Something like this seems to have happened with E-BUSINESS.

fixed pie myth   An American version of a ZERO-SUM GAME that does not in fact exist in a given situation.

flat organization   An ORGANIZATION with relatively few levels in its HIERARCHY. An oft-quoted example is the Catholic church, a global organization with only five levels from parish priest to pope. Compare with TALL ORGANIZATION.

flexible firm   A company that follows a model of 'flexibility' in dealing with its employees. This has three aspects: [1] *functional* – the division of employees into essential core workers and the peripheral remainder; [2] *numerical* – varying the number of employees as and when required; [3] *financial* – varying pay and fringe benefits with supply and demand in the labour market.

flexible time   Under a system of FLEXIBLE WORKING HOURS, flexible time refers to those periods during which an employee may choose whether to be at work or not, in contrast to CORE TIME, when attendance is mandatory.

flexible working hours   A method of organizing working hours which has no fixed starting or finishing times and which allows people some latitude in deciding when they will work, provided their daily, weekly or monthly total of hours worked is that contracted for. The working day is divided into CORE TIME and FLEXIBLE TIME. Extra hours worked within a given period may be credited to the next period or given as time off.

flexitime Popular term for FLEXIBLE WORKING HOURS.

float [1] To launch a new company. [2] A small amount of cash used for expenses or in making change. [3] To allow a currency to find its own EXCHANGE RATE in the MARKET, as opposed to maintaining a particular rate by CENTRAL BANK intervention. [4] Used in NETWORK ANALYSIS to denote the amount of time that can be added to a given activity without extending the total time of the whole project.

floppy A small magnetic disk inserted into a COMPUTER or WORD PROCESSOR and used for the storage of data. It is called 'floppy' to distinguish it from a hard disk, which is a permanent fixture with a much higher storage capacity.

flow chart A diagram showing all the parts of a SYSTEM or the stages in a process, and the interrelationships between them; for example, a map of the London Underground or a plan of a self-assembly wardrobe.

flow production See CONTINUOUS PROCESS PRODUCTION.

fmcg An acronym for FAST-MOVING CONSUMER GOODS.

followership A research focus that began in the 1980s on why people follow leaders as an attempt to overcome dissatisfaction with existing theories of LEADERSHIP that concentrated largely on leaders and their behaviour.

Ford, Henry (1863–1947) The founder of the Ford Motor Company, who is celebrated in the study of MANAGEMENT for inventing the ASSEMBLY LINE form of manufacturing in 1913.

Fordism An ideology named after HENRY FORD, who first put the principles of SCIENTIFIC MANAGEMENT into action on his ASSEMBLY LINE.

forecasting A series of techniques for trying to predict the future on the basis of known data, usually with regard to the economy or some aspect of it like sales, demand or the need for MANPOWER PLANNING. Sometimes a QUALITATIVE METHODOLOGY like the DELPHI METHOD may be used, but more often a QUANTITATIVE METHODOLOGY is used employing a mathematical or statistical technique like REGRESSION analysis. See also MODEL and OPERATIONAL RESEARCH.

foreman A FIRST-LINE SUPERVISOR responsible for a group of workers on the SHOP FLOOR. Usually one level above CHARGEHAND.

formal communication Any COMMUNICATION between people through the official channels of an ORGANIZATION, following the official procedure. Usually contrasted with INFORMAL COMMUNICATION.

formal group A group set up by the MANAGEMENT of an ORGANIZATION with a written mandate and a well-defined purpose. Usually compared with an INFORMAL GROUP.

formal organization The 'face' of an ORGANIZATION, as exhibited in its brochure, annual report, rule book, ORGANIZATION CHART and so forth. It represents the official structure of the organization and the way it is *supposed* to function. Compare with INFORMAL ORGANIZATION.

forming A term sometimes applied to the initial stage of group formation within an ORGANIZATION. The individuals concerned are intent on finding out what they can about each other (and making a good impression) and do not yet see themselves as a distinct group. See also STORMING, NORMING and PERFORMING.

form letter   A standard letter used for repetitive kinds of correspondence, such as rejection slips from publishers.

FORTRAN (Formula Translation)   A SYSTEM of words and symbols used in science and TECHNOLOGY to instruct a COMPUTER in its TASK of INFORMATION PROCESSING. See COMPUTER LANGUAGE.

four P's of marketing   See MARKETING MIX.

framing effect   A psychological effect based on human COGNITION in which we make judgements based on the cognitive framework within which a situation or proposition is put to us. Putting such a proposition to us on behalf of a client is the mainstay of ADVERTISING. For example, a statement like 'nine out of ten lager drinkers prefer Plonker' sounds impressive at first hearing but begs some important questions, like 'prefers it to what? Bleach?' Or 'how were these intrepid lager drinkers chosen?' and 'were they paid for their views?' and so on.

free enterprise system   An ideal of CAPITALISM in which supply and demand are the only influences on the MARKET and government intervention is minimal, or even less.

free market   The kind of MARKET that would exist under a FREE ENTERPRISE SYSTEM.

frequency distribution   In STATISTICS, this is a tabulation of the number of times something occurs in a body of data.

Freud, Sigmund (1856–1939)   A Viennese neurologist and psychologist. Freud's work may be divided into three areas: his invention of PSYCHOANALYSIS as a therapeutic technique, his theory of PERSONALITY (EGO, ID and SUPEREGO), and his social philosophy. While each of Freud's ideas is still hotly debated, few people would dispute his enormous and widespread influence in making the twentieth century more aware than any previous age of the POWER of the irrational and the UNCONSCIOUS in human affairs.

fringe benefit   A REWARD beyond the basic PAY for the job. Examples can range from subsidized meals and travel to pensions, holidays and sickness benefits.

functional   Referring to a specialized aspect or function of an ORGANIZATION, like PERSONNEL or MARKETING. Often used more broadly in the sense of something in the organization that is working efficiently.

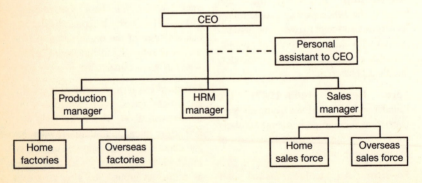

Figure 15 Functional organization.

functional authority The AUTHORITY that is associated with a particular job.

functional organization A form of ORGANIZATIONAL STRUCTURE in which specialists carry out their own particular function in an ORGANIZATION (like RESEARCH AND DEVELOPMENT or QUALITY CONTROL) but without any AUTHORITY over people in LINE MANAGEMENT. (See Figure 15.)

fundamental attribution error The tendency to make an erroneous attribution about the causes of someone's behaviour by overestimating the effects of her or his personal characteristics and underestimating those of the social ENVIRONMENT.

future shock A term introduced by the American writer Alvin Toffler in the 1970s to denote the growing difficulty many people have in our society of coping with, and adapting to, what he considered to be an increasingly rapid pace of social change.

G

gain–loss theory of interpersonal attraction An attempt in SOCIAL PSYCHOLOGY to formulate a theory that takes account of changes in people's liking for each other. It suggests that increases or decreases in the rewarding behaviour we receive from another person has more effect on us than a constant level of liking or disliking. Thus we like best someone who starts out negatively in our estimation and becomes more positive, and we like least a person who starts out positive and becomes negative.

gainsharing A form of PAYMENT BY RESULTS, like the SCANLON PLAN, where employees are paid extra for increasing productivity or decreasing costs. It can thus be used in either commercial or non-profit ORGANIZATIONS.

Gallup poll The first and the best-known QUESTIONNAIRE technique for the mass SAMPLING of public opinion. It was developed by the American social scientist George Gallup.

game theory A mathematical appr-oach to the study of CONFLICT and decision-making which treats conflict situations as though they were games, with set tactics and strategies and totally rational players. Some of the simpler situations studied, like the PRISONER'S DILEMMA, have been of interest to people in SOCIAL PSYCHOLOGY looking for a MODEL that would generate ideas about social behaviour.

Gantt chart A type of BAR CHART developed by HENRY GANTT which is widely used in the PLANNING and CONTROL of PRODUCTION. The chart depicts the progress of a project over time in terms of scheduled PERFORMANCE as compared to actual performance. (See Figure 16.)

Gantt, Henry (1861–1919) An American engineer, and colleague of F.W. TAYLOR, who was a pioneer of MAN-AGEMENT CONSULTANCY and developed the GANTT CHART, emphasized the importance of employees as HUMAN RESOURCES in an ORGANIZATION and the need to understand their MOTIVATION. He also urged that more social responsibility be shown by business to society.

garbage in, garbage out A slogan coined by American operatives in the COMPUTER industry, but widely adopted outside it, implying that the QUALITY of the output from a SYSTEM depends upon the quality of the input to it.

GAS See GENERAL ADAPTATION SYNDROME.

gatekeeper [1] In SOCIOLOGY, this term is used for someone with the POWER to decide who will join a select group. [2] In ORGANIZATIONAL THEORY, the term is used for someone with the power to decide what information will flow into or out of an ORGANIZATION.

Gaussian curve The BELL-SHAPED CURVE of a NORMAL DISTRIBUTION, named in honour of the nineteenth-century German mathematician K.F. Gauss.

GDP See GROSS DOMESTIC PRODUCT.

gender roles See SEX ROLES.

general adaptation syndrome The body's non-specific response to STRESS that consists of three stages: the *alarm*

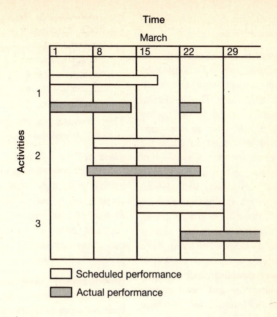

Figure 16 Gantt chart.

reaction, when the body responds with the heightened physiological reactivity of the 'fight or flight' response to meet the demands of the STRESSOR; *resistance*, when the body tries to cope with the stressor and outwardly appears to have returned to normal but inwardly is releasing high levels of stress hormones; and *exhaustion*, where resources are depleted and the body's defence against disease and illness is decreased.

generalized other   According to the American sociologist G.H. Mead, this is the concept an individual has of how other people expect her or him to behave in a given situation. Compare this with SIGNIFICANT OTHER.

general manager   The MANAGER responsible for the whole range of ADMINISTRATION in an ORGANIZATION and not just a specific function within it.

generic   Having a general application to a group or class of things rather than to a specific individual. [1] It is widely used in MARKETING and examples can include the ADVERTISING of materials like wool, or the sale of non-branded products like eggs, or in reference to a class of product like wine. [2] In HUMAN RESOURCE MANAGEMENT, it can refer to a class of SKILL such as accountancy, law or computing which is not job-specific and can be transferred from one employer to another.

genotype   An individual's genetically inherited potential. Usually contrasted with PHENOTYPE.

gentleman's agreement   A verbal contract which is not legally binding and depends for its implementation on the sense of honour of the 'gentlemen' involved. In practice, this kind of agreement often works as well as, if not better than, the written kind. A good example of this is the diamond business.

geodemographic segmentation   As the name suggests, this is a combination of GEOGRAPHIC SEGMENTATION and DEMO-GRAPHIC SEGMENTATION. This particular market segment is based on the finding that consumers who live in the same neighbourhood will tend to have the same SOCIO-ECONOMIC STATUS and each of the factors making up this status (income, education and occupation) will also be similar. Thus, people in a particular neigh-bourhood will often have similar needs, wants and preferences and a similar amount of money to spend on them. It is a way of identifying ready-made clusters of households with similar lifestyles and pat-terns of consumption, and therefore pro-vides a useful tool for marketers who have clearly identified and detailed targets.

geographic segmentation   A form of MARKET SEGMENTATION where the market is segmented by location on the assump-tion that consumers living in a particular location will have similar needs, wants and preferences, and that these will differ systematically from those of consumers living in other locations. It has been argued that the process of GLOBALIZATION and the worldwide MARKETING of famous brands like Microsoft and Coca-Cola has reduced the importance of this form of segmentation outside of a particular national market.

gestalt   A German word meaning a form, a configuration or a whole, which has properties that are more than just the sum of its parts; for example, the way the brain organizes dots of light into visual patterns, or musical notes into melodies. See also CLOSURE.

GIGO   An acronym for GARBAGE IN, GARBAGE OUT.

Gilbreth, Frank (1868–1924)   An American MANAGEMENT scientist who pioneered TIME-AND-MOTION STUDY and contributed generally to the SCIENTIFIC MANAGEMENT movement. Gilbreth was an engineer and worked with his wife Lillian, a psychologist, on many projects. They invented, among other things, the SIMO CHART and the THERBLIG.

glass ceiling   A real though invisible barrier that may be present in an ORGANI-ZATION preventing women from rising above a certain level in the organizational HIERARCHY. Its origin lies in the ATTI-TUDES of the men who run the organiza-tion about the idea of women being in positions of AUTHORITY.

globalization   The process of ever-increasing worldwide integration of cul-tures, societies and, especially, economies. This process has been made possible by high-speed electronic COMMUNICATIONS and has led to a global marketplace in goods, services and CAPITAL as well as the emergence of a global workforce.

GNP   See GROSS NATIONAL PRODUCT.

goal setting   A term used in the theory of MOTIVATION. It has been found that the PERFORMANCE of a TASK is aided if people agree to accept specific GOALS for them-selves which are stretching but attainable.

gofer   An office junior, one of whose duties is to go for ('gofer') things and run errands.

golden handcuffs   A financial induce-ment to an employee to stay, which is so favourable that he or she would find it difficult to leave the ORGANIZATION.

golden handshake   A relatively large sum of money given in the form of SEV-ERANCE PAY for a departure that is usually ahead of normal RETIREMENT or comes at the end of a contract.

golden hello   A relatively large payment made to an individual as an inducement to leave one ORGANIZATION and come to another.

golden parachute   [1] An American GOLDEN HANDSHAKE. [2] A relatively large sum paid to the directors of the losing company in a TAKE-OVER bid should they suffer REDUNDANCY. No such provision is made for any other employees.

goodwill   Any INTANGIBLE ASSET of a business, which includes its reputation, the LOYALTY of its employees or customers, its location, and so on.

go-slow   A form of INDUSTRIAL ACTION, short of a STRIKE, where workers do not withdraw their labour but instead slow down the rate at which the work is done, usually by meticulously following the rule book. See also WORK-TO-RULE.

graphology   The study of handwriting in an attempt to gain a quick insight into someone's PERSONALITY. Often used (or misused) in business as a kind of 'quick and dirty' PROJECTIVE TECHNIQUE, especially in the SELECTION of new staff.

graveyard shift   In SHIFT WORK practice this is a colloquial term for the night shift.

great man theory   The idea that the course of events is influenced at crucial times by the actions of outstanding men, often because of their CHARISMA. As a way of understanding history it is a gross oversimplification. Despite this, it is still popular in the study of LEADERSHIP and the place of leadership within the functioning of an ORGANIZATION.

green audit   See ENVIRONMENTAL AUDIT.

greenfield site   A location for a new commercial or industrial development on which there is no existing or previous development. Originally, these locations were, and sometimes still are, green fields on the outskirts of urban areas. A move to such a site is often accompanied by new forms of INDUSTRIAL RELATIONS practices that attempt to overcome traditional confrontations between MANAGEMENT and TRADE UNIONS.

green pound/dollar   A term used to describe consumer spending on products identified as environmentally friendly.

greenwash   Similar to 'whitewash' when applied to a company's PUBLIC RELATIONS efforts to obtain credit for ethical or environmentally friendly policies when in fact it is conducting business as usual.

grey economy   Part of the INFORMAL ECONOMY. Unlike the BLACK ECONOMY, WORK in the grey economy is unpaid. It consists of work done within households or communities. Usually, this takes the form of an informal arrangement between family, friends or neighbours, but in some places it may be more systematically organized; for example, in the form of LETS. It has been estimated that work done in the grey economy accounts for over half of all work done in the FORMAL and INFORMAL ECONOMIES combined.

grey market   A term sometimes used to describe the MARKET SEGMENTATION by age that identifies older consumers (usually over the age of fifty) as a separate group.

grey pound/dollar   A term used to describe consumer spending on products identified as being particularly appropriate to elderly people, or simply the total consumer spend of elderly people.

grid training   See MANAGERIAL GRID.

grievance procedure   In INDUSTRIAL RELATIONS, this is a series of arrangements for settling grievances that employees have against their employers, either directly or between their MANAGEMENT and TRADE UNION representatives.

gross domestic product   In ECONOMICS, this is the total value of all business activity (all goods and services produced) within a country's economy over a given period of time. See also GROSS NATIONAL PRODUCT.

gross national product   In ECONOMICS, this is the value of the GROSS DOMESTIC PRODUCT plus the value to a country's residents of all foreign investments.

group cohesiveness   In SOCIAL PSYCHOLOGY, this term refers to the tendency of a group to maintain itself in the face of external threats or pressures, based on the attraction the group has for each of its members, which acts as a binding force.

group dynamics   In SOCIAL PSYCHOLOGY, this term refers to the study of the way people behave in a GROUP, especially a small FACE-TO-FACE GROUP. This field is closely associated with the pioneering work of KURT LEWIN.

grouping   In STATISTICS, this is the process of combining individual scores into categories or putting them in RANK ORDER; for example, as PERCENTILES.

group mind   A hypothetical entity (see HYPOTHESIS), sometimes given mystical qualities, which has been suggested as the agency for crowds acting in unison. It is a way of saying we don't understand very much about crowd behaviour.

group norm   Behaviour expected of all the members of a group. In a WORK GROUP the HAWTHORNE STUDIES discovered that this can mean an individual

keeping to the same level of PRODUCTIVITY as the other group members, regardless of MANAGEMENT instructions or INCENTIVES. See also NORM.

group polarization   The tendency of a group to become more extreme in its decision-making than its individual members. Thus, cautious individuals will spark an even more CAUTIOUS SHIFT and risk-taking individuals a more RISKY SHIFT.

group process   A term used to describe the interactions within a group and the changes that occur over time in the relationships between its members. See also ENCOUNTER GROUP and T-GROUP.

group selection methods   Techniques of SELECTION which aim to assess the ABILITY of individuals to work with other people in a group. They usually involve the observation of a group of candidates in a discussion or a problem-solving situation.

group structure   The way in which a group is designed and organized. It forms the framework for the GROUP PROCESS and for the PERFORMANCE of the group's TASK. Especially important in this context is the COMMUNICATION NETWORK within the ORGANIZATION.

group therapy   A form of PSYCHOTHERAPY which involves several people at the same time. The assumption here is that people can benefit from the experiences and companionship of other people, as well as experiencing the GROUP PROCESS itself.

groupthink   The English writer George Orwell's term for the totalitarian imposition of authorized thoughts on all the members of a society. The term has been introduced into SOCIAL PSYCHOLOGY by the American scientist Irving Janis, where it is sometimes used to describe the way that members of a very cohesive group can become so preoccupied with maintaining a group consensus of thought that their critical faculties become dulled – sometimes to the point of making a catastrophic decision. Contrast with SYNERGY. See also CONSENSUAL VALIDATION.

group training methods   These are TRAINING techniques which use the properties of a group to help individual members learn. The point of the training may be to have the members learn from each other's expertise in tackling a particular problem together, or the point of the group might be the GROUP PROCESS from which the members would be encouraged to learn about themselves and how they are perceived by others, as well as about group behaviour in general. See also COVERDALE TRAINING, ENCOUNTER GROUP, SENSITIVITY TRAINING and T-GROUP.

group working   An attempt to increase JOB SATISFACTION (as well as PRODUCTIVITY), especially among ASSEMBLY-LINE workers, by forming individuals into a coherent WORK GROUP and allowing them more autonomy over, and responsibility for, their work than they would have as a series of individuals. This process often involves JOB RESTRUCTURING of individual jobs.

growth   [1] In ECONOMICS, this is the expansion of a business ORGANIZATION or the economy in general. The rate of growth in the latter is usually measured by the rate of change in the GROSS DOMESTIC PRODUCT. [2] In PSYCHOLOGY, the term refers to an increase in maturity as shown by evidence of intellectual or emotional development.

growth needs   An important aspect of theories of MOTIVATION, especially that of ABRAHAM MASLOW. After the basic physiological needs in his HIERARCHY OF NEEDS have been met the psychological or growth needs can potentially be satisfied.

H

habit A learned response to a given situation which occurs in such a regular fashion that it appears to be virtually automatic. Thus, it may at times be mistaken for innate behaviour and considered an instinct.

habituation In PSYCHOLOGY, this refers to a decreasing response to a stimulus as it becomes more familiar through repeated presentation. With reference to drug use, habituation is the condition, resulting from repeated use of a drug, where there is a psychological, though not a physical, dependence on the drug but with little or no desire to increase the dose; for example, the two-Martini lunch as opposed to ALCOHOLISM.

hacking Unauthorized breaking into the DATABASE of a COMPUTER.

hall test In MARKET RESEARCH, this is the technique of asking people their opinions of the ADVERTISING, packaging and presentation of a product (originally done on the spot in a supermarket 'hall').

halo effect In SOCIAL PSYCHOLOGY, this refers to the tendency to generalize in judging a person from just one characteristic (usually positive) to a total impression. Compare with HORN EFFECT.

handbook A book of instructions on how to operate some machine or procedure. In a more academic sense it is used of a survey of a particular field that is intended to be authoritative and comprehensive.

hard copy A copy on paper, often in the form of print-out, of data stored electronically in a COMPUTER or WORD PROCESSOR.

hard currency A national currency used in international trade because it has a stable or rising EXCHANGE RATE and is generally accepted as being easily convertible into other currencies; for example, the American dollar or Swiss franc.

hard sell A colloquial term for the aggressive ADVERTISING, MARKETING, PROMOTION and SELLING of a product.

hardware The physical components of electronic and mechanical equipment that make up a COMPUTER; for example, the disk drives, keyboard, printer, VISUAL DISPLAY UNIT and so on. These components must be in place before any SOFTWARE can be added to the SYSTEM.

Hawthorne effect The finding in INDUSTRIAL PSYCHOLOGY that paying attention to people at work improves their PERFORMANCE. Part of the series of HAWTHORNE STUDIES done at the Hawthorne works of the Western Electric Company in Illinois between 1927 and 1932. Various attempts were made to improve workers' conditions, including changes in lighting, rest breaks, hours of work and methods of payment. Each of these changes resulted in an increase in PRODUCTIVITY, and so did a return to the original conditions of work. The investigators concluded that the changes in the external ENVIRONMENT had not influenced the workers' PERFORMANCE as much as had their PERCEPTION that the MANAGEMENT of the ORGANIZATION was interested in them and their work. This is an example of SOCIAL FACILITATION.

Hawthorne studies A series of investigations carried out at the Hawthorne plant of the Western Electric Company in Illinois between 1927 and 1932, under the direction of ELTON MAYO, which marked a turning point in the history of INDUSTRIAL PSYCHOLOGY. The scale of the research was vast – in one phase over 20,000 employees were interviewed – and it explored various aspects of the way in which the employees regarded their work, their colleagues and their supervisors. Apart from the HAWTHORNE EFFECT, one other major finding that attracted great attention was that a WORK GROUP could set its own rate of PRODUCTION regardless of external financial INCENTIVES offered by MANAGEMENT to the group or to the individuals in it.

head-hunting The process of looking systematically for talented people and offering them an INCENTIVE to move to another ORGANIZATION. A more general form of EXECUTIVE SEARCH.

health and safety at work An area of work subject to a great deal of detailed legislation in most industrialized countries because of the importance of labour to PRODUCTIVITY.

hearing loss The degeneration of an individual's hearing ability. Apart from physical damage or disease it can be caused by prolonged exposure to NOISE. Legislation on HEALTH AND SAFETY AT WORK has reduced the serious risk of hearing loss in HEAVY INDUSTRY, though there are still dangers there and in LIGHT INDUSTRY, and even in daily life. (See Figure 17.)

heavy industry The term applied to traditional industries, like steelmaking, coalmining and shipbuilding, which were the basis of Western INDUSTRIALIZATION in the nineteenth century and have always required heavy physical labour. Compare with LIGHT INDUSTRY.

hedonism In PSYCHOLOGY, this refers to the idea that all our behaviour stems

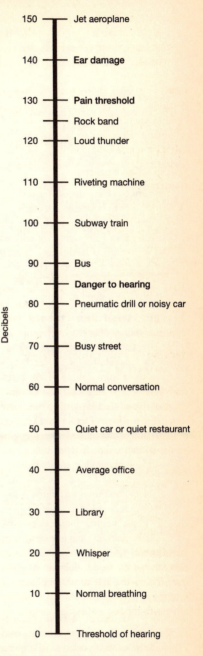

Figure 17 Hearing loss and the loudness of some familiar sounds.

from the MOTIVATION to pursue pleasure and avoid pain; in philosophy, the doctrine that it is our ethical duty to do so. The one does not, of course, imply the other.

helicopter factor   A term sometimes used in the study of LEADERSHIP to describe the ABILITY to rise above the immediate situation one is in, get a broader perspective on it, and see how it relates to the ORGANIZATION in general.

herd instinct   Used as a description of the way people in business will often follow a trend simply because other people in their PEER GROUP are doing so, without thinking it through or having any rational reasons for their behaviour. The indiscriminate buying of INTERNET stocks in the late 1990s is a good example.

Herzberg two-factor theory   An influential theory of MOTIVATION proposed in the late 1950s by Fred Herzberg, an American psychologist. Herzberg's theory resulted from a study of JOB SATISFACTION in which he found that satisfaction and dissatisfaction with WORK were caused by different factors. Satisfaction resulted from 'motivators' like recognition and increased responsibility, but dissatisfaction resulted from the working ENVIRONMENT itself and factors like poor physical conditions or relatively low PAY. Herzberg referred to these as 'hygiene factors'. Thus, neither interesting work nor a good working environment was sufficient by itself – though each was necessary – to ensure job satisfaction. Herzberg's work led to an emphasis on JOB ENRICHMENT schemes.

heuristic   An idea or method of teaching that stimulates further thinking and discovery. Now widely used to describe a rule of thumb for making a decision. See also ALGORITHM.

hidden agenda   Things which are not listed on the formal agenda of a meeting but which influence the meeting none the less. These may be unspoken (or even UNCONSCIOUS) ATTITUDES that individuals hold on the subjects under discussion, or they may form a quite conscious attempt at manipulating the meeting on behalf of the hidden agenda of an individual or group interest.

hierarchical task analysis   A form of TASK ANALYSIS used in assessing TRAINING needs, which describes a TASK in terms of a HIERARCHY of the operations necessary for its PERFORMANCE, ranging from the broadest down to the most detailed.

hierarchy   [1] Any ORGANIZATIONAL STRUCTURE containing different levels of AUTHORITY, and often responsibility. [2] Any arrangement of things in succeeding levels, each one subsuming all preceding levels.

hierarchy of needs   A theory of MOTIVATION proposed by the American psychologist ABRAHAM MASLOW in the 1940s. He suggested there were five distinct levels of human need arranged in a HIERARCHY (see Figure 18), starting with the basic physiological needs for food and shelter. As one level of need is satisfied another is reached, until by the fifth level the individual is concerned with the need for SELF-ACTUALIZATION.

histogram   In STATISTICS, this is a form of BAR CHART on which a FREQUENCY DISTRIBUTION can be represented graphically. (See Figure 19.)

homeostasis   A physiological term for the maintenance of balance or equilibrium within a complex SYSTEM like the human body, or its subsystems like temperature and oxygen level. See also SERVOMECHANISM.

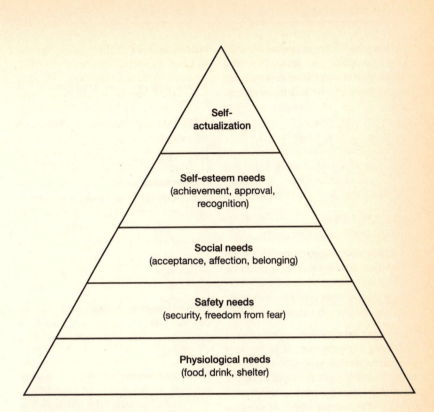

Figure 18 Maslow's hierarchy of needs.

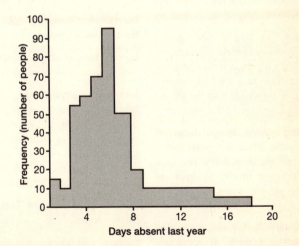

Figure 19 Histogram.

home-worker   A person who works for an ORGANIZATION at home. This form of working was very common at one time but declined markedly with the twentieth-century growth of BUREAUCRACY. But with the development of the ELECTRONIC OFFICE, and a trend towards DECENTRALIZATION, home working is increasing again both as a way of making a living and as a way of cutting down on commuting to the office. See also NETWORKING.

homo economicus   The Latin ancestor of the modern ECONOMIC MAN.

horizontal communication   Any COMMUNICATION between people at the same level of the HIERARCHY in an ORGANIZATION. Compare with DOWNWARD COMMUNICATION and UPWARD COMMUNICATION.

horizontal integration   The process whereby a company extends its business interests into other geographical areas of the same (or a similar) MARKET. This is usually accomplished by some form of MERGER with, or TAKE-OVER of, another firm in the same business, though sometimes a company is able to extend its PRODUCTION of goods and services by itself. Compare with VERTICAL INTEGRATION.

horn effect   In SOCIAL PSYCHOLOGY, this is the tendency to make a generalization in judging a person from one negative characteristic to a total impression. (The 'horn' is associated with the Devil.) This is a negative form of HALO EFFECT.

hot desking   A system used in ORGANIZATIONS whose STAFF are often away from headquarters. Instead of having their own office space in the headquarters building, people will use whatever desk and equipment is available when needed.

house journal   A magazine or newsletter, produced for members of an ORGANIZATION and other interested parties, containing news of the organization and its STAFF.

house organ   An American HOUSE JOURNAL.

HRM   See   HUMAN   RESOURCE MANAGEMENT.

HTA   See HIERARCHICAL TASK ANALYSIS.

human asset accounting   An attempt to measure the value to an ORGANIZATION of its HUMAN RESOURCES by treating them as ASSETS as well as costs to the organization and assessing, for example, RECRUITMENT and TRAINING policies and funding in this light. Associated with the work of the American psychologist RENSIS LIKERT.

human capital   That part of an ORGANIZATION'S CAPITAL represented by the ABILITY, experience and SKILL of its workforce.

human communication   [1] Simply referring to the process of COMMUNICATION between people. [2] A relatively new field of study involving contributions from COMPUTER science, linguistics, logic, PSYCHOLOGY and SOCIAL SCIENCE.

human engineering   An American term for ERGONOMICS.

human factors engineering   Another American term for ERGONOMICS.

humanistic psychology   A school of PSYCHOLOGY which emphasizes the positive qualities that differentiate human beings most from other animals, particularly creativity, play and psychological growth in general. LIKERT, MASLOW and MCGREGOR are among its proponents.

human performance factors   Still another American term for ERGONOMICS.

human relations   An approach to ORGANIZATIONAL THEORY that arose in the

1930s in opposition to the SCIENTIFIC MANAGEMENT school. The human relations approach was greatly influenced by the HAWTHORNE STUDIES and the other work of ELTON MAYO, and later by KURT LEWIN and DOUGLAS MCGREGOR. It emphasizes the importance of MORALE in an ORGANIZATION and the need for good working relationships between MANAGEMENT and the people managed, in the quest for organizational effectiveness and high PRODUCTIVITY.

human resource accounting See HUMAN ASSET ACCOUNTING.

human resource management The responsibility for making the best use of an ORGANIZATION's employees. One of the major functions of PERSONNEL MANAGEMENT.

human resource planning See MANPOWER PLANNING.

human resources All the people who work for an ORGANIZATION in any capacity.

hurry sickness The classic disease of a TYPE A PERSONALITY.

hypertext A technique for linking INFORMATION SYSTEMS, which is used on the INTERNET. The term itself means 'over text' and implies that a given text contains links to other texts. Its use on the Internet dates from 1992 when the British COMPUTER scientist Tim Berners-Lee produced a BROWSER which linked the user with the sources of information available. Essentially, this transformed what had previously been an academic network into the generally accessible WORLD WIDE WEB.

hypothesis An explanation which has been put forward to account for observed data, but which has still to be tested.

I

id From the Latin word for 'it'. According to FREUD the id houses the deepest unconscious drives, which are most in touch with the biological nature of the body, and is one of the three main aspects of the PERSONALITY. The id is dominated by the 'pleasure principle' and causes problems for the EGO when its drives are blocked. See also SUPEREGO.

identification In general terms, this implies recognizing the IDENTITY or nature of someone or something. In PSYCHO-ANALYSIS, it refers to the phenomenon of emulating the behaviour of a person with whom one has a powerful emotional bond.

identity Having essentially unchanging characteristics. When applied to an individual it is usually considered to be the basic content of someone's PERSONALITY, especially his or her SELF-IMAGE.

identity crisis The acute feeling that one's IDENTITY and sense of SELF have lost their normal stability and continuity over time, leaving one disoriented and having difficulty in recognizing oneself.

ideology In SOCIOLOGY, this term refers to a SYSTEM of beliefs that embodies the values of a large group of people. The espousal of the ideology by the group members helps to strengthen the GROUP COHESIVENESS; for example, businesspeople having the ideology of the FREE ENTERPRISE SYSTEM.

idiographic An approach to the study of human behaviour that emphasizes the uniqueness of the individual rather than general laws or principles. Contrast with NOMOTHETIC.

IKBS See INTELLIGENT KNOWLEDGE-BASED SYSTEM.

illumination In ERGONOMICS, the provision of appropriate lighting in the workplace is a very important aspect of HEALTH AND SAFETY AT WORK.

impersonality A form of MANAGEMENT that is mechanical in its approach and lacks the personal involvement of a HUMAN RELATIONS emphasis.

implicit personality theory In PSYCHOLOGY, this refers to the unquestioned assumptions an individual uses in thinking about the PERSONALITY of another person. More specifically the term refers to the characteristics that tend to be associated with each other in judging someone's personality. For instance, '*warm*' usually goes with 'outgoing', 'sociable' and 'good-humoured', '*cold*' tends to go with 'withdrawn', 'reserved' and 'humourless'.

impression formation In SOCIAL PSYCHOLOGY, this refers to the process of putting together the various bits of information about someone which we gather in the course of INTERPERSONAL CONTACT, making sense of her or him in one coherent impression of that person.

impression management In SOCIOLOGY, this is a term introduced by the Canadian sociologist Erving Goffman, which describes the attempt to present oneself (one's SELF) to other people in such a way that they will react in a controllable or predictable fashion. See also PRESENTATION OF SELF.

impulse buying When a consumer purchases goods or services without having planned to do so beforehand. The encouragement of impulse buying is the point of displays at supermarket check-out counters.

incentive In ECONOMICS, this term is almost synonymous with MOTIVATION. In PSYCHOLOGY, it is the basis of *external* motivation only and can refer to any kind of REWARD or inducement. In an ORGANI-ZATION, especially a business organiza-tion, the term is most often applied to financial rewards, although PROMOTION and enhanced STATUS may also be used.

incidental learning LEARNING that takes place without one making a con-scious effort to do so; for example, learn-ing the names of shops on the way to the bus stop.

income This term is usually reserved for money received by an individual, whether *earned* through WORK or *unearned* through dividends, interest and so on.

increment [1] In PERSONNEL MAN-AGEMENT, this is a regular, and usually automatic, increase in a scale of PAY. [2] In ERGONOMICS, it may refer to an increase in a stimulus from the ENVIRON-MENT of a standard amount; for example, of ILLUMINATION.

incremental innovation A form of INNOVATION that is really part of the prin-ciple of KAIZEN, where the improvements made to a product are small and continu-ous in nature rather than spectacular step-changes.

incremental learning LEARNING that takes place in a series of regular and orderly steps rather than following flashes of INSIGHT LEARNING.

index linking A mechanism for offset-ting changes in the value of money by mak-ing systematic adjustments to payments,

such as pensions, in line with changing prices, usually as reflected in the RETAIL PRICE INDEX.

indirect discrimination A form of DISCRIMINATION which does not specifi-cally single out particular targets but operates as the by-product of some other measure; for example, the requirement of residential mobility for job PROMOTION invariably discriminates against women.

indirect labour costs The costs associated with those members of the workforce not directly involved in the PRODUCTION of goods and services, but whose labour is essential to the running of the ORGANIZATION; for example, mainte-nance and secretarial staff. Usually com-pared with DIRECT LABOUR COSTS.

indirect taxation A form of TAXATION which is not paid directly to the govern-ment, as in DIRECT TAXATION, but added to the cost of goods and services; for example, Value Added Tax or the tax on cigarettes and petrol in the United Kingdom.

individual differences The compa-rison of people's characteristics and PER-FORMANCE on certain dimensions which are considered socially important, and especially of their INTELLIGENCE and INTEL-LIGENCE TEST scores.

induction The process of introducing new members into an ORGANIZATION. The aim of induction is to provide them with an overview of the whole organization and their place in it, and to give them a taste of the ORGANIZATIONAL CULTURE and the nature of the PSYCHOLOGICAL CON-TRACT they will be expected to make with the organization.

industrial action Any form of collec-tive action taken by the employees of an ORGANIZATION – usually organized by a TRADE UNION – most often to do with PAY or conditions of EMPLOYMENT. Action taken may include a GO-SLOW, STRIKE or WORK-TO-RULE. In some cases, employers may take industrial action against their employees by organizing a LOCK-OUT.

industrial democracy A situation in which the MANAGEMENT in an ORGANIZATION or an industry shares POWER with the workers or their representatives in making decisions about their work and about the organization in general. See also COLLECTIVE BARGAINING, EMPOWERMENT, LEARNING ORGANIZATION, WORKER-DIRECTORS and WORKS COUNCILS.

industrial disease A disease whose origin is directly attributable to conditions in the ENVIRONMENT of the work being done; for example, the lung diseases of silicosis in miners, asbestosis in building workers and REPETITIVE STRAIN INJURY in keyboard workers.

industrial dispute A CONFLICT between MANAGEMENT and workers or between their representatives, usually about PAY or conditions of EMPLOYMENT.

industrial engineering An American term for a kind of applied ERGONOMICS which concentrates on the SYSTEM of PRODUCTION and draws on various fields, including INDUSTRIAL PSYCHOLOGY, OPERATIONAL RESEARCH and TIME-AND-MOTION STUDY, as well as physics and mathematics.

industrial espionage Spying on an ORGANIZATION to obtain information of economic (or sometimes, in an INDUSTRIAL DISPUTE, *political*) value that the organization wishes to keep to itself. In the United Kingdom, stealing a TRADE SECRET is not in itself a criminal offence. Other countries have different laws on industrial espionage.

industrialization The term used to describe the process of change in a society

from being a largely agricultural economy to an economy dominated by machines, with a concomitant change in the way work is organized, featuring a DIVISION OF LABOUR, MASS PRODUCTION and STANDARDIZATION.

industrial medicine Medical research and PRACTICE carried out in an industrial working ENVIRONMENT and specializing in INDUSTRIAL DISEASE.

industrial psychology The branch of PSYCHOLOGY that deals with the world of work, including COUNSELLING, the ENVIRONMENT, HUMAN RELATIONS, JOB ANALYSIS, JOB SATISFACTION, MOTIVATION, RECRUITMENT, SELECTION, TRAINING and, especially, ERGONOMICS. The term is now used interchangeably with OCCUPATIONAL PSYCHOLOGY and both are being superseded by the broader term WORK PSYCHOLOGY.

industrial relations This term is now used to describe the web of relationships that exists between employees, or their TRADE UNION representatives, MANAGEMENT and government. Its usage is therefore much broader than its original industrial or manufacturing context and extends to issues and procedures concerning employment in any WORK ENVIRONMENT. See also CLOSED SHOP, COLLECTIVE BARGAINING, INDUSTRIAL ACTION and INDUSTRIAL DEMOCRACY.

Industrial Revolution The name given to the historical process beginning in the late eighteenth century (and usually dated from James Watt's invention of the steam engine) that led to the INDUSTRIALIZATION of the United Kingdom, making it the first industrialized nation and the richest economy the world had ever seen.

industrial sociology The study of the effects of societal processes on the

ENVIRONMENT of work and on the economy, such as the BLACK ECONOMY, or social change and its effects on economic life.

industrial training In PERSONNEL MANAGEMENT, this term usually refers to the TRAINING of new workers in a particular industry or sector of the economy, at all levels of ABILITY and SKILL.

industrial tribunal The SYSTEM of industrial tribunals was established in the United Kingdom in 1964, originally to deal with INDUSTRIAL TRAINING disputes. It now deals with a wide variety of disputes between employees and employers, such as unfair dismissal or DISCRIMINATION. Each tribunal consists of three members, including a legally qualified chairman and one nominee from each side of industry. Parties to the dispute may be represented by anyone (e.g. a TRADE UNION official) and not necessarily someone with a legal qualification.

inertial marketing A way of MARKETING goods and services which relies on the inertia of an existing customer in preferring to leave arrangements unchanged. This is done either by sending unsolicited products to people on a sale-or-return basis or by automatic renewal of existing agreements on an anniversary date.

inertia selling See INERTIAL MARKETING.

inferential statistics In STATISTICS, these are procedures by which generalizations can be made from findings on REPRESENTATIVE SAMPLES to the large groups from which they are drawn.

inferiority complex According to the Viennese psychoanalyst Alfred Adler, this is an UNCONSCIOUS condition where an individual feels inadequate and resentful, often because of some physical feature regarded as a defect. This complex leads to distorted behaviour, the most striking of which is OVERCOMPENSATION for the perceived defect – a mechanism often invoked to explain aggressiveness in small men.

inflation In ECONOMICS, this term describes a situation in which prices are rising relatively quickly, as measured for example, by the RETAIL PRICE INDEX, thus causing a fall in the real (as opposed to the nominal) value of money.

inflationary spiral In ECONOMICS, this is a situation arising from INFLATION where price rises lead to higher PAY demands, which, if satisfied, lead to higher PRODUCTION costs and therefore to still higher prices, and so on.

informal communication Any COMMUNICATION between people that takes place outside official channels within an ORGANIZATION; for example, through the GRAPEVINE. Usually contrasted with FORMAL COMMUNICATION.

informal economy The official name for what is widely known as the BLACK ECONOMY, though it also includes the GREY ECONOMY and alternative trading media like LETS.

informal group Unlike a FORMAL GROUP, an informal group is not set up by the MANAGEMENT of an ORGANIZATION but arises spontaneously in the workplace – where it may not be wholly, or even partly, connected with work.

informal organization Unlike the outward face of the FORMAL ORGANIZATION this reflects the *inner life* of the ORGANIZATION, where COMMUNICATION proceeds via the GRAPEVINE, where life is lived in INFORMAL GROUPS, and PRODUCTIVITY is determined by the GROUP NORM of a particular WORK GROUP.

informal theories of motivation The guidelines – often UNCONSCIOUS – that people use to account for each other's behaviour. Managers in a business ORGANIZATION often use THEORY X or THEORY Y.

informal theories of personality The guidelines – often UNCONSCIOUS – that people use to form a general overview of someone's PERSONALITY. These are contained in IMPLICIT PERSONALITY THEORY and IMPRESSION FORMATION.

information gathering This is the essential first step in setting up an INFORMATION SYSTEM, which requires a procedure for identifying and collecting information.

information highway An electronic network which links ORGANIZATIONS or homes with providers of information, in its broadest sense (like telephone or television companies), by means of cable.

information management This is concerned with applying INFORMATION TECHNOLOGY to the flow of information in an ORGANIZATION with the intention of ordering it in the best way to achieve ORGANIZATIONAL GOALS.

information overload A situation in which the sheer amount of information in an INFORMATION SYSTEM is simply too great to be coped with by the INFORMATION MANAGEMENT available.

information processing A key term in the study of COGNITION, which is used to denote what happens mentally between the stimulus and the response to it, including PERCEPTION, MEMORY, thinking, decision-making and problem-solving. By 'information' is usually meant any stimulus with a mental content – an image, idea, fact, opinion and so on.

information retrieval The process of recovering data from a DATABASE. This process lies at the heart of a MANAGEMENT INFORMATION SYSTEM. The most common example of information retrieval is probably the checking by an airline booking clerk of the availability of seats on a particular flight.

information system Any systematic way of organizing the handling of information, from INFORMATION GATHERING to INFORMATION RETRIEVAL and use.

information technology A field that combines the TECHNOLOGY of the COMPUTER with that of COMMUNICATION. It is concerned with the gathering, recording, storage, processing and dissemination of information and represents the latest form of MAN–MACHINE INTERFACE. See also ARTIFICIAL INTELLIGENCE and SYSTEMS THEORY.

information theory The study of information and the way it is communicated. It originated with mathematicians and engineers and draws heavily on concepts from these fields, but with advances in brain research it has also been used in linguistics and PSYCHOLOGY.

infrastructure The network of essential services supporting a modern society that has undergone the process of INDUSTRIALIZATION, especially education, health, gas, electricity, transport and water.

inhibition In PSYCHOLOGY generally, this term refers to the blocking of one physiological or psychological process by another; for example, the response to one sense receptor (the eyes) inhibiting response to another (the ears), or fear inhibiting escape from danger. In PSYCHOANALYSIS, inhibition is used specifically to describe an impulse from the ID being blocked from entering consciousness by the SUPEREGO. This is not the same as REPRESSION, where the impulse is actively held back.

initiating structure The way in which the TASK LEADER of a group organizes it in pursuit of its objectives.

innovation The development of something new. It is most often applied to the introduction of new goods and services to the MARKET, particularly those incorporating some advance in TECHNOLOGY.

input–output analysis This is a set of STATISTICS used in a general sense in ECONOMICS, and more specifically in MARKETING and MARKET RESEARCH, in which patterns of buying and selling between industries or sectors of an economy are analysed to study changes in their trading relationships over a given period of time. This technique is particularly useful in spotting changing trends in consumer choices.

in-service training The TRAINING of STAFF, as a normal part of their job, by the ORGANIZATION they work for in order to enhance their value to the organization.

INSET See IN-SERVICE TRAINING.

insider dealing Making a PROFIT, or avoiding a loss, in financial transactions as a result of having access to confidential information not available to the general investing public.

insight learning A form of LEARNING in which there appears understanding – usually sudden – in dealing with a problem. Insight learning involves both COGNITION, in finding a solution to a practical problem, and the SELF-KNOWLEDGE that can be achieved in PSYCHOTHERAPY. It is usually compared with TRIAL AND ERROR LEARNING or ROTE LEARNING.

institution In SOCIAL SCIENCE, this term refers to a social, cultural, economic or political arrangement that may be of greater or lesser importance to people's lives – like the family or the monarchy – but which usually endures over time and reflects some basic values of the society. When an individual ORGANIZATION has endured long enough it is often accepted as an institution; for example, the Bank of England or the BBC.

institutional investor An ORGANIZATION that invests in shares and other securities with funds obtained from a large number of individual savers; for example, a bank, insurance company or TRADE UNION.

institutional racism Behaviour exhibiting racial PREJUDICE which has not been adopted by individual choice, but is simply the consequence of a general CONFORMITY to the NORMS and conventions of a society whose INSTITUTIONS of law, government and business systematically discriminate against particular racial groups.

instrumental aggression A term used in SOCIAL PSYCHOLOGY to describe behaviour that is aggressive not for its own sake but as a means to an end; for example, the difference between killing an enemy in a face-to-face confrontation and pressing a button in a missile site a thousand miles away.

intangible assets ASSETS which have no physical existence (unlike, say, machinery or property) but which are still presumed to be of some financial value to a business ORGANIZATION; for example, COPYRIGHT, GOODWILL, PATENT or TRADEMARK.

integration The process of organizing different parts into a whole of a higher order. It is used widely in science, from the ORGANIZATION of nervous impulses necessary for any kind of behaviour up to the organization of a whole society. In both individual PSYCHOLOGY and ORGANIZATIONAL PSYCHOLOGY integration is widely regarded as the key criterion of healthy functioning.

integrative bargaining   A form of BARGAINING whose objective is to achieve an outcome in which both parties gain. That is, the attempt to organize a win–win situation.

intellectual capital   The collective knowledge and brainpower to be found within the STAFF of an ORGANIZATION. The value of this form of CAPITAL has increased enormously with the development of INFORMATION MANAGEMENT and the rise of the KNOWLEDGE WORKER.

intellectual property right   For many years, this referred to the ownership of a COPYRIGHT, PATENT or TRADEMARK. More recently, the term has been extended to include the right to any kind of published or broadcast intellectual endeavour in industry, commerce, science or the arts, or even of any commercially confidential information.

intelligence   Although this concept has been discussed in PSYCHOLOGY since the 1870s there is no universally accepted agreement on what intelligence is. Most psychologists would probably agree that heredity sets the limits of a person's intelligence, and most would also agree that the ABILITY to think in one form or another (handling abstract ideas, adapting to new situations, perceiving complex relationships) is a sign of high intelligence – which may not get us very far, but has never prevented psychologists from designing new INTELLIGENCE TESTS.

intelligence test   A TEST that is supposed to measure INTELLIGENCE, whatever that may be. Its purpose is to discriminate between people who score high and people who score low (i.e. high and low IQ), for the purpose of assigning them to various educational, occupational and social categories. High scores are supposed to denote high intelligence and vice versa, but in the absence of an agreed definition of intelligence the OPERATIONAL DEFINITION becomes circular – people score high on intelligence tests because they are highly intelligent because highly intelligent people score high on intelligence tests. There is also a great deal of evidence that intelligence tests, which are usually highly verbal, tend to be biased in favour of white, urban, middle-class people in their SELECTION of test items.

intelligent knowledge-based system The branch of ARTIFICIAL INTELLIGENCE whose objective is to develop computer systems resembling various aspects of human INTELLIGENCE; for example, language ABILITY and LEARNING capacity.

interaction process analysis   A technique for recording and analysing the interactions between people in a FACE-TO-FACE GROUP.

intercorrelations   A table of CORRELATIONS between each and every one of a series of variables.

interference   This term has two principal meanings in PSYCHOLOGY: the change in perception when two light or sound waves out of phase come together, and, more commonly, where one kind of LEARNING disturbs another or leads to INHIBITION of it.

intergroup relations   In SOCIAL PSYCHOLOGY, this term refers to the relation *between* one group and any other groups. Compare with INTRAGROUP RELATIONS. See also SUPERORDINATE GOAL.

internalization   In PSYCHOLOGY, this is the process of accepting external ideas or values as one's own to the point of not being aware of their origins. The best-known example of this concept is the SUPEREGO, where the values of the parents and the parent society are internalized into the developing PERSONALITY.

internal justification In SOCIAL PSYCHOLOGY, this is a way of resolving COGNITIVE DISSONANCE and underlies the most powerful kind of ATTITUDE change. For example, if you feel, on reflection, that you have an awful job, you can resolve (psychologically) the dissonance between the COGNITIONS 'I am a sensible person' and 'I choose to work in an awful job' either externally or internally. An *external* justification might be 'I do it for the money', but that wouldn't change your opinion of the JOB. However, if you began to consider the job in a different light and saw its more positive aspects you would be justifying your decision to stay in an awful job *internally*. You would in fact be persuading *yourself*, the most powerful way of changing anyone's attitudes.

internal validity The extent to which a psychological test or research finding is valid in its own terms. That is, how far does a test measure what it is supposed to measure; how far does an experiment deal with the factor it is supposed to deal with?

internet A global network of electronic COMMUNICATIONS which grew out of a group of academic and military research networks established in the United States during the 1960s. Among other services, it now includes ELECTRONIC MAIL and the WORLD WIDE WEB.

interpersonal attraction The general term for an area of SOCIAL PSYCHOLOGY concerned with why people are attracted to each other. For a more specific term see GAIN–LOSS THEORY OF INTERPERSONAL ATTRACTION.

interpersonal conflict The general term for any kind of CONFLICT between individuals (as opposed to groups).

interpersonal contact The general term for any kind of contact, of any type or duration, between individuals (as opposed to groups).

interpersonal relations The general term for any kind of relationship or form of COMMUNICATION between individuals (as opposed to groups).

interpersonal skills development A GROUP TRAINING METHOD which emphasizes the SKILLS involved in COMMUNICATION with other people and in listening to their replies. These skills are obviously important throughout the life of an ORGANIZATION but are perhaps most visible (on both sides of the table) in an INTERVIEW, especially a PERFORMANCE APPRAISAL INTERVIEW.

interpretivists A school of consumer research that regards the act of buying as being only a small part (however important) of a consumer's activities. It holds that buying behaviour has to be *interpreted* in the light of a person's entire consumer experience, and indeed his or her entire life experience.

interview In essence, an interview is a form of conversation, between an interviewee and one or more interviewers, which is structured to a greater or lesser extent. It is probably the technique most widely used (and misused) in ORGANIZATIONS for the ASSESSMENT of a person's ABILITY, despite the fact that its RELIABILITY and VALIDITY in the SELECTION of staff are usually very low. However, sensitive and well-trained interviewers *can* still make use of the method quite successfully.

interview bias The effects on an INTERVIEW of the conscious and UNCONSCIOUS biases (assumptions, expectations) of the interviewer. See also SELF-FULFILLING PROPHECY.

intragroup relations   In SOCIAL PSY-CHOLOGY, this term refers to the relations between its members *within* the group. Compare with INTERGROUP RELATIONS. See also SUPERORDINATE GOAL.

intranet   An information network derived from the INTERNET but which is limited to authorized members of a given ORGANIZATION. Compare with EXTRANET.

intrapreneur   A member of a large ORGANIZATION who displays the ATTITUDES and behaviour of an ENTREPRENEUR.

in-tray exercise   A form of SIMULA-TION used in the SELECTION of candidates for a managerial job where people are required to deal with the typical daily tasks of the job (as represented by the contents of the in-tray). It is usually considered to have more RELIABILITY than most other selection methods because it is part of what the job itself actually entails.

intrinsic motivation   Doing something for its own sake, because the activity itself constitutes a REWARD. Always contrasted with EXTRINSIC MOTIVATION.

introversion   According to the Viennese psychoanalyst Carl Gustav Jung, this is a basic PERSONALITY dimension of being withdrawn, inward-looking and passive that is usually contrasted with EXTRAVERSION.

inventory   In ACCOUNTING, this term has three related uses: [1] a list of items in stock; [2] a list of raw materials; [3] the cost of materials currently being processed.

investment   In ECONOMICS, this is the general term for spending money, usually from current INCOME, on the ASSETS of a business ORGANIZATION (including its human assets) in order to expand and increase PRODUCTION in the future.

invisible hand   In ECONOMICS, this refers to the term invented in the eighteenth century by ADAM SMITH to support the policy of free trade as opposed to government intervention in the workings of the MARKET. The pursuit of self-interested economic behaviour by each individual was supposed to lead naturally, when aggregated, to the best interests of the whole society being served – as if by the workings of an 'invisible hand'. This idea is frequently claimed as the basis of the modern IDEOLOGY of the FREE MARKET.

IQ   The intelligence quotient; a score obtained from an INTELLIGENCE TEST by dividing the mental age (MA) obtained on the test by the actual or chronological age (CA) and multiplying by 100; that is, IQ = MA/CA $\times$ 100. An IQ score by itself is meaningless. It does not measure intelligence the way a tape measures height, for instance. It is only a measure of comparison between all the people who have taken that particular test, with the average score being placed arbitrarily at around 100.

ISO 9000   A standard of QUALITY set by the International Standardization Organization (ISO) and based on the BS5750.

IT   See INFORMATION TECHNOLOGY.

item analysis   In STATISTICS, this is a technique to determine the effectiveness of different items on a TEST in its DISCRIMINATION among the people who take it.

iterative process   [1] In OPERATIONAL RESEARCH, this refers to a mathematical technique for making successive approximations in the search for a solution by the method of repeated calculations. [2] In a BUREAUCRACY, especially in the PUBLIC SECTOR, the term is used to denote a dialogue or a series of consultations back and forth in the formulation of a policy document.

J

Japanization The adoption by Western companies of Japanese policies and work practices, such as JUST-IN-TIME PRODUCTION, TOTAL QUALITY MANAGEMENT and WORK TEAMS. But see also the entry on W. EDWARDS DEMING for some background to this process.

jargon A private language, spoken by a GROUP in the conduct of its affairs, which is usually impenetrable – intentionally – to outsiders, that is, the 'lay public'. It serves to enhance GROUP COHESIVENESS and the SELF-ESTEEM of its members if they use, for example, *computerese* or *legalese*. See also PROFESSION.

J-curve [1] In PSYCHOLOGY, this term denotes a FREQUENCY DISTRIBUTION of conforming behaviour, portraying on a graph that the behaviour of most people in a given situation will fall at or near the behaviour expected. (See Figure 20.) The curve looks roughly like a capital J, or a reverse J, in shape. [2] In ECONOMICS,

the curve depicts a small decrease in some variable followed by a large and rapid increase.

jet lag The physiological effects and psychological STRESS caused by having to adjust one's CIRCADIAN RHYTHM to the disorienting effects of rapid long-distance air travel that involves passing through different time zones.

JIT See JUST-IN-TIME PRODUCTION.

j.n.d. See JUST-NOTICEABLE DIFFERENCE.

job analysis A key ROLE for practitioners of INDUSTRIAL PSYCHOLOGY, where the elements making up a job are studied in an attempt to match the TASKS and SKILLS necessary for successful PERFORMANCE with the ABILITY of the worker to perform them. Job analysis is an essential prerequisite for the study of jobs and job-holders and is therefore an important tool of PERSONNEL MANAGEMENT.

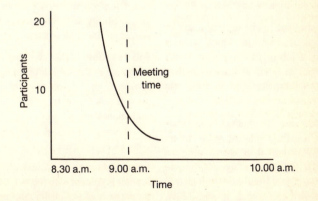

Figure 20 J-curve.

job characteristics model   A technique for evaluating the effectiveness of a JOB ENRICHMENT scheme. Devised by J.R. Hackman and G.R. Oldham, it focuses on the JOB SATISFACTION provided by five key characteristics: [1] SKILL variety, [2] TASK IDENTITY, [3] task significance, [4] AUTONOMY and [5] FEEDBACK.

job costing   A method for calculating costs in an area where each job constitutes a separate order or finite unit of work. This is considered particularly appropriate for CONSULTANCY work; for example, in building or in qualitative MARKET RESEARCH.

job demands   The requirements that a job has, and therefore the PERFORMANCE that will be expected of the person doing it.

job description   The broad outline of what TASKS a job consists of; delineating its duties and responsibilities and the position of the job within the ORGANIZATION.

job design   The process of relating all the TASKS to be performed within an ORGANIZATION to specific jobs.

job enlargement   Expanding the content of a job to include new responsibilities that will usually require TRAINING and the acquisition of new SKILLS.

job enrichment   The desired result of JOB RESTRUCTURING, in which various aspects of a job or its component TASKS are changed in order to help strengthen employee MOTIVATION and increase JOB SATISFACTION.

job evaluation   A method of comparing jobs for their relative value to an ORGANIZATION and then determining on this basis a HIERARCHY of PAY appropriate to each one. The method uses such factors as complexity, experience, responsibility, SKILL and so on.

job fragmentation   Splitting an existing job up and dividing it among other jobs, or creating a new series of smaller jobs.

job longevity   The concept that length of time spent in a job is an important factor in determining what contributes most to an individual's JOB SATISFACTION. For example, there is evidence that, after five years in a job, factors in the organizational ENVIRONMENT like PAY, FRINGE BENEFITS and relationships with colleagues and supervisors are more important than the PERFORMANCE of the job itself.

job mobility   The extent to which workers are prepared to change job, especially if a change requires geographical relocation.

job redesign   Doing a new JOB DESIGN as part of a wider process, like JOB ENLARGEMENT or JOB ENRICHMENT, and preparatory to JOB RESTRUCTURING.

job restructuring   Marking changes in the TASKS and responsibilities of an *individual's* job rather than a change in ORGANIZATIONAL STRUCTURE or GROUP WORKING practices, though the latter would lead to job restructuring. The addition of similar tasks as a result of job restructuring would mean JOB ENLARGEMENT; an increase of responsibility and different types of task would be JOB ENRICHMENT.

job rotation   The systematic moving of people at the same level in an ORGANIZATION from one job to another. On the SHOP FLOOR it is done to relieve boredom and monotony; as part of MANAGEMENT DEVELOPMENT it is done to give MANAGERS a broader experience of the ORGANIZATION.

job satisfaction   The extent to which a worker is content with the REWARDS she or he gets out of her or his job, particularly in terms of INTRINSIC MOTIVATION.

job security   The right to continued EMPLOYMENT, usually until RETIREMENT. Contractually, this is now quite rare; psychologically, the feeling of security varies with the job and the employee.

job segregation   See OCCUPATIONAL SEGREGATION.

job sharing   The procedure whereby two (or more) part-time workers make up one full-time job between them and share the accompanying PAY on a pro rata basis.

job simplification   The process of using people like machines by reducing their job to consist of the smallest TASK possible with the least amount of discretion in it. It is particularly associated with WORK on an ASSEMBLY LINE. Compare with WORK SIMPLIFICATION.

job specification   A much more detailed version of a JOB DESCRIPTION, stating as exactly as possible what a job entails. It is usually drawn up on the basis of a JOB ANALYSIS.

job transition   The process of moving from one job to another, either within the same ORGANIZATION or between organizations. A time of heightened psychological activity and STRESS.

Johari Window   A technique used in COUNSELLING to help people give and receive FEEDBACK about the effects of their behaviour. The 'window' is actually a 2 × 2 table. (See Figure 21.) The whole window is meant to represent the whole truth about someone and each quadrant therefore represents a particular aspect of the truth. 'Johari' is derived from the first names of the two men who developed the technique, Joseph Luft and Harry Ingham.

joint consultation   A procedure whereby both employees and employers in an ORGANIZATION (or their representatives) have a forum for discussing such common concerns as DISCIPLINE, TRAINING, or the WELFARE FUNCTION.

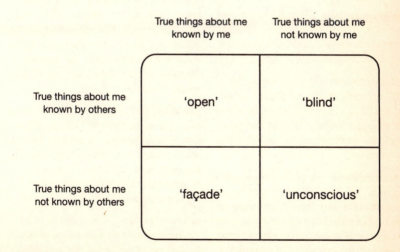

Figure 21 Johari Window.

journeyman   The traditional term for a skilled worker who has completed a craft or trade APPRENTICESHIP but is not yet a master craftsman in SELF-EMPLOYMENT. In previous times, such a worker would need to *journey* around offering his SKILLS to a master until such time as he could set up in business for himself.

junior management   The term applied to MANAGERS who are relatively low in the HIERARCHY of an ORGANIZATION because they are junior in age and/or level of responsibility and AUTHORITY.

just-in-time production   A Japanese approach to the process of PRODUCTION, which emphasizes tight scheduling of materials into and out of the process, with a very low INVENTORY of stock carried on-site. The aim of the process is to prevent bottlenecks in production and ensure a smooth flow of THROUGHPUT. It is also claimed that this approach reduces costs, increases JOB SATISFACTION and improves QUALITY.

just-noticeable difference   In ERGONOMICS, this is the minimum amount of difference that a subject can detect between two stimuli.

just-world hypothesis   The term used in SOCIAL PSYCHOLOGY for the unquestioned assumption that the world is a just place where the deserving receive a proper REWARD and the undeserving are punished. It therefore follows that if people are punished they must have done something to deserve it, and this is how the HYPOTHESIS accounts for people who blame victims for their own misfortunes. See also DISTRIBUTIVE JUSTICE.

K

k A common abbreviation for one thousand, derived from the French 'kilo'. It is used especially of money; for example, $50K = $50,000.

kaizen The Japanese concept of 'continuous improvement'. It is based on the related assumptions that a product can always be improved and that this must be done in accordance with customer needs. It applies to both HUMAN RESOURCES and the use of machinery and underpins such concepts as KANBAN, QUALITY CIRCLE and TOTAL QUALITY MANAGEMENT.

kanban The basis for the Japanese SYSTEM of JUST-IN-TIME PRODUCTION. It involves requesting items only as they become necessary in the PRODUCTION process.

karoshi The Japanese term for 'death by overwork'.

keiretsu Name given to an interlocking and mutually supportive group of giant Japanese companies. Also known as ZAIBATSU.

Kelly repertory grid A technique used in MARKET RESEARCH to obtain opinions from respondents about products and their BRAND IMAGE. The materials are presented in threes and the respondents are asked to say why one is different from the other two and why these two are similar. Nobody seems quite sure who Kelly was.

Keynes, John Maynard (1883–1946) A highly influential British economist who believed that an economy could not regulate itself in the interests of the society as a whole via the FREE MARKET. He suggested that general prosperity, and full EMPLOYMENT in particular, required government spending and INVESTMENT.

key success factors See CRITICAL SUCCESS FACTORS.

kinaesthetics The study of body movements. It is used in TIME-AND-MOTION STUDY and WORK STUDY.

kinesics The study of body movements in NON-VERBAL COMMUNICATION.

KISS principle An acronym for Keep It Short and Simple. KISS is a valuable aid in human COMMUNICATION (but then you knew that already, didn't you?).

knowledge-based industry A term used of a field that deals in the COMMUNICATION of information and particularly in INFORMATION MANAGEMENT.

knowledge engineering A term sometimes used of a group of techniques, based on theories of ARTIFICIAL INTELLIGENCE, which are concerned with the design of INTELLIGENT KNOWLEDGE-BASED SYSTEMS.

knowledge management The MANAGEMENT of KNOWLEDGE WORKERS as well as the information they deal with.

knowledge of results The process of giving people FEEDBACK on their PERFORMANCE of a TASK. In the study of LEARNING this has been found to increase someone's MOTIVATION to perform better.

knowledge worker A term sometimes used of a person working in the COMMUNICATION of information, particularly in INFORMATION MANAGEMENT.

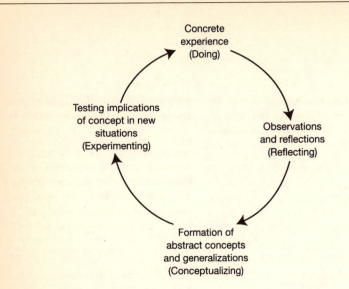

Figure 22 Kolb's learning cycle.

Kolb's learning cycle A formulation of different ways of LEARNING and of stages in the learning process that is widely used in MANAGEMENT TRAINING. It was developed by an American psychologist called David Kolb. There are four aspects of Kolb's cycle: *doing, reflecting, conceptualizing* and *experimenting*. (See Figure 22.) Ideally, fully integrated learning requires the whole cycle to be completed, though the theory is that everyone has a particular preference for one of the four modes of learning.

Kondratieff cycle The term given in ECONOMICS to a phenomenon first noticed by the nineteenth-century Russian economist Nikolai Kondratieff. This was the appearance of long, but regularly occurring, cycles or waves in economic activity that oscillated between boom and RECESSION every fifty years or so. Their existence is a matter of some debate.

Kuder Preference Record This is a QUESTIONNAIRE technique, used in OCCUPATIONAL PSYCHOLOGY, which is designed to elicit a subject's areas of vocational interest. It is named after its designer, the American psychologist George Kuder.

L

labelling theory   In PSYCHOLOGY, this is a way of explaining DEVIANCE by focussing on the reactions of other people to the person whom they have labelled deviant. When combined with SELF-FULFILLING PROPHECY, labelling theory has also been used to account for very disturbed, or psychotic, behaviour. Thus, if a person is labelled paranoid, everything he or she does is interpreted in the light of his or her paranoia, and invariably then taken as evidence for the correctness of the original diagnosis.

labour-intensive   The term used for relying mainly on labour in the PRODUCTION of goods and services, as opposed to the INVESTMENT of CAPITAL in the process of AUTOMATION; for example, as in teaching or tailoring. It is therefore the opposite of CAPITAL-INTENSIVE.

labour mobility   See JOB MOBILITY.

labour relations   See INDUSTRIAL RELATIONS.

labour turnover   The percentage of the total labour force of an ORGANIZATION leaving its EMPLOYMENT and being replaced over a given period of time, usually a year.

laissez-faire **economy**   From the French for 'let do'. This is the term used in ECONOMICS for the traditional doctrine that a government should not intervene in the workings of its country's economy. The basis for the FREE ENTERPRISE SYSTEM.

laissez-faire **leadership/management**   A form of LEADERSHIP or MANAGEMENT in which the input of the leader/manager is minimal and has little direct effect on an ORGANIZATION. This often leads to

infighting by subordinates who attempt to make use of the POWER vacuum thus created to further their own interests.

last in, first out   [1] A method of valuing stock or taking INVENTORY in which the prices of the newest items purchased are applied to the entire stock. Items received last are then first to be sold. [2] A method of choosing people for REDUNDANCY in an ORGANIZATION, where the last to be hired are the first to be made redundant.

late-entry strategy   The business strategy of seeking COMPETITIVE ADVANTAGE by coming late into a MARKET. See LATE-MOVER ADVANTAGE.

late-mover advantage   The supposed advantage for a company of entering a new MARKET relatively late and thereby learning from the mistakes of its predecessors. This may be happening with E-BUSINESS.

lateral communication   See HORIZONTAL COMMUNICATION.

lateral integration   See HORIZONTAL INTEGRATION.

lateral mobility   Sideways JOB MOBILITY in the same ORGANIZATION at the same level of AUTHORITY and responsibility.

lateral thinking   A term suggested by the British psychologist Edward de Bono to describe an attempt to solve a problem by any means other than the usual straight-line method of thinking, thus allowing the problem to be reconceptualized, and perhaps solved, by a previously unacceptable or unthought-of solution.

LCU   A LIFE CHANGE UNIT.

leadership   [1] A widely applied term that usually refers to the PERSONALITY characteristics and the behaviour of people with AUTHORITY, influence and responsibility for leading groups. See also CHARISMA, GREAT-MAN THEORY, LEADERSHIP STYLE and TRANSFORMATIONAL LEADERSHIP. [2] The term is also used to refer to the group of people officially responsible for running an ORGANIZATION.

leadership style   This term usually refers to the adoption of an AUTHORITARIAN MANAGEMENT or a DEMOCRATIC MANAGEMENT style by an individual in an ORGANIZATION, depending on which style is more comfortable to his or her PERSONALITY.

leadership substitutes   Research into FOLLOWERSHIP has raised the question of whether leaders are always necessary, and has suggested substitutes like special TRAINING for STAFF or having a variety of experienced people adopt the leadership ROLE in turn.

lead time   The time taken to complete a cycle of activity. The term is usually used in reference to the PRODUCTION process, from the initial idea to the finished product, although it can also refer to the time-lag in supplying an order.

lean production   The process of reducing the costs and wastage involved in the production of a product in an attempt to maximize both efficiency and effectiveness. It usually involves JUST-IN-TIME PRODUCTION, KAIZEN and DOWNSIZING.

learning curve   The curve obtained by plotting on a graph measured changes in the PERFORMANCE of LEARNING over time.

learning organization   An ORGANIZATION whose ORGANIZATIONAL CULTURE encourages individual LEARNING as well as collective learning about the organization itself. This would encompass such HUMAN RELATIONS approaches as CUSTOMER SERVICE, EMPOWERMENT, TEAM-BUILDING and TOTAL QUALITY MANAGEMENT.

learning plateau   A flattening of the LEARNING CURVE due to a temporary halt in LEARNING progress.

learning set   Sometimes described as 'learning how to learn', this is a generalized approach to problems in which people carry over into a new LEARNING situation the responses and strategies they learned in a previous situation. TRANSFER OF TRAINING results from a learning set.

learning theory   In PSYCHOLOGY, this refers to the systematic attempt to explain the process of LEARNING.

least preferred co-worker   A technique developed by the American psychologist Fred Fiedler to assess the extent to which someone in a position of LEADERSHIP is predisposed to deal more with the TASK confronting the group or the INTERPERSONAL RELATIONS of its members. The technique involves asking people about their 'least preferred co-worker'. Someone with negative views of this colleague has a low LPC score and, it is assumed, is predominantly a TASK LEADER. Someone with a more positive view would therefore have a high LPC score and be more concerned with maintaining harmony and cordiality within the group (i.e. a SOCIO-EMOTIONAL LEADER) than with the PERFORMANCE of a task.

left brained   A term sometimes used to describe people who are verbal in their thinking rather than visual or intuitive. The origin for this rather sweeping generalization is that the major speech centre is apparently on the left side of the brain cortex. Usually contrasted with RIGHT BRAINED.

legitimacy A term sometimes used of the LEADERSHIP of a group or ORGANIZATION when it is fully accepted by the group members.

legitimate power This form of POWER is what is usually meant by having AUTHORITY as a consequence of one's position in the ORGANIZATION. It implies, very importantly, that a willingness to accept that authority is shown by people in positions subordinate to it.

LETS An acronym for Local Exchange Trading System. This is an attempt to organize systematic trading relationships within the GREY ECONOMY, which started in Canada in 1982. LETS has since spread successfully to a number of other countries, especially the United States and the United Kingdom. Members of a LETS form a network and trade their services and products with each other on the basis of a notional LETS currency, which cannot be converted into cash. Thus ten LETS might be enough to get your windows washed and 100 might get you the use of a garage for a few months. In some places local traders outside the scheme have been willing to accept LETS units as part payment for their own goods and services.

level of aspiration The GOALS or standards of PERFORMANCE a person sets for herself or himself.

levels of significance See STATISTICAL SIGNIFICANCE.

Levitt's total product concept A concept introduced to MARKETING by the American writer Theodore Levitt. It deals with the psychological gap that may exist between the producer's view of a particular product and that of the consumer. This is particularly true of NEW PRODUCT DEVELOPMENT. Levitt sees a product as a combination of various attributes that increase in complexity as they develop through four different levels. (See Figure 23, p86.) Products go from being *generic* to being *potential*, containing possibilities that have not yet been attained.

Lewin, Kurt (1890–1947) A German psychologist who escaped from the Nazis and went to the United States in the 1930s. He was a student of the early GESTALT psychologists who applied much of their thinking to SOCIAL PSYCHOLOGY, in which he pioneered the field of GROUP DYNAMICS as well as the HUMAN RELATIONS school of MANAGEMENT. See, for example, his work on LEADERSHIP STYLE.

Life Change Unit An item in a rating scale of stressful incidents drawn up by a team of American psychologists. The bigger the event, or change, in a person's life the greater the likely STRESS. Top of the scale is the death of a spouse. But stressful events (LCUs) are not necessarily, or entirely, painful; marriage is also high on the list. The very fact of change itself, which of course is quite unavoidable, seems to contribute to the experience of stress.

life space A term introduced by KURT LEWIN to describe the totality of the physical and psychological factors in the ENVIRONMENT of an individual or group at any given time.

life stage See FAMILY LIFE CYCLE.

lifestyle segmentation The attempt to divide people into different consumer groups on the basis of the typical spending patterns that underlie their lifestyle. This is closely related to their SOCIO-ECONOMIC STATUS.

LIFO See LAST IN, FIRST OUT.

light industry The term applied to industries like electronics or clothing,

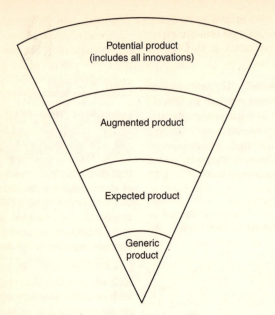

Figure 23 Levitt's total product concept. (Adapted from *The Marketing Imagination*, Theodore Levitt, Free Press, New York, 1986.)

which tend to be smaller in scale and to require less physical labour than HEAVY INDUSTRY.

Likert Rensis (1903–81)　An American psychologist whose contributions to the study of MANAGEMENT and ORGANIZATIONAL THEORY include the concepts of HUMAN ASSET ACCOUNTING, the LIKERT SCALE, the LINKING-PIN MANAGEMENT STRUCTURE and SYSTEM 4.

Likert scale　A QUESTIONNAIRE scale developed by the American psychologist RENSIS LIKERT, which allows respondents to indicate how much they agree or disagree with a series of statements on a three- or five-point scale, as opposed to the more simplistic choice of either/or responses. It is widely used in ATTITUDE studies.

line and staff concept　A term used in ORGANIZATIONAL THEORY to denote the different functions performed in an ORGANIZATION by MANAGERS who are directly responsible for achieving the organization's GOALS ('line') and those who perform supportive functions like MARKETING or PERSONNEL ('staff'). This distinction becomes somewhat blurred in practice. See also LINE MANAGEMENT and STAFF MANAGEMENT.

linear programme　A mathematical technique used in OPERATIONAL RESEARCH to help the DECISION-MAKER where there is a direct, straight-line relationship between two variables; for example, where the shortest route means the lowest cost.

linear relationship　The relationship between two or more jobs in an ORGANIZATION as plotted on an ORGANIZATION CHART.

linear time　Our most salient view of time, which perceives it as flowing in a straight line from the past to the future via the present. Our most common experience of it is as CLOCK TIME. Compare with CYCLICAL TIME.

line management   The term used to describe MANAGERS who are responsible for an ORGANIZATION carrying out its basic functions, such as MARKETING, PRODUCTION and so on, and who give and receive orders via the CHAIN OF COMMAND, within the organizational HIERARCHY. Compare with STAFF MANAGEMENT, and see also LINE AND STAFF CONCEPT.

line of command   See CHAIN OF COMMAND.

line relationship   A LINE MANAGEMENT relationship between a superior and a subordinate in the HIERARCHY of the ORGANIZATION.

linking-pin management structure A way of conceptualizing ORGANIZATIONAL STRUCTURE, developed by the American psychologist RENSIS LIKERT, where an ORGANIZATION consists of a series of interlocking groups connected up into a coherent SYSTEM by key individuals, each of whom has overlapping group membership. These members are the 'linking pins' in the system.

liquid assets   Any ASSETS that are in cash and immediately available, or that are easily convertible into cash, like securities or bank deposits.

lock-out   Action taken by employers in the course of an INDUSTRIAL DISPUTE, which involves denying the workers access to the workplace by locking them out; its consequences are the same as a STRIKE.

locus of control   A dimension of PERSONALITY in which people who have an *internal* focus feel they have control over

Figure 24 Logo.

what happens to them, and people with an *external* locus tend to attribute their experiences to outside forces or other people.

logistics   A term that was originally used in the military sphere to describe the organizing and moving of troops and equipment. It is now often applied to any detailed planning process in an ORGANIZATION which entails the DISTRIBUTION or redistribution of resources.

logo   [1] Short for 'logotype', the TRADEMARK or other identifying symbol of an ORGANIZATION, often including the name. (See Figure 24.) [2] A high-level COMPUTER LANGUAGE.

longitudinal research   Repeated study of the same people over a period of time. By its nature this form of research is more difficult to carry out than CROSS-SECTIONAL RESEARCH, and it is much more rarely done. But because the *same* subjects are being compared at different points in time its findings are considered more powerful in illustrating the effect being studied. See also COHORT EFFECT.

long-range planning   What a CORPORATE PLAN is supposed to be used for.

long-term unemployment   A term normally reserved for a period of UNEMPLOYMENT of twelve months or longer.

longwall method   A method of PRODUCTION in the UK coal-mining industry which led to a change in SHIFT WORK and other practices as the result of the introduction of new mining TECHNOLOGY. These changes meant there was one long coalface of two hundred yards being worked by three shifts of miners with different TASKS, as opposed to one team on a ten-yard face who did the whole job. This resulted in social and PSYCHOSOMATIC DISORDERS, which were dealt with by treating the new workplace as a SOCIO-TECHNICAL SYSTEM.

loss leader   In MARKETING, this refers to a product or service sold at a loss for the seller in order to attract customers to buy her or his other products or services.

loyalty   Usually defined within an ORGANIZATION as the dedication of people to a group and its objectives – rarely the other way round. See also BRAND LOYALTY and ORGANIZATIONAL LOYALTY.

LPC   See LEAST PREFERRED CO-WORKER.

Luddite   The term used to describe workers who are obstinately opposed to the introduction of NEW TECHNOLOGY into their workplace. It derives from the activities of British textile workers during the INDUSTRIAL REVOLUTION, supposedly following the example of one Ned Lud, who saw new machinery as a threat to their traditional craft SKILLS and working PRACTICES and opposed its introduction violently.

M

Machiavellianism A PERSONALITY characteristic in which a person manipulates others for his or her own gain. The term is named after the political theories of the fifteenth-century Italian statesman and writer Niccolò Machiavelli, whose book *The Prince* has been used as source material by psychologists in the construction of the MACH-V SCALE.

machine bureaucracy An ORGANIZATION that is run like a machine, with a dominant BUREAUCRACY which is particularly rigid and inflexible.

machine controls The knobs, wheels, switches and so on that provide energy or information to a machine.

machine dynamics In ERGONOMICS, this term refers to the set of factors involved in the design of the MAN–MACHINE INTERFACE.

machine readable Information presented in such a form that it can readily be identified and processed by a machine.

macho management A term that arose in the Reagan–Thatcher era of the 1980s. It represents the extreme aggressiveness towards the workforce associated with the slogan 'management's right to manage', at a time when SENIOR MANAGEMENT in business ORGANIZATIONS generally felt they had enough POWER and CONTROL of the SHOP FLOOR to ignore the interests of their employees and disdain any HUMAN RELATIONS approaches. This is a good example of the ABC School of Management – Authoritarian, Brutal and Crass.

Mach-V Scale A PSYCHOLOGICAL TEST that is intended to identify and measure MACHIAVELLIANISM.

macroeconomic model In ECONOMICS, this is a computer model of the workings of a whole economy, usually a national economy. It is extensively used by both academics and government ministries to test the implications of changes in different aspects of the economy, such as interest rates or TAXATION.

macroeconomics The part of ECONOMICS that deals with the overall working of an economy – usually a national economy – and the interrelations, between its different factors, including GROSS DOMESTIC PRODUCT and GROSS NATIONAL PRODUCT, EMPLOYMENT and UNEMPLOYMENT, INVESTMENT patterns and national MARKETS. It is usually compared with MICROECONOMICS.

magic thinking Any attempt to understand and manipulate the human condition by recourse to supernatural powers. In particular, the term is used to describe the belief that there is a causal link between one's wishes and the real world – that 'wishing can make it so'. It is said to be typical of children, psychotics and 'primitive' peoples, but it is not entirely unknown among NORMAL adults in our own society.

Maier's Law If the data do not fit the theory, the data must be disposed of. In other words, if the facts do not fit your preconceived notion then it's the facts that must be wrong. This was suggested by the American psychologist Norman Maier, in exasperation at fellow psychologists' slavish adherence to their pet theories regardless of the evidence. But it is much more widely applicable, of course, than academic PSYCHOLOGY. It may well, indeed, be a firmly rooted part of the way in which we make sense of the world.

mail order   A form of trading conducted mainly through a postal or delivery SYSTEM which connects buyers and sellers.

mailshot   An American term for a one-off ADVERTISING circular sent to prospective customers.

mainframe   A large, powerful, centralized COMPUTER.

make-work   WORK created to keep STAFF or equipment occupied and not because there is any real need for it. This is not supposed to happen in a time of REDUNDANCY and RIGHTSIZING.

management   [1] All that is involved in making the most effective use of available resources, whether in the form of machines, money or people. [2] A collective term for the people responsible for the management of an ORGANIZATION; that is, for the directing, PLANNING and running of its operations, for the implementation of its policies and the attainment of its objectives.

management accounting   The preparation of ACCOUNTING information for use by the MANAGERS of an ORGANIZATION in budgeting, decision-making, PLANNING and formulating policy.

management audit   An AUDIT of all aspects of MANAGEMENT in an ORGANIZATION to review the use of all resources and see whether any improvements in efficiency can be made. It includes an examination of CAREER DEVELOPMENT, MORALE of STAFF, the effects of PERSONNEL policies, financial PERFORMANCE, PLANNING effectiveness and the SKILLS of the organization's MANAGERS.

management buyout   A situation in which the MANAGERS of a business ORGANIZATION make a bid to own it, in whole or in part, by buying out the original shareholders and then operating as a separate ENTERPRISE on their own behalf.

management by crisis   A MANAGEMENT STYLE that tends to favour crash programmes to deal with problems as they arise in an ORGANIZATION rather than focussing on long-term PLANNING or on the overall objectives of the organization. It is a style that suits a MANAGER inclined to AUTHORITARIAN MANAGEMENT and is a way of turning short-term CRISIS MANAGEMENT into a permanent arrangement.

management by exception   A form of managerial CONTROL that requires subordinates to inform SUPERVISORS only when something happens which is sufficiently exceptional to require their attention.

management by objectives   A term proposed by the American MANAGEMENT writer PETER DRUCKER in the 1950s to emphasize the importance of setting objectives for – and by – each individual member of an ORGANIZATION as well as the various branches of the organization. Drucker also emphasized the element of self-control and taking responsibility for one's own work. As an objective and a quantifiable measure of PERFORMANCE this technique has since become very popular with SENIOR MANAGEMENT, though its application in PRACTICE has often been more top-down and formalized than Drucker had intended.

management by walking about   A technique suggested by some specialists in MANAGEMENT SCIENCE for keeping SENIOR MANAGEMENT, and especially the chief executive, in touch with what is actually happening in the ORGANIZATION.

By walking about where people are actually doing the work MANAGERS are able to get information and opinions at first hand and undistorted by passing through the channels of UPWARD COMMUNICATION.

management charter initiative This was established in Britain in 1988 by a group of large companies to promote national standards of COMPETENCIES in MANAGEMENT development.

management consultant Someone who offers a CONSULTANCY service in any area of MANAGEMENT or the running of an ORGANIZATION.

management development The process of identifying, TRAINING and generally equipping relatively junior MANAGERS with the experience or SKILL necessary for SENIOR MANAGEMENT positions with an ORGANIZATION in the future. It is a process that, ideally, should be an integral part of a coherent PERSONNEL policy going from initial RECRUITMENT to ultimate RETIREMENT.

management education Any course of instruction in MANAGEMENT and related fields – which is often known as BUSINESS ADMINISTRATION. Success in such a course is usually rewarded with an academic qualification, whether the setting is an institution of higher education or an in-house programme tailored to a particular ORGANIZATION. The term is often used interchangeably with MANAGEMENT TRAINING, though the emphasis of management education is generally more formal and academic.

management game A BUSINESS GAME used in MANAGEMENT TRAINING.

management information system A centralized, and usually computerized, INFORMATION SYSTEM for use by the MANAGERS of an ORGANIZATION in making decisions.

management science [1] The application of scientific methods, and particularly QUANTITATIVE METHODOLOGY, to the practice of MANAGEMENT. [2] The application of a specifically BEHAVIOURAL SCIENCE or SOCIAL SCIENCE perspective to the study of MANAGEMENT.

management service Any service intended to help MANAGEMENT function more effectively, such as DATA PROCESSING or MARKET RESEARCH.

management style The general approach a MANAGER has to dealing with other people at work, and in particular the exercising of his or her AUTHORITY with subordinates. This style is often characterized as tending towards AUTHORITARIAN MANAGEMENT or DEMOCRATIC MANAGEMENT, depending on the PERSONALITY of the individual manager, but people can also have somewhat different approaches when faced with different situations. See also THEORY X and THEORY Y.

management training Any form of TRAINING in the practices and techniques of MANAGEMENT. One important form of management training is to have MANAGERS deal with CASE STUDIES of real-life (or even fictitious) issues in ORGANIZATIONS and work on solutions to problems; another is to play BUSINESS GAMES designed to deal with particular aspects of management. The term is often used interchangeably with MANAGEMENT EDUCATION, though the emphasis of management training is generally more focussed and less formal or academic.

manager Anyone involved in the ADMINISTRATION of an ORGANIZATION with the AUTHORITY to use organizational resources, whether money, labour or equipment, in furtherance of the organization's objectives.

managerial accounting See MANAGEMENT ACCOUNTING.

managerial economics The application of ECONOMICS to the kind of practical business decision that a MANAGER has to take. As well as economics the field draws on OPERATIONAL RESEARCH, MANAGEMENT ACCOUNTING and MARKETING.

managerial grid A technique used in MANAGEMENT DEVELOPMENT that was devised by two American SPECIALISTS in ORGANIZATIONAL PSYCHOLOGY, Robert Blake and Jane Mouton, building on previous contributions to the study of HUMAN RELATIONS by psychologists like ARGYRIS, LEWIN and LIKERT. The technique consists of scoring managers on two dimensions at right angles to each other to form a grid. The dimensions are *concern for PRODUCTION* (or the TASK in hand) and *concern for people*. Each individual's scores are then plotted on this grid to see how much of each concern they express. The grid also forms the basis for a seminar exploring various aspects of the WORK GROUP. (See Figure 25.)

managerial psychology The systematic study of the ROLE of the MANAGER in an ORGANIZATION and in particular the relationships between SUPERVISORS and supervisees. This area of study is a part of INDUSTRIAL PSYCHOLOGY.

managerial viewpoint The view of an ORGANIZATION that SENIOR MANAGEMENT

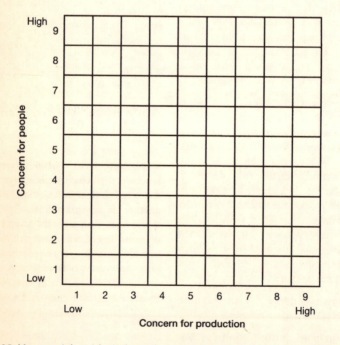

Figure 25 Managerial grid. (Adapted from *The Managerial Grid*, Blake and Mouton (1964)).

have and which reflects their interests. It is by far the dominant view – and often regarded as the only one – compared to, say, that of SHOP FLOOR workers, part-time employees or even shareholders.

man–machine interface In ERGONOMICS, this refers to all those points of contact in the workplace between people and the equipment they use. The term now has a particular reference to INFORMATION TECHNOLOGY.

man–machine system This is at the heart of ERGONOMICS where the workplace is regarded as a SYSTEM within which workers and machines are to be fully integrated.

manpower analysis An analysis of the employees in an ORGANIZATION that attempts to identify patterns and trends in their EMPLOYMENT. It will examine, for instance, the DISTRIBUTION of employees by age, sex, SKILL, JOB TITLE and length of service. It is the first stage of systematic MANPOWER PLANNING.

manpower audit See MANPOWER ANALYSIS.

manpower forecasting See MANPOWER PLANNING.

manpower planning The process of FORECASTING both the numbers and the kinds of employees that an ORGANIZATION will require over a given period of time and taking steps to ensure their supply. Ideally, this should be an integral part of an organization's PERSONNEL policy from RECRUITMENT to RETIREMENT, including SELECTION, PROMOTION and TRAINING.

manual skill A SKILL that requires physical rather than mental ABILITY.

manual worker Someone employed on the SHOP FLOOR of an ORGANIZATION doing physical rather than mental work, whether the work is skilled or unskilled.

marginal cost The extra costs of PRODUCTION of a unit additional to those already produced or planned.

marginality A term used in SOCIAL SCIENCE to denote the effects on an individual or a group of being excluded from the mainstream life of a society. It is now applied to life within an ORGANIZATION as well. See also DEVIANCE.

margin of error The range of error or inaccuracy usually regarded as acceptable; for example, in operating machinery or making calculations. See also STANDARD DEVIATION and TOTAL QUALITY MANAGEMENT.

market [1] A situation where buyers and sellers are in COMMUNICATION with each other. This may take several forms; for example, in person (as in a cattle auction), electronically (as in the stock exchange) or through the MASS MEDIA, as in newspaper ADVERTISING columns. [2] The nature of the demand for a particular product.

market forces The factors determining supply and demand in a given MARKET. See also PRICING.

marketing The complex series of processes by which demand for goods and services is identified, supplied, anticipated or manipulated by a producer. While now often regarded as part of the responsibility of every aspect of the business and, indeed, every employee it relies heavily on such functions as ADVERTISING, MARKETING RESEARCH and NEW PRODUCT DEVELOPMENT. See also DIRECT MARKETING, MARKET SEGMENTATION, MARKETING MIX and PROMOTION.

marketing concept The fundamental philosophy of MARKETING that emphasizes the supreme importance of the customer to any provider of goods or services. Essential to this philosophy is an understanding of what the customer wants in any given MARKET, and this is usually ascertained by extensive MARKET RESEARCH. It should be contrasted with the PRODUCTION ORIENTATION.

marketing environment   The set of external factors that affect the MARKET in which an ORGANIZATION operates; that is, cultural, economic, legal, political, geographical and so on.

marketing mix   The combination of different aspects of a business ORGANIZATION's strategy for MARKETING a product; for example, ADVERTISING, MARKET RESEARCH, PRODUCTION and PUBLIC RELATIONS. The guidelines for the most appropriate mix are sometimes expressed as the 'four Ps': [1] product, [2] price (MARKET), [3] promotion and [4] place.

marketing research   The collection and analysis of a wide range of information that can aid in the formulation of a MARKETING policy for the products of an ORGANIZATION. It usually includes the use of MARKET RESEARCH on specific product ideas.

market leader   The business ORGANIZATION with the largest share in a given MARKET.

market niche   A unique place or gap in the MARKET for a given product. See also UNIQUE SELLING POINT.

market penetration   The amount of demand in a given MARKET that is supplied by a particular ORGANIZATION.

market research   Work carried out in the course of MARKETING RESEARCH, either by a business ORGANIZATION itself or by SPECIALISTS from an external

CONSULTANCY, to assess the likely MARKET for a given product or the effects of past or prospective ADVERTISING of that product on consumers. Depending on the kind of information required, the research may use either QUANTITATIVE METHODOLOGY, with SURVEY RESEARCH on large numbers of people, or QUALITATIVE METHODOLOGY, with DEPTH INTERVIEWS of individuals and families and GROUP interviews of 5–10 people in a FACE-TO-FACE GROUP.

market segmentation   The analysis of buyers or potential buyers in a given MARKET along various dimensions. These usually include DEMOGRAPHICS like age, sex and SOCIO-ECONOMIC STATUS, buying patterns with respect to price and QUALITY, and PERSONALITY factors like conservatism–radicalism, NEED FOR ACHIEVEMENT or NEED FOR AFFILIATION. The objective is to divide a market into segments comprising similar kinds of people so that MARKETING efforts can be targeted more precisely, and the most effective approach used with each segment. For specific forms of market segmentation see under BENEFIT SEGMENTATION, DEMOGRAPHIC SEGMENTATION, GEOGRAPHIC SEGMENTATION, PSYCHOLOGICAL SEGMENTATION and USAGE SEGMENTATION.

market share   The amount of total demand in a MARKET which a particular business ORGANIZATION supplies over a given period of time.

market value   The current price that a particular item would fetch in the MARKET.

Marx, Karl (1818–83)   Economist and theorist of SOCIALISM who lived and worked (and died) in London and based much of his thought on his analysis of the effects of the INDUSTRIAL REVOLUTION and the British factory SYSTEM. He believed in ECONOMIC DETERMINISM and argued that social harmony and individual happiness lay in changing the economic relationships between people in society, and in particular that labour should not be exploited and workers should own the means of PRODUCTION.

masking In ERGONOMICS, this refers to the blocking of one sensory stimulus or process by another.

Maslow, Abraham (1908–70) An American PERSONALITY theorist and leading exponent of HUMANISTIC PSYCHOLOGY. He is closely associated with the terms HIERARCHY OF NEEDS, PEAK EXPERIENCE and SELF-ACTUALIZATION.

mass customization A recent development in MARKETING which takes advantage of the increased sophistication of computers to combine mass production techniques with individual customization of a product. For example, Levi jeans, though still manufactured in the traditional way, can also now be tailored to an individual customer's measurements thus reaching the ultimate in MARKET SEGMENTATION, a SEGMENT OF ONE.

massed practice A technique of LEARNING in which the lessons or periods of PRACTICE follow each other without a break. Generally speaking, and for most purposes, this is considered a less effective method of learning than DISTRIBUTED PRACTICE, with which it is usually contrasted.

mass marketing The promotion of a given product by a company in large quantities in order to facilitate its MASS PRODUCTION.

mass media Forms of COMMUNICATION between producers and consumers that reach a large – usually nationwide – audience; that is radio, television and newsprint.

mass production The PRODUCTION of identical items on a very large scale. It requires the processes of AUTOMATION, DIVISION OF LABOUR, JOB SIMPLIFICATION, SPECIALIZATION and STANDARDIZATION. In the twentieth century the prototype for mass production was the ASSEMBLY LINE developed in the car manufacturing industry by HENRY FORD. For comparison, see also BATCH PRODUCTION and CONTINUOUS PROCESS PRODUCTION.

matrix organization A flexible form of ORGANIZATIONAL STRUCTURE often used in situations which require a mix of people with different SKILLS and experience to be focussed on a particular TASK, or an unusual project that crosses existing departmental boundaries in an ORGANIZATION. The people involved in this kind of TASK FORCE will continue to report officially to LINE MANAGEMENT, but in their day-to-day work they will be responsible to the project leader.

Mayo, Elton (1880–1949) An Australian psychologist and MANAGEMENT specialist who worked at the Harvard Business School and had a great influence, during the 1920s and 1930s, on the development of INDUSTRIAL PSYCHOLOGY. He is associated particularly with the HAWTHORNE STUDIES, which were carried out under his direction. Mayo stressed the importance of HUMAN RELATIONS in the workplace and regarded INTERPERSONAL RELATIONS within the WORK GROUP as the key factor. He encouraged MANAGEMENT to listen to workers on the SHOP FLOOR and take their views seriously – a reaction to the SCIENTIFIC MANAGEMENT advocated by F.W. TAYLOR and the dominant industrial image of the ASSEMBLY LINE.

MBO See MANAGEMENT BY OBJECTIVES.

MBWA See MANAGEMENT BY WALKING ABOUT.

McClelland, David (1917–98) An American psychologist and leading contributor to the study of MOTIVATION, and particularly the part played by UNCONSCIOUS needs. He has suggested that one very important human need is the NEED FOR ACHIEVEMENT and has provided historical and cross-cultural evidence to support this view. An ENTREPRENEUR will be more concerned with the need for achievement than other people. McClelland also suggested the importance of the NEED FOR POWER, a need that is of particular relevance to the MANAGEMENT of an ORGANIZATION.

McGregor, Douglas (1906–64) An American psychologist and leading contributor to ORGANIZATIONAL THEORY from the HUMAN RELATIONS perspective. He classified the assumptions about human nature made by supporters of the RATIONAL-ECONOMIC view as a rather cynical THEORY X, which he rejected in favour of his own, more optimistic, THEORY Y.

MCI See MANAGEMENT CHARTER INITIATIVE.

MDW See MEASURED DAYWORK.

mean In STATISTICS, this is the most commonly used MEASURE OF CENTRAL TENDENCY. It is the arithmetic average, found by summing the values of a series of numbers and dividing this by the total number in the series.

measured daywork A MANAGEMENT procedure where a daily PRODUCTION target is defined for all the workers on the SHOP FLOOR, whose PAY is then made up of a fixed, regular amount for each day that the target is met – as opposed to PAYMENT BY RESULTS.

measure of central tendency One of three STATISTICS which can each be used as a central value to describe a series of numbers: the MEAN, the MEDIAN and the MODE.

mechanistic organization A term introduced by two British sociologists and MANAGEMENT theorists, Tom Burns and George Stalker. It denotes a relatively closed and formal type of ORGANIZATION with a high degree of BUREAUCRACY, in contrast to an ORGANIC ORGANIZATION.

median In STATISTICS, this is a MEASURE OF CENTRAL TENDENCY which divides a group of scores in half, with half the score falling above the median score and half below.

mediation An alternative term for ARBITRATION.

membership group In SOCIAL PSYCHOLOGY, this term is used to denote the particular group to which an individual belongs. Compare with REFERENCE GROUP.

memory [1] A function of COGNITION which refers to the storage of information. [2] With reference to a COMPUTER, this is an electronic form of storing information.

mental health Mental and emotional well-being, harmony and INTEGRATION of an individual's thoughts, feelings and behaviour. In the workplace, JOB SATISFACTION and PEER GROUP support are crucial to mental health, as is the ability to manage STRESS when it arises.

mental set An expectation of, or readiness for, a particular experience.

mentoring A SYSTEM in an ORGANIZATION whereby an experienced senior member of STAFF coaches, advises and counsels a junior member (or members) as they progress through the organization.

mere exposure In SOCIAL PSYCHOLOGY, this is a term introduced in the 1960s by the American psychologist Robert Zajonc to explain the phenomenon that, other things being equal, the more familiar people become with objects, words or pictures of faces they don't know, the more they like them. Mere exposure may thus help to explain the influence of frequent ADVERTISING on buying habits and even political preferences.

merger An amalgamation of two or more business ORGANIZATIONS into a single new organization by mutual agreement – as opposed to a TAKEOVER by one company of another.

meritocracy A social SYSTEM in which advancement is based on ABILITY rather than birth or background.

merit rating A form of REWARD for members of an ORGANIZATION, based on an assessment of their worth beyond the normally expected PERFORMANCE of their JOB, on the grounds that different people doing the same job can have a different value to the organization. The kinds of factor usually taken into account are ABSENTEEISM, APTITUDE, ATTITUDE towards MANAGEMENT, length of service, punctuality and so on.

'me-too' product A new product whose PROMOTION deliberately attempts to model it on, or even mimic, the MARKET LEADER in the hope that potential consumers will conflate the two in their minds and choose the former by mistake, thereby eating into the leader's market share.

micro Shortened, colloquial form of MICROCOMPUTER.

microchip A tiny piece of silicon, containing a complete electrical circuit, used extensively in the manufacture of the MICROCOMPUTER.

microcomputer A relatively small and cheap COMPUTER that has been designed for specific applications.

microeconomics The part of ECONOMICS that deals with small-scale issues like the prices of individual products, the PERFORMANCE of individual companies, or even a family BUDGET. Compare with MACROECONOMICS.

micromarketing A form of MARKETING that targets very small, narrowly defined, groups of people as part of a MARKET SEGMENTATION process. The ultimate form of micromarketing might be a SEGMENT OF ONE.

microprocessor The MICROCHIP containing the central processing unit of a MICROCOMPUTER. Also used of the microcomputer itself.

middleman An individual or an ORGANIZATION acting as a link between others, especially between producers of goods and services on the one hand and consumers or retailers on the other; for example, a furniture wholesaler or a literary agent. See also WHOLESALING.

middle management Any MANAGER whose position in the HIERARCHY of an ORGANIZATION is higher than JUNIOR MANAGEMENT and lower than SENIOR MANAGEMENT is part of middle management, and this accounts for most managers in most organizations. Middle managers are typically in charge of the constituent units that make up an organization, responsible for the work of other people but with little or no say in the making of policy or the taking of organization-wide decisions. They were particularly vulnerable to the enthusiasm for DELAYERING and DOWNSIZING that swept the 1980s and the early 1990s.

mid-life crisis The term applied to the process of reassessing one's personal and work life that people typically go through around middle age (from about 35–55). It is inevitably accompanied by ANXIETY, and sometimes by DEPRESSION. It may also manifest itself in the form of an IDENTITY CRISIS.

Milgram, Stanley (1933–84) An American psychologist who made several notable contributions to SOCIAL PSYCHOLOGY, particularly in the study of CONFORMITY to AUTHORITY. His best-known finding was that most people could be persuaded to give other people electric shocks when told to do so by an authority figure.

mindguards In GROUPTHINK, these are the group members who guard the group against outsiders and prevent their disturbing ideas from getting through.

minimax strategy In GAME THEORY, this is the strategy of choosing to minimize loss rather than maximize gain.

Minnesota Multiphasic Personality Inventory For many years this was widely considered to be the leading PAPER-AND-PENCIL TEST of PERSONALITY, though it is now somewhat out of fashion. It contains 550 statements which the subject responds to as being true or false about herself or himself. The pattern of responses is intended to reveal certain personality characteristics, particularly those associated with a tendency towards psychological disturbance.

Mintzberg, Henry (1939–) A Canadian MANAGEMENT theorist, best known for his empirical observations of MANAGERS at work, highlighting the differences between what they are supposed to do, or what they think they do and what they actually do.

MIS See MANAGEMENT INFORMATION SYSTEM.

mission statement [1] A brief explanation (usually no more than a couple of sentences) of what an ORGANIZATION exists to do, its purpose and objectives, that can act as a guide to key groups in its ENVIRONMENT like STAFF and customers. [2] A brief statement that every organization now feels it has to make about itself and thus often bland, or meaningless, or misleading and best understood as a PUBLIC RELATIONS exercise.

mixed economy In ECONOMICS, this refers to the kind of economy in which the ownership of the means of PRODUCTION is partly in the PRIVATE SECTOR and partly in the PUBLIC SECTOR.

MMPI See MINNESOTA MULTIPHASIC PERSONALITY INVENTORY.

mnemonic Any trick to aid the MEMORY, such as the use of the phrase 'Every Good Boy Deserves Favour' (EGBDF) in learning musical notation.

modality In ERGONOMICS and PSYCHOLOGY, this term usually refers to a particular form of sensory experience, like vision or hearing.

mode In STATISTICS, this is a MEASURE OF CENTRAL TENDENCY; the most frequently occurring value in a series of numbers.

model [1] Any representation of an object, situation or ORGANIZATION. It may be physical, verbal, mathematical or produced by COMPUTER SIMULATION. [2] In SOCIAL PSYCHOLOGY, it is used of a person whose behaviour is closely observed. See also MODELLING.

modelling In SOCIAL PSYCHOLOGY, this is a form of LEARNING from observing a MODEL which goes much further than copying or imitating. Children, especially, may generalize from the model's behaviour to a wide range of similar behaviours of their own invention.

modem From the term 'modulator–demodulator'. It is an electronic device that converts information from a COMPUTER into a form suitable for transmission by telephone, thus enabling COMMUNICATION with other computers.

monetarism In ECONOMICS, this refers to the theory that the successful MANAGEMENT of an economy depends crucially on CONTROL of the MONEY SUPPLY, because too rapid a rise in the supply of money can lead to INFLATION.

monetary policy In ECONOMICS, this refers to a government's position on the regulation of the amount of spending power available in an economy and the cost of borrowing money; for example, deciding whether or not to impose a CREDIT SQUEEZE.

money supply In ECONOMICS, this refers to the total amount of money circulating within an economy at any given time, in the form of notes, coins, bank deposits and so on.

monochronic culture A concept developed by the American anthropologist Edward Hall. It refers to a CULTURE in which time is divided up sequentially into segments and where the SOCIAL NORM is to do one thing at a time. Such cultures tend to be found in the Anglo-Saxon countries of North America and Northern Europe, where doing business revolves around strict timetabling and punctuality. Contrast with POLYCHRONIC CULTURE.

monoculture Any CULTURE whose SOCIAL NORMS include the assumption that there is only one right way of doing things and one correct SYSTEM of values and beliefs – your average ORGANIZATION, in fact. See also NIH SYNDROME.

monopoly A situation in which a MARKET is under the CONTROL or domination of a single ORGANIZATION. This condition is generally considered to be met at one-quarter to one-third of the market in question. A monopoly is contrary to the ideal of the FREE MARKET and is therefore subject to legal sanctions in all industrialized countries with a capitalist or MIXED ECONOMY. Monopolies can occur in both the PRIVATE SECTOR and the PUBLIC SECTOR. See also DUOPOLY and OLIGOPOLY.

monopsony A situation in which one buyer can CONTROL, or greatly influence, the price of a product through being the only buyer, or the most powerful buyer, in a particular MARKET. A country's Ministry of Defence is a common example.

Monte Carlo methods A technique of SIMULATION, including COMPUTER SIMULATION, that deliberately introduces an element of randomness, for reasons discussed in CHAOS THEORY.

moonlighting Doing a second (or even third) job, usually in the BLACK ECONOMY, in addition to one's normal EMPLOYMENT.

Moore's Law Named after Gordon Moore, the co-founder of the computer company Intel. In 1965, he observed that each new microchip, produced roughly every two years, had about twice as much capacity as its predecessor. This doubling effect meant that over time computer power would rise exponentially. To date, Moore's Law seems to be holding.

morale An indicator of how much IDENTIFICATION the members of an ORGANIZATION have with its aims and values and how much JOB SATISFACTION they derive from belonging to it.

mores The customs, conventions and PRACTICES of a group, an ORGANIZATION or a society.

motivation   In PSYCHOLOGY, this is a general term for any part of the hypothetical psychological process which involves the experiencing of needs and DRIVES, and the behaviour that leads to the GOAL which satisfies them. In more popular usage, motivation refers to those factors that predispose people to act in one way rather than another. See also HERZBERG TWO-FACTOR THEORY, MASLOW, MCCLELLAND and MCGREGOR.

motive hierarchy   See HIERARCHY OF NEEDS.

motor skill   Any SKILL that depends on muscular CONTROL and co-ordination.

multimodal distribution   In STATISTICS this term refers to a DISTRIBUTION with several MODES.

multinational company   A commercial ORGANIZATION which operates in more than one country and moves its resources and activities between them, in such a way as to maximize its trading advantages in areas like labour costs or TAXATION benefits.

multiple-activity chart   A CHART which records the activities and interrelationships of workers or machines on the same time scale.

multiplier effect   In ECONOMICS, this is an idea, associated with JOHN MAYNARD KEYNES, that emphasizes the powerful effect of even small increases in INVESTMENT.

multi-sensual marketing   Product MARKETING that makes use of as wide a range of sensory stimuli as possible. For example, an upmarket bookstore may have a spacious appearance, piped classical music, soft carpeting and a coffee shop to provide a pleasant aroma.

Murphy's Law   An Irish version of the more general SOD'S LAW.

N

n Ach The abbreviation for NEED FOR ACHIEVEMENT.

Nader, Ralph (1934–) An American lawyer and campaigner whose exposure of shoddy practices in the Detroit car industry of the early 1960s heralded the broad movement of concern for the quality of CONSUMER GOODS known generally as CONSUMERISM.

n Aff The abbreviation for NEED FOR AFFILIATION.

NAFTA See NORTH AMERICAN FREE TRADE AREA.

nationalization The process – now virtually extinct – by which a state takes over the ownership of a private company or industry and brings it within the CONTROL of the PUBLIC SECTOR. This may be due to practising the IDEOLOGY of SOCIALISM or to the attempt to save a strategic part of the economy from collapse or from foreign ownership. DENATIONALIZATION has been much more popular since the Reagan–Thatcher years of the 1980s and the collapse of the Soviet Union.

nationalized industry An industry that has undergone NATIONALIZATION.

natural wastage The reduction in the number of people employed in an ORGANIZATION through resignation, RETIREMENT or death (rather than a policy of dismissal or REDUNDANCY), who are not then replaced.

near-market research Scientific research with an evident potential for commercial applications.

need for achievement A concept associated particularly with the American psychologist DAVID MCCLELLAND. It is the strongly felt MOTIVATION to achieve, to accomplish ambitions and to be successful that is commonly found in the ENTREPRENEUR, for example. McClelland suggested that this motivation is inculcated by careful child-rearing patterns, and especially the encouragement of early ACHIEVEMENT (like walking and talking) by mothers. This may hold good especially for the relationship between mothers and first-born sons.

need for affiliation As used in SOCIAL PSYCHOLOGY, this term refers to the need to be with other people, particularly when facing an unpleasant experience. There is some evidence that this need may be related to birth order, with last-born children having least need and first-born children (especially males) having most.

need for power An aspect of MOTIVATION suggested by DAVID MCCLELLAND. It is a need to influence other people and have them do things they would not otherwise do. Such people tend to be very concerned with their position and status in the organizational HIERARCHY. They may also be prone to MACHIAVELLIANISM.

need hierarchy See HIERARCHY OF NEEDS.

need to make sense This is a tendency observed time and again throughout all the diverse areas of PSYCHOLOGY. People apparently have a very deep-rooted need to make sense of themselves, their thoughts and feelings, and their ENVIRONMENT. This is true whether the environment is physical or social; whether the person is alone in it or with other people. In particular, people are threatened by evidence of ambiguity, disorder or unpredictability and will try very hard to reduce these and feel psychologically more comfortable, even at the expense of the truth. See also COGNITIVE DISSONANCE, EGO DEFENCE and SELF-FULFILLING PROPHECY.

negotiation   In INDUSTRIAL RELATIONS, this is the essence of the COLLECTIVE BARGAINING process. It refers to the discussion of terms and conditions of EMPLOYMENT by employers and employees, or their representatives, with a view to reaching a mutually acceptable outcome.

Neo-Human Relations School   A development of the HUMAN RELATIONS approach to ORGANIZATIONAL THEORY which arose in the 1950s and 1960s and emphasized more of a WORK PSYCHOLOGY orientation. It accepted, for instance, that conflicts of interest were endemic to ORGANIZATIONS and had to be managed rather than banished, or wished away. Closely associated with the work of HERZBERG, MASLOW and MCGREGOR.

neologism   Literally, 'a new word'. It is found in scientific and scholarly writing where common words are used in a new way, like BUG or MOUSE, or where new words are concocted, like BRAINSTORMING or WORKAHOLIC.

nepotism   The PRACTICE of a business owner or member of SENIOR MANAGEMENT of an ORGANIZATION showing favouritism towards a relative regardless of his or her ability. Standard practice in many private companies but severely frowned upon (officially) in public organizations.

network analysis   See CRITICAL PATH ANALYSIS.

network-building   Any systematic attempt to link people and resources round a common goal or shared interests and values, like the OLD SCHOOL TIE and what it represents.

networking   Linking people who are scattered geographically into a single WORK GROUP by electronic means; for example, TELEWORKING.

network organization   A sexier way of describing an INFORMAL ORGANIZATION.

neurolinguistic programming   A fashionable technique for influencing interpersonal COMMUNICATION, aimed at changing someone's behaviour or beliefs, whose content and purpose are difficult to pin down despite the scientific-sounding name. It is concerned with patterns of relations between bodily movement, memory and the use of language. It originated as a form of PSYCHOTHERAPY, based apparently on GESTALT psychology, but is now widely applied to the world of work despite (or perhaps because of) the lack of evidence that it actually does anything.

neurotic organization   The idea that the irrational and dysfunctional behaviour of a key individual at the top of a HIERARCHY can affect those around him to the extent that the ORGANIZATION itself comes to mirror his neurosis. HENRY FORD was a good example. See also CEO DISEASE.

new product development   The very expensive process of bringing to MARKET new products and, much more frequently, INNOVATIONS to existing products. Many thousands of such products appear every year but it is estimated that as few as 10 per cent of them may be commercially successful.

new technology   The term often used to describe the applied microelectronic devices to be found in the ELECTRONIC OFFICE.

NGO See NON-GOVERNMENTAL ORGANIZATION.

NGT See NOMINAL GROUP TECHNIQUE.

niche marketing The systematic search for a MARKET NICHE, usually by a small specialist ORGANIZATION. Its basic principle is the attempt to create a new MARKET rather than to increase its MARKET SHARE of an existing market.

NIH (not invented here) syndrome The syndrome that militates against copying from, or even LEARNING from, others in the same field. It is usually regarded in MANAGEMENT SCIENCE as a sign of insecurity or inertia masquerading as arrogance (for instance, 'if it wasn't invented here how good can it be?') and was widely used (in the past) by Western companies to denigrate the Japanese, whose business PRACTICES were enthusiastically opposed to the NIH syndrome.

NLP See NEUROLINGUISTIC PROGRAMMING.

noise [1] Any sound that the listener does not want to hear. Prolonged noise can cause STRESS and even HEARING LOSS, as well as a drop in PRODUCTION. [2] Anything that distracts from the message in a SYSTEM of COMMUNICATION.

nominal group technique Any method for eliciting the ideas of group members on a given topic.

nomothetic An approach to the study of human behaviour that emphasizes general or universal principles rather than the uniqueness of the individual. Contrast with IDIOGRAPHIC.

non-directive therapy A form of PSYCHOTHERAPY which accepts an individual's expression of his or her needs and conflicts on his or her own terms, without any preconceived system of interpretation for steering the person in a particular direction. Compare with BEHAVIOUR MODIFICATION and PSYCHOANALYSIS.

non-employment The state of neither being in paid EMPLOYMENT nor seeking it – other than being in RETIREMENT; for example, married women with no paid employment.

non-executive director A director of an ORGANIZATION who is not a full-time employee and who does not have any EXECUTIVE form of AUTHORITY.

non-governmental organization This term is usually applied to an ORGANIZATION that operates internationally but is not supported, in the main, by direct governmental funding; for example, Amnesty International or the Red Cross.

non-parametric statistics Statistical methods that may be used when the data do not conform to a NORMAL DISTRIBUTION; for example, most data in studies of human behaviour.

non-profit organization Any ORGANIZATION whose ownership resides entirely with its members and whose financial operations are not intended to yield a PROFIT for shareholders; for example, clubs, neighbourhood associations or charities.

non-verbal behaviour Any form of human behaviour that does not employ speech or writing.

non-verbal communication Direct, face-to-face COMMUNICATION between people by any means other than the spoken word. This would include facial expressions, body gestures, hand gestures, body posture and eye contact.

norm In STATISTICS, this is a single value representative of a whole set of numbers, such as one of the MEASURES OF

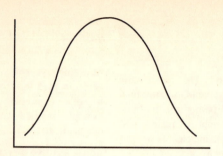

Figure 26 Normal distribution.

CENTRAL TENDENCY (MEAN, MEDIAN and MODE). See also GROUP NORM and SOCIAL NORM.

normal Literally, CONFORMITY to the NORM or standard. As applied to human behaviour it usually refers to what is expected (the SOCIAL NORM) or what is generally considered right, proper or correct under the given circumstances.

normal distribution The DISTRIBUTION of data from a RANDOM SAMPLE of the POPULATION. When these data are plotted on a graph they show up as a symmetrical BELL-SHAPED CURVE with scores clustered around the average and declining towards either extreme. (See Figure 26.)

normative Any behaviour, idea or opinion that pertains to a particular NORM or expectation.

normative influence In SOCIOLOGY, this is the process by which other people's anticipated judgements of what is right and wrong influence someone's behaviour.

norming A term sometimes used for the third stage of group formation within an ORGANIZATION where the GROUP NORMS of expected behaviour and appropriate roles for all the members are being worked out. Members now see themselves as belonging to the group and GROUP COHESIVENESS is emphasized. See also FORMING, STORMING and PERFORMING.

North American Free Trade Agreement A treaty, originally between Canada and the United States and extended to Mexico in 1994, which aims to set up a free trade area where tariffs and other barriers to trade between member nations may be removed.

n Pow Abbreviation for NEED FOR POWER.

numeracy Literally, the ability to count – the numerical equivalent of literacy. The term is used more widely to include people with no fear of dealing with STATISTICS or mathematics and the ABILITY to handle QUANTITATIVE METHODOLOGY.

O

O & M See ORGANIZATION AND METHODS.

OB Mod An abbreviation for organizational BEHAVIOUR MODIFICATION.

occupational choice Having a choice of occupation is largely confined to middle-class people with education and/or connections. Within this constraint, choice is determined partly by interests and ABILITIES and partly by SELF-IMAGE and an idea of what is appropriate to the people concerned.

occupational health The study of people's health in their work environment, including the factors that contribute to ill-health such as STRESS. This field draws mainly on PSYCHOLOGY and other branches of SOCIAL SCIENCE, as well as medicine.

occupational medicine See INDUSTRIAL MEDICINE.

occupational psychology Used interchangeably with the older usage of INDUSTRIAL PSYCHOLOGY, though strictly speaking it should have a wider remit covering all occupations regardless of setting.

occupational segregation A situation where certain jobs or occupations are filled by certain groups, often regardless of their being theoretically open to all. DISCRIMINATION is usually by sex, religion and social background. The OLD SCHOOL TIE might make an appearance.

Occupational Stress Indicator A PSYCHOLOGICAL TEST that tries to measure the degree of JOB SATISFACTION and (dissatisfaction) that an individual is experiencing. Produced in 1987 by a leading expert on STRESS, Cary Cooper, and his associates.

occupational therapy An adjunct to PSYCHOTHERAPY in hospitals, which involves patients in performing useful TASKS to help improve their SELF-ESTEEM and feelings of worth.

OD See OPERATIONAL DEFINITION.

office politics A term widely used for the games people play in their attempts, whether as individuals or groups, to advance their own interests within an ORGANIZATION, whether legitimately or not.

office technology See ELECTRONIC OFFICE.

off-line That part of a COMPUTER system which is not under the immediate CONTROL of the central processing unit and cannot therefore be accessed directly. It is used to produce data that is only required at relatively long intervals, like a monthly bank statement or a quarterly electricity bill. Compare with ONLINE.

OJT See ON-THE-JOB TRAINING.

old school tie A long-established form of NETWORKING. In this case, chaps who went to the same English public school (and are therefore entitled to wear the same tie) practise various forms of mutual aid in later life.

oligopoly In ECONOMICS, this is a situation in which a few sellers can CONTROL or dominate a MARKET. Such a situation is widely regarded as an INCENTIVE for the sellers to form a CARTEL. See also DUOPOLY and MONOPOLY.

OM See OPERATIONS MANAGEMENT.

omnibus survey   In MARKET RESEARCH, this is a wide-ranging form of survey that seeks to obtain data on many different topics at the same time, usually for a number of different clients.

180° evaluation   A technique used in PERSONNEL MANAGEMENT where opinions about someone's work are obtained from all of his or her equal status colleagues. Compare with 360° EVALUATION.

one-trial learning   LEARNING that occurs after a single trial or PRACTICE.

online   That part of a COMPUTER system which is under the immediate CONTROL of the central processing unit and can make information immediately accessible to the user by being linked directly to a MAINFRAME and operating in REAL TIME. The most common example is that of an airline seat reservation SYSTEM. Compare with OFF-LINE.

on-the-job training   A form of TRAINING that is given to people at their place of WORK, and usually during working hours. In the United Kingdom, it often involves SITTING NEXT TO NELLIE, and in the United States, the use of the BUDDY SYSTEM.

open-plan office   A single large room divided into various workstations but with no fixed walls or barriers between them. It has been associated with a reduction in JOB SATISFACTION.

operational audit   See MANAGEMENT AUDIT.

operational definition   A definition of something which is based on the operation of the factors which produced it; for example, INFLATION is defined by the movement of prices and the real value of money. The term is also used more loosely to mean a 'working definition' or a 'rule of thumb'.

operational research   A branch of MANAGEMENT SCIENCE that applies mathematics to a series of techniques, like CRITICAL PATH ANALYSIS, which an ORGANIZATION may use in its PLANNING and decision-making. In essence, operational research is used to see whether the efficiency and COST EFFECTIVENESS of a SYSTEM can be improved by developing a scientific MODEL to study that system and including within it the factors of change and RISK.

operations management   Traditionally, operations management has been concerned with all the processes that go into the physical PRODUCTION of the goods that an ORGANIZATION is set up to provide. With the balance of economic activity in developing countries changing inexorably, since the late 1950s, from the manufacturing to the service sector, OM has had to become less concerned with material processes and more involved with MARKETING (and therefore customers) and HUMAN RESOURCE MANAGEMENT (and therefore staff).

operations research   The American term for OPERATIONAL RESEARCH.

operations strategy   A plan that attempts to put the CORPORATE STRATEGY of an ORGANIZATION into a practical format which can be acted upon.

opinion leader   A term used in SOCIOLOGY to denote a person of STATUS within a given group, whose opinions are highly thought of and who can therefore influence the opinions of other members of the group. See also TWO-STEP FLOW OF COMMUNICATION.

opinion polling   A form of SURVEY RESEARCH in which respondents are asked their opinions about goods, services or political candidates.

opportunity cost   In ECONOMICS, this refers to the lost INCOME, PROFIT or time involved in forgoing an alternative course of action; that is, this is an economic cost and would not be included as an ACCOUNTING cost.

optimization   The process of weighing up all the factors in a given situation with the aim of producing the most effective or optimum PERFORMANCE, given unavoidable constraints. Compare with SATISFICING.

OR   See OPERATIONAL RESEARCH.

organic organization   A term introduced by two British sociologists and MANAGEMENT theorists, Tom Burns and George Stalker. It denotes a relatively open and informal type of ORGANIZATION displaying flexibility in people's JOB DESCRIPTIONS, for example, and encouraging COMMUNICATION and the flow of new ideas outside the formal CHAIN OF COMMAND. This is in striking contrast to what happens in a MECHANISTIC ORGANIZATION. See also BUREAUCRACY.

organization   A group of people brought together for the purpose of achieving certain objectives. As the basic unit of an organization is the ROLE rather than the person in it, the organization is maintained in existence, sometimes over a long period of time, despite many changes of members. See also BUREAUCRACY, DIVISION OF LABOUR, FORMAL ORGANIZATION, HIERARCHY, INFORMAL ORGANIZATION, ORGANIZATIONAL THEORY and SPECIALIZATION.

organizational audit   An AUDIT of all aspects of an ORGANIZATION's operations. In PRACTICE, this is usually the same as a MANAGEMENT AUDIT.

organizational behaviour   The behaviour of an ORGANIZATION acting as an entity, rather than that of any individual member.

organizational buying   The process of buying goods and services on behalf of ORGANIZATIONS rather than individual consumers. Far more money is spent, in total, on organizational buying than individual buying. Organizational buyers and sellers usually operate in a much smaller market than individuals and, indeed, may well know each other personally. The arms trade is a well-known example.

organizational change   The term that describes the process of change within an ORGANIZATION.

organizational climate   The ethos of, or commonly perceived feelings about, an ORGANIZATION. It is based on tangible factors like the prevailing MANAGEMENT STYLE, the clarity of GOALS and values, the time horizons and so on.

organizational commitment   The extent to which people feel committed to the ORGANIZATION they work in. It is an important component of employee MORALE and MOTIVATION and is mainly concerned with how emotionally attached someone is to their organization.

organizational conflict   A clash of interests, values or GOALS between individuals or groups within an ORGANIZATION.

organizational convenience   A course of action that meets the (usually financial) interests of the ORGANIZATION as a whole (i.e. SENIOR MANAGEMENT) rather than the interests of staff or customers; for example, moving to a cheaper but less accessible location.

organizational culture   This denotes 'CULTURE' as the term is used in both ANTHROPOLOGY and PSYCHOLOGY; that is, not only the shared beliefs, values, ATTI-TUDES and expectations of its members that make up the life of an ORGANIZATION, but also the unquestioned assumptions about its traditions and ways of doing things. See also NIH SYNDROME.

organizational design   The extent to which an ORGANIZATION has been deliber-ately structured to achieve its stated goals and the form which that structure takes. It includes the set of roles and responsibili-ties set out in the official documents of the FORMAL ORGANIZATION.

organizational development   A process that affects the ORGANIZATION as a whole as well as its individual members. It involves the application of BEHAVI-OURAL SCIENCE to the process of improv-ing the functioning and the MANAGEMENT of the organization, especially in response to changes in the ENVIRONMENT.

organizational goals   The formally stated objectives which are the basis for the existence and the maintenance of an ORGANIZATION.

organizational learning   Learning that is not limited to particular members of an ORGANIZATION but is retained within the organization as a whole and that would remain even if the individuals who did the actual learning were to leave. The learning has therefore been institutional-ized, through either the FORMAL ORGANI-ZATION or, probably more effectively, through the INFORMAL ORGANIZATION.

organizational loyalty   The basis of the PSYCHOLOGICAL CONTRACT between an ORGANIZATION and its members. It is usu-ally assumed to be something the individ-ual owes the organization – rarely the other way round.

organizational man   A term, used both approvingly and pejoratively, applied to someone who has the kind of PERSONALITY which allows him or her to fit relatively comfortably into an ORGANI-ZATION, particularly a FORMAL ORGANIZA-TION with some degree of BUREAUCRACY.

organizational pathology   Writers on ORGANIZATIONAL THEORY from a HUMAN RELATIONS viewpoint (such as ARGYRIS and MCGREGOR) have proposed that an ORGAN-IZATION can be healthy or unhealthy, just like any of its individual members. Their criteria for judging organizational health parallels accepted criteria for individual MENTAL HEALTH, as follows: [1] *reality testing* – the ABILITY to perceive what is really happening in the ENVIRONMENT and how this is likely to affect the organiza-tion; [2] *adaptability* – the ability to react to a changing environment; [3] *identity* – the extent to which members are clear on what the organization is, what it stands for and what its goals are. Underpinning these criteria is the crucial need for INTEGRATION so that different parts of the organization are not in conflict with each other – a sure sign of both individual and organizational pathology.

organizational politics   Another term for OFFICE POLITICS.

organizational psychology   Often used interchangeably with the older term INDUSTRIAL PSYCHOLOGY but without the connotation of being limited to ORGANI-ZATIONS in industrial, or indeed work, settings.

organizational shape   The profile of the levels of HIERARCHY in an ORGANIZA-TION; the extent to which it is a FLAT ORGANIZATION or a TALL ORGANIZATION.

organizational size   The number of members which an ORGANIZATION has can have a direct effect on its ORGANIZATIONAL CLIMATE, ORGANIZATIONAL CULTURE and

ORGANIZATIONAL STRUCTURE. The larger the number the greater the pressure to operate as a FORMAL ORGANIZATION with a high level of BUREAUCRACY, a relatively fixed CHAIN OF COMMAND, and increased levels in a HIERARCHY of AUTHORITY.

organizational structure The arrangement of the work of an ORGANIZATION into the different functional roles and management roles.

organizational symbols Symbols uniquely associated with a particular ORGANIZATION. These may be internal (annual dinner, founder's picture or slogan) or external (LOGO or TRADEMARK).

organizational theory The systematic study of the ORGANIZATION, its structure and functioning, and its relationships to the people who comprise it. This area of study draws heavily on PSYCHOLOGY and SOCIOLOGY.

organizational tree See ORGANIZATION CHART.

organizational types Any attempt to classify or categorize ORGANIZATIONS along one or more dimensions with the aim of identifying characteristic differences between them; for example, formality, as a way of distinguishing MECHANISTIC ORGANIZATIONS from ORGANIC ORGANIZATIONS.

organization and methods The application of WORK STUDY techniques to the structure and procedures of an ORGANIZATION in order to improve the efficiency of the organization's SYSTEMS.

organization chart A CHART outlining the relationships between the direct functions, responsibilities and titles in an ORGANIZATION and often the people who actually perform them. (See Figure 27, p110.) This is an important guide to the workings of the FORMAL ORGANIZATION.

orientation programme See INDUCTION.

OSI See OCCUPATIONAL STRESS INDICATOR.

outplacement The process of helping people to find new jobs after giving them notice of REDUNDANCY but while they are still employed.

outsourcing Obtaining supplies of material and HUMAN RESOURCES outside the ORGANIZATION.

outworker See HOME-WORKER.

overachiever A person who exceeds the level of ACHIEVEMENT expected of her or him. The term is sometimes used in the field of education to describe someone who tries too hard; that is, a person whose ambitions appear to outstrip his or her ABILITY. Contrast with UNDERACHIEVER.

overcompensation Producing a greater effort than is needed to overcome a difficulty or resolve a defect. The term is often used in connection with attempts to overcome an INFERIORITY COMPLEX.

overconforming This term is sometimes used to describe a person who is excessively slavish to the demands of AUTHORITY or the conventions of a SOCIAL NORM.

overhead Any recurrent day-to-day expenditure incurred in running an ORGANIZATION other than the costs of labour and material; for example, rent, heating and lighting.

overlearning LEARNING in which PRACTICE or repetition continues beyond the point required for adequate mastery of the TASK. Overlearning is not usually considered harmful; that is, it is not thought possible to learn something too well.

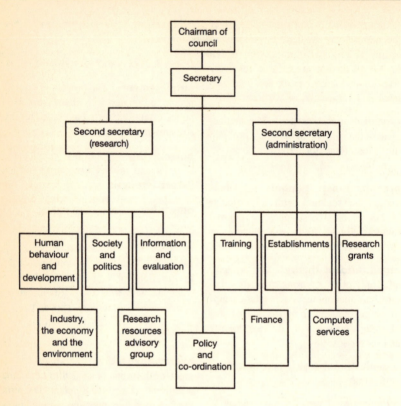

Figure 27 Organization chart.

overmanning   A situation in which there are more people employed by an ORGANIZATION than are necessary for the efficient PERFORMANCE of its work. Compare with UNDERMANNING. See also UNDEREMPLOYMENT.

overtime   Any time worked outside normal working hours for which people may be paid at a higher rate than the basic level of PAY, usually DOUBLE TIME or TIME-AND-A-HALF.

Owen, Robert (1771–1858)   The owner of a textile mill at New Lanark, Scotland, who is sometimes credited with being the first modern MANAGER, because he addressed the issues of MOTIVATION and PRODUCTIVITY and was particularly interested in the ATTITUDES of people to their work and the MANAGEMENT of that work.

own brand   The PRACTICE of a retailer putting its own name on a product as opposed to that of the producer; for example, 'Statt's Baked Beans' as opposed to 'Heinz Baked Beans'. It has been standard practice for a number of years for most leading retailers to buy in generic products like food or clothing from the same group of suppliers – often in cheaper labour MARKETS – and then to put their own label on them. This tendency appears to be growing, at the expense of the well-known BRANDS.

P

pacing The process of allowing a fixed amount of time for the PERFORMANCE of an operation, or an entire job, on a moving ASSEMBLY LINE. Usually the time allowed (or pace) is set by machinery under the CONTROL of a SUPERVISOR.

PAI See PERFORMANCE APPRAISAL INTERVIEW.

paired comparisons A method of assessing a series of items and putting them in RANK ORDER by comparing each one with all the others in turn. This method can be used in JOB EVALUATION; for example, in comparing the PERFORMANCE of a number of MARKET RESEARCH interviewers.

panacea A universal remedy for all problems in an ORGANIZATION. Ideally, it should be cheap, painless and change nothing important, which is why *re-organization* is such a great favourite.

panel testing See CONSUMER PANEL.

paper-and-pencil test Any kind of TEST or PROJECTIVE TECHNIQUE that requires written answers. Now usually computerized.

PAQ See POSITION ANALYSIS QUESTION-NAIRE.

paradigm A detailed example or MODEL of a particular process.

Parameter Mathematically, this is a constant in an equation that defines the form of the curve. In PSYCHOLOGY, it is a constant that defines the curve of a psychological function like LEARNING. In STATISTICS, it takes the form of a measure of a total POPULATION of scores. The term is sometimes used loosely, and wrongly, as if it were 'perimeter'.

parametric statistics STATISTICS that deal with a NORMAL DISTRIBUTION or other POPULATION of scores.

Pareto analysis A technique for identifying and concentrating on the minority of things, both positive and negative, that are thought to contribute most to the operations of an ORGANIZATION. It is sometimes referred to as the '80 : 20 rule', or 'the law of the trivial many and the critical few'. Examples include 20 per cent of customers accounting for about 80 per cent of the sales, or 20 per cent of stock accounting for 80 per cent of the value of an INVENTORY. The analysis is named after Vilfredo Pareto, the late nineteenth-century Italian engineer, economist and sociologist who first suggested the idea.

parity [1] Equal rates of PAY between individuals or groups of people. [2] The perceived fairness of equal rates of pay between individuals or groups of people. When used in this sense it has the same value, connotation and importance for MOTIVATION as the term EQUITY.

Parkinson's Law Work expands to fill the time available for its completion. C. Northcote Parkinson, the British writer, introduced this concept in the 1950s as a humourous observation, but it has since become a serious contribution to MANAGE-MENT SCIENCE (like the PETER PRINCIPLE). Parkinson later introduced a variant of his law that is just as familiar in private life as it is in the life of the ORGANIZATION – expenditure rises to meet INCOME.

participant observation   A research technique in SOCIAL SCIENCE where an observer becomes an accepted member of the group he or she wishes to study.

participation   The term used to describe the involvement of people in the PERFORMANCE of the ORGANIZATION they work for; for example, by EMPLOYEE OWNERSHIP or PROFIT SHARING.

participative management   The kind of MANAGEMENT which emphasizes INDUSTRIAL DEMOCRACY, active worker PARTICIPATION in running an ORGANIZATION and the importance of HUMAN RELATIONS at WORK. The opposite of RATIONAL MANAGEMENT.

part-time job   Any job that takes up less than the NORMAL full-time hours of work in any given situation.

patent   A MONOPOLY right, awarded by law to an individual or group, granting sole right to make, use or sell an article or process they have invented. In the United Kingdom, a patent normally lasts for twenty years, during which time the patent holder is protected from any attempts by others to copy the invention.

paternalism   The process of treating adults like children in an ORGANIZATION by withholding from them any POWER to make decisions affecting their own work lives.

path–goal theory   A type of CONTIN-GENCY THEORY OF LEADERSHIP which is based on the EXPECTANCY THEORY OF MOTIVATION. It concentrates on maximiz-ing the PERFORMANCE of subordinates in a given situation, with the leader or MAN-AGER having an enabling function of clearing a path for his or her subordinates towards their personal goals at work.

Paula Principle   This is not a female version of the PETER PRINCIPLE but the inverse of it. It states that women in an ORGANIZATION are held below their level of competence. As the argument behind this principle is that incompetent men are particularly threatened by competent women, it also *complements* the Peter Principle.

Pavlov, Ivan (1849–1936)   A Russian physiologist who won the Nobel Prize in 1904 for his work on the digestive SYSTEM of dogs. In the course of his research he chanced upon a phenomenon he could not explain and followed it (reluctantly) out of physiology and into PSYCHOLOGY. What puzzled him was that his dogs began to salivate not only when they were presented with food but even before they were fed, when they recognized the man coming to feed them – the essence of CONDITIONING. Though Pavlov thought he had found a way of studying the brain, rather than behaviour, his work inspired a new American school of PSYCHOLOGY called BEHAVIOURISM.

pay   An amount of money paid on a regular basis to people in regular EMPLOY-MENT. Payment may be of wages or salary, in cash or by cheque, or by direct bank transfer.

payment by results   A SYSTEM of remuneration in which PAY is linked to PRODUCTIVITY. See also PIECEWORK and WORK STUDY.

payment in kind   Payment for work done in goods and services rather than money.

PBR   See PAYMENT BY RESULTS.

PC   See PERSONAL COMPUTER.

peak experience   In HUMANISTIC PSY-CHOLOGY, this term refers to a rare moment of great emotional POWER in which a person feels something akin to ecstasy, where she or he is at one with herself or himself and with the world – a moment of SELF-ACTUALIZATION, in fact.

pecking order The HIERARCHY of STATUS relationships formed among farm-yard hens by their PRACTICE of pecking each other. The most pecked hen has the lowest status. The term is now routinely (and therefore dangerously) applied to status relationships in human groups. Similarly, the term 'henpecked' has long been part of everyday speech – though it is applied to males rather than females.

peer group Any group of people with whom one associates on more or less equal terms. It is used of both a social group and a WORK GROUP.

people-oriented culture An ORGANI-ZATIONAL CULTURE which emphasizes most the meeting of the professional and psychological needs of an ORGANIZA-TION's members. Usually found in small, non-traditional organizations. Often compared with TASK-ORIENTED CULTURE.

percentile In STATISTICS, this is one-hundredth of the total number of scores in a ranked DISTRIBUTION; for example, the ninetieth percentile is the point below which lie 90 per cent of the scores.

perception The mental process by which the brain receives the flow of infor-mation about the ENVIRONMENT from the sense organs (eyes, ears and so forth) and uses this raw material to help us make sense of that environment.

perceptual defence The process of defending oneself (one's SELF), or one's EGO, from the awareness of unpleasant perceptions, either by misperceiving them as being pleasant or inoffensive or by not perceiving anything at all.

performance The way a job or TASK is done by an individual, a group or an ORGANIZATION.

performance appraisal interview An INTERVIEW between an employee and his or her line MANAGER, usually con-ducted once a year, at which an ASSESS-MENT is made of the individual's job performance and how it relates to TRAIN-ING needs, PROMOTION opportunities and so on.

performance-related pay See PAY-MENT BY RESULTS.

performing A term sometimes used for the fourth stage of group formation within an ORGANIZATION. This is ideally the group in its mature form (although not all groups achieve this stage) where it works most effectively. Interdependence of members is emphasized at this stage. See also FORMING, STORMING and NORMING.

peripheral route to persuasion It is widely accepted in CONSUMER PSYCHOL-OGY that there are two different 'routes to persuasion' for a COMMUNICATION aimed at prospective purchasers. The peripheral route, which does not require rational thought by the consumer, is followed when the consumer's involvement and MOTIVATION in assessing the product are low. That is, the receiver of the message may respond to cues, like background music, that do not involve much assess-ment of the message itself. Compare with the more effective CENTRAL ROUTE TO PERSUASION.

perk An abbreviation of the word 'perquisite' whose use is largely synony-mous with that of FRINGE BENEFIT, although it has overtones of more specifi-cally job-related kinds of benefit, like free meals for restaurant workers or cheap travel for airline employees. See also PAYMENT IN KIND.

personal computer   A MICROCOMPUTER used only by a single individual.

personality   The sum total of all the factors that make an individual human being both individual and human; the thinking, feeling and behaving that all human beings have in common, and the particular characteristic pattern of these elements that makes every human being unique. Psychologists often emphasize the INTEGRATION and the dynamic nature of an individual's personality, and the important ROLE of UNCONSCIOUS processes that may be hidden from the individual but are at least partly perceptible to other people.

personality test   See PSYCHOLOGICAL TEST.

personality types   Names given to what appear to be distinct patterns of individual tendencies and behaviour; for example, AUTHORITARIAN PERSONALITY, TYPE A, TYPE B.

personal space   In SOCIAL PSYCHOLOGY, this is the idea that the area immediately surrounding an individual is felt to be his or her own. The amount of space claimed in this way varies from CULTURE to culture, but any invasion of it is taken as a hostile or threatening act.

person–job fit   The extent to which the PERSONALITY of an individual fits harmoniously with the job he or she does. On the goodness of fit between the two will depend the crucial factors of work, like JOB SATISFACTION, PRODUCTIVITY and STRESS.

personnel   [1] The people employed in an ORGANIZATION. [2] The function of dealing with an organization's employees as its HUMAN RESOURCES.

personnel audit   See MANAGEMENT AUDIT.

personnel economics   The use of financial INCENTIVES and disincentives in the RECRUITMENT, SELECTION and MANAGEMENT of STAFF. Economists often call this 'motivation' but most psychologists would regard it as only a part of MOTIVATION, the part that deals with external (as opposed to internal) incentives.

personnel management   A specialized function concerned with all aspects of the MANAGEMENT of HUMAN RESOURCES in an ORGANIZATION from RECRUITMENT to RETIREMENT, including conditions of EMPLOYMENT, SELECTION, TRAINING, PLACEMENT, PROMOTION and the WELFARE FUNCTION.

personnel specification   See EMPLOYEE PROFILE.

person perception   The process by which people form impressions of others, then flesh these impressions out and make them more coherent – though not necessarily more accurate. See also NEED TO MAKE SENSE.

PERT   See PROGRAMME EVALUATION AND REVIEW TECHNIQUE.

PEST Analysis   A review of a company's business environment in terms of four major factors: [1] Political, [2] Economic, [3] Social and [4] Technological.

Peter Principle   In a HIERARCHY, every employee tends to rise to her or his level of incompetence – and stick there. Laurence Peter, the Canadian educational psychologist, introduced this concept in the 1960s as a humorous observation but it has since become a serious contribution to MANAGEMENT SCIENCE (like PARKINSON'S LAW). The Peter Principle deals mainly with the experience of men, as might be expected, but see the related PAULA PRINCI-PLE for women. It is perhaps most applicable where people are promoted out of a SPECIALIST job they are good at (like sales, car mechanics or teaching) into a MANAGEMENT position which usually requires a different set of skills, and for which they have received no TRAINING.

phenotype   The result of the interaction between the GENOTYPE of inherited genetic tendencies and the social ENVIRONMENT. There is no way of seeing a person's genotype, for genetic potentialities can only appear in actual behaviour. All the behaviour that we can observe from before birth right throughout life is therefore a phenotype.

picket   A person or group posted outside their workplace as a TRADE UNION presence during an INDUSTRIAL DISPUTE. The picket will try to persuade other workers to support their side of the dispute by not crossing the picket line and going in to work.

pictogram   A CHART which uses pictures or symbols to represent numerical data. (See Figure 28.)

piecework   A form of PAYMENT BY RESULTS where workers are paid for each piece of work they do rather than the number of hours they put in. It was based originally on the SCIENTIFIC MANAGEMENT principles of F.W. TAYLOR.

pie chart   A circular CHART with sections representing proportions of some total entity as slices of a pie. (See Figure 29, p116.)

pilot study   A term sometimes used in MARKET RESEARCH or SURVEY RESEARCH; for example, when a proposed QUESTIONNAIRE may be tested on a few respondents before being used on a large-scale study, to see whether the questionnaire needs revising and whether the study itself is worth doing.

pink pound/dollar   A term used to describe consumer spending on products identified as being particularly appropriate to gay and lesbian people, or simply the total consumer spend of homosexuals.

placement   The process of placing someone in a job, ideally with a perfect PERSON–JOB FIT. This is an important aspect of PERSONNEL MANAGEMENT.

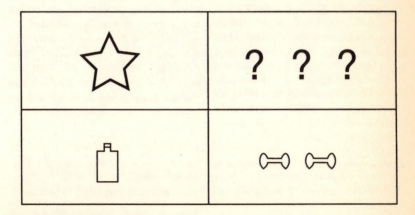

Figure 28 Pictogram.

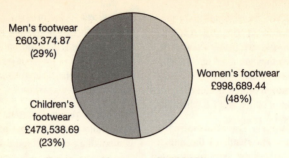

Men's footwear
£603,374.87
(29%)

Women's footwear
£998,689.44
(48%)

Children's
footwear
£478,538.69
(23%)

Total sales of footwear = £2,080,603

Figure 29 Pie chart.

planned economy   An ECONOMY under the central direction and CONTROL of the state (e.g. under the IDEOLOGY of SOCIALISM), which would decide on matters like PAY and PRODUCTION in the absence of MARKET FORCES.

planned obsolescence   See BUILT-IN OBSOLESCENCE.

planning   Any attempt systematically to organize the future PERFORMANCE of people, money, or goods and services, within a given set of constraints and TIME HORIZON.

planning, programming and budgeting system   A widely used technique of ACCOUNTING which, like ZERO-BASED BUDGETING, originated in the United States. It usually follows five steps: [1] set overall objectives for the ORGANIZATION; [2] compare alternatives for effectiveness in achieving objectives; [3] compare alternatives for cost efficiency; [4] select most effective and efficient programmes; and [5] review and assess programme performance.

plant   The buildings, equipment and machinery used in the running of an ORGANIZATION, especially in manufacturing industry.

plateau   See LEARNING PLATEAU.

pluralistic ignorance   A social situation in which each individual believes himself or herself to be the only exception to the accepted beliefs or behaviour of his or her group.

point-of-sale advertising   A form of ADVERTISING material that is BELOW THE LINE and placed in retail outlets; that is, the point at which the sale is actually made.

polychronic culture   A concept developed by the American anthropologist Edward Hall. It refers to a CULTURE in which time is organized 'horizontally' along parallel tracks, rather than sequentially, so that people may do several things at the one time. In this kind of culture social and interpersonal relationships are usually more important than timetabling and punctuality. Such cultures are commonly found in Southern Europe, Latin America, Africa and the Middle East. Contrast with MONOCHRONIC CULTURE.

population   In STATISTICS, this is the total number of cases or individuals from which a sample is drawn for study and about which inferences are to be made.

Porter's Five Forces Model   A technique for analysing the competitive forces in a given MARKET and on a given company. Invented by the American MARKETING guru Michael Porter. The five forces Porter identified are: [1] competitors, [2] potential entrants, [3] buyers, [4] substitutes and [5] suppliers. (See Figure 30.)

Position Analysis Questionnaire A written technique which asks people to keep a diary, along certain detailed and standardized lines, about what they *actually* do in their job as opposed to what they think they do or what they're supposed to do. It is now widely regarded as an important element of a JOB ANALYSIS.

positioning A technique of MARKETING that is closely allied to MARKET SEGMENTATION. The position of a product in the MARKET reflects the way consumers see it in relation to its competitors. The particular attributes of the product, and the way it is promoted, form the ingredients of the strategy a marketer will use in positioning it for its target segment of the market. This implies, therefore, that the marketer has first segmented the market and identified the preferred target. There would be little point in attempting to position a product without having done so first.

post-decision dissonance A form of COGNITIVE DISSONANCE that is experienced after making a difficult decision. The closer the alternatives one has to choose from in their desirability the greater will be the dissonance experienced. This is an important concept to MARKETING in terms of a consumer's post-purchase behaviour. The theory predicts that in order to reduce dissonance following a difficult choice between two desirable alternatives, the consumer will emphasize the positive aspects of the product she chose and the negative aspects of the one she didn't.

post-industrial society A concept associated with the American sociologist Daniel Bell, in which the SERVICE SECTOR could become an alternative basis to manufacturing industry for the creation of

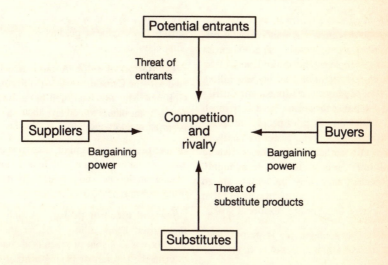

Figure 30 Porter's Five Forces Model.

wealth in society, following the adoption of NEW TECHNOLOGY.

post-modernism   The view that the detached objective observer – a key assumption in traditional Western science and scholarship – doesn't exist. In terms of consumer behaviour it has been suggested by the application of this theory that rather than having an objective IDENTITY people obtain their identity, and are identified by others, from their purchases; that we are what we consume, in a sense.

post-purchase behaviour   See POST-DECISION DISSONANCE.

power   The ABILITY to make things happen by exerting influence over people or things. The most commonly recognized sources of power are physical strength, knowledge, or position in the HIERARCHY of an ORGANIZATION. But there are also less concrete sources of power, such as exist in PERSONALITY factors like CHARISMA or the relationships between people in an organization. See also COERCIVE, EXPERT, LEGITIMATE, REFERENT and REWARD POWER.

power distance   An individual's orientation to AUTHORITY. The extent to which people at the lower levels of an ORGANIZATION, or of a society, are willing to accept that POWER is unequally distributed and that they don't have very much of it. In some countries people are apparently willing to forgo power for clarity in lines of authority: in others, where authority seems to be less highly respected, they may be willing to go against official authority in pursuit of an important social or organizational goal.

PPB   An acronym for PLANNING, PROGRAMMING AND BUDGETING SYSTEM.

PR   See PUBLIC RELATIONS.

practical intelligence   A suggested form of INTELLIGENCE that may not be picked up on a standardized INTELLIGENCE TEST. As the name suggests it is about having an ABILITY to solve problems in practical rather than abstract situations.

practice   [1] In PSYCHOLOGY, this term refers to the repetition of certain behaviour during the process of LEARNING some SKILL. [2] In ANTHROPOLOGY, and in general usage, the term is usually applied to a particular custom or tradition.

predatory pricing   The practice of pricing a product at such a low level that competitors cannot compete and are forced out of the MARKET, whereupon the predator raises the price substantially.

predictive validity   See CONSTRUCT VALIDITY.

prejudice   An ATTITUDE, opinion or belief with a strong emotional underpinning that makes it largely impervious to reason or evidence to the contrary. The term is usually (though not always) used in a negative sense.

premium   A term widely used in MARKETING to describe a product as 'rare', 'first-class' or 'expensive'.

presentation of self   A term associated with the Canadian sociologist Erving Goffman, who was interested in the way people want others to perceive them. See IMPRESSION MANAGEMENT.

presenteeism   A form of ABSENTEEISM while remaining in the job. It is found among employees who are seriously disaffected from their ORGANIZATION.

price and incomes policy   A policy that governments follow whether their IDEOLOGY is in favour of STATE INTERVENTION in the MARKET or having a *LAISSEZ-FAIRE* ECONOMY. The object of the policy is to reduce INFLATION and UNEMPLOY-MENT, and the means of achieving it is to have a reduction in PAY and in prices, or in their rate of increase.

price discrimination In ECONOMICS, this is a PRICING situation where two units of the same product are sold at different prices, whether to the same consumer or to different consumers. In PSYCHOLOGY, the term would refer, in this context, to an aspect of PERCEPTION; the consumer's ABILITY to perceive that there was in fact a difference in price.

pricing The decisions made by an ORGANIZATION in setting a price for the goods or services it provides, taking into account the cost of PRODUCTION and the nature of the MARKET. See also MARKET FORCES.

primacy effect The finding that, under certain conditions in the process of LEARNING, the first one of a series to be learned is remembered best. See also RECENCY EFFECT.

primary group A small group (such as the family) characterized by direct, intimate, personal relationships between people who depend on each other for support and for satisfaction of emotional needs.

prioritizing Making a list of priorities. Not so much a NEOLOGISM as a distortion of the English language.

Prisoner's Dilemma A situation developed out of GAME THEORY and used in SOCIAL PSYCHOLOGY in the study of BARGAINING behaviour. In this particular game two suspects are caught by the police and questioned separately about a crime. If one prisoner confesses and the other does not, the squealer is set free and the fall guy takes the rap. If both confess, both are convicted but dealt with

leniently. If neither confesses, both benefit, because they cannot then be convicted.

private sector The part of a MIXED ECONOMY which is controlled by individuals or companies rather than the state. Compare with PUBLIC SECTOR.

privatization The process of transferring the ownership of an ORGANIZATION or an industry from the PUBLIC SECTOR to the PRIVATE SECTOR, usually by the public sale of shares.

privatized industry An industry that has undergone PRIVATIZATION.

PRIZM An acronym for Potential Rating Index by Zip Market. It is used in MARKETING research on GEODEMOGRAPHIC SEGMENTATION to rank neighbourhoods by SOCIO-ECONOMIC STATUS. Developed by the Claritas Corporation in the United States, PRIZM established an SES ranking (or 'zip quality') of all neighbourhood clusters throughout the country, ranging from ZQ1 ('blue-blood estates') where the most affluent Americans live, to ZQ40 ('public assistance') where the poorest people in the inner cities live. The term is the American equivalent of ACORN.

proactive inhibition The detrimental effect of previous LEARNING on the recall of later learning. Compare with RETRO-ACTIVE INHIBITION.

probability In STATISTICS, this refers to the likelihood that a given event will occur as compared with the likelihood of alternative events occurring. For example, the probability of obtaining a given number when throwing a six-sided dice is one in six.

problem recognition This is the first stage in the process of CONSUMER DECISION-MAKING, which is triggered by consumers perceiving that they have some need which is not being met. The consumer's 'problem' is therefore to close the gap between the actual state they are currently in and the desired state they would like to be in. (See Figure 31.)

process production   See CONTINUOUS PROCESS PRODUCTION.

process theories   Theories of MOTIVATION which are concerned with the process of *how* people decide on what behaviour to engage in. These include theories of EQUITY, EXPECTANCY and GOAL-SETTING. Often contrasted with content theories of motivation, mainly concerned with needs, such as NEED FOR ACHIEVEMENT, NEED FOR AFFILIATION and NEED FOR POWER.

product champion   A key member of an ORGANIZATION who gives devoted support to an innovative idea or product.

product cycle   See PRODUCT LIFE CYCLE.

product differentiation   [1] The packaging and ADVERTISING of different BRANDS of virtually identical products in order to create differences between them in the mind of the consumer. [2] The process of designing and producing a range of the same basic products in order to appeal to different segments of the MARKET; for example, breakfast cereals with or without fibre, fruit, sugar and so on.

product innovation   A product whose PRODUCTION breaks new ground for an ORGANIZATION, either because of the process involved in producing it or the MARKET it is aimed at.

production   All the processes involved in providing goods and services to the MARKET, from the extraction of raw materials to the RETAILING of finished products.

production orientation   A view of the marketplace often held by producers when the demand for their product

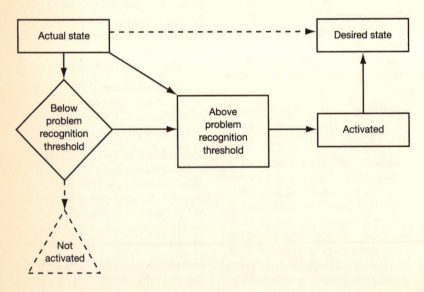

Figure 31 Problem recognition.

exceeds the supply and consumers are forced to buy what there is rather than what they may really want. Under these conditions producers 'sell whatever they can produce', as opposed to the MARKETING CONCEPT where they 'produce whatever they can sell'.

productivity   The rate of output of a worker or a machine.

product life cycle   A term used in MARKETING to describe the different stages that every product goes through from its initial development and introduction to the MARKET, via its initial sales and its established sales, to its eventual decline and withdrawal from the market. (See Figure 32.)

product mix   The range of products, and the particular combination of them at any given time, that an ORGANIZATION produces.

product obsolescence   The final stage of a PRODUCT LIFE CYCLE, when it is superseded by other products. Its identification necessitates the withdrawal of the product from the MARKET.

profession   [1] 'An occupation possessing high social STATUS and characterized by considerable SKILL and knowledge, much of which is theoretical and intellectual in nature' (*The Penguin Management Handbook*). [2] 'A conspiracy against the laity' (George Bernard Shaw).

professional socialization   The process of SOCIALIZATION that a new recruit to a PROFESSION has to undergo.

profit   Any financial gain resulting from business activity. It is basically the excess of INCOME over expenditure for a given period of time.

profit centre   A unit of ORGANIZATION which is treated as a separate entity for purposes of financial CONTROL, and which is allocated designated INCOME targets that allow its PROFIT to be calculated over a given period of time. This unit may be a department, a place, a person or even a machine. Contrast with COST CENTRE.

profit-related pay   A type of PROFIT SHARING for employees who used to have UK tax advantages if they took part of their earnings in this form. However, as

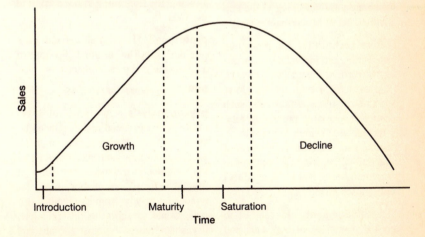

Figure 32 Product life cycle.

PRP often did not follow the more volatile movements of company profits, the tax advantages have been phased out.

profit sharing   An INCENTIVE involving the DISTRIBUTION of some of the PROFIT made by a business to its employees, over and above their normal PAY, in the form of cash or shares.

programmed learning   A form of LEARNING involving a SYSTEM of self instruction, based on CONDITIONING, where a TASK to be mastered is broken down into small steps. The subject is given FEEDBACK about his or her mastery of each step as he or she goes along.

Programme Evaluation and Review Technique   The name of a particularly popular technique in CRITICAL PATH ANALYSIS.

progress chasing   Monitoring each stage of the PRODUCTION process for QUALITY, cost and punctuality.

projection   In PSYCHOANALYSIS, this refers to an EGO DEFENCE where an individual (at the UNCONSCIOUS level) attributes to other people feelings she or he has, but which are too threatening to the EGO to admit into her or his consciousness.

projective technique   A procedure for uncovering an individual's UNCONSCIOUS MOTIVATION, ANXIETY or CONFLICT. Like the RORSCHACH TEST, the 16PF TEST or the THEMATIC APPERCEPTION TEST, such a procedure consists of presenting relatively unstructured stimuli to the subject, designed to encourage the PROJECTION of the material, which would be inadmissible to consciousness, in a relatively direct and undisguised form.

project management   In contrast to the normal operations of both LINE and STAFF MANAGEMENT, projects are intended to pursue specific, time-limited objectives that cross the usual departmental boundaries of an ORGANIZATION. Both the staffing and the LEADERSHIP of such projects will also cross these boundaries. Project management uses both practical techniques like CRITICAL PATH ANALYSIS and HUMAN RELATIONS approaches like TEAM-BUILDING.

promotion   [1] Any attempt to publicize an ORGANIZATION, its products or its interests, by ADVERTISING or PUBLIC RELATIONS. [2] The process of moving within the same organization to a job of greater AUTHORITY, PAY and STATUS. See also the PETER PRINCIPLE.

proprietor   The sole owner of an establishment or business.

Protestant Work Ethic   The idea that work is both an end in itself and a good in itself. This was central to the view of society held by leading Protestant reformers like Calvin and Luther. Together with other values they held, like thrift and an emphasis on ACHIEVEMENT, this ethic is widely believed to have been the major contribution to the INDUSTRIAL REVOLUTION and the rise of INDUSTRIALIZATION in the West.

prototype   [1] A trial version of a product. [2] The original version of a product as compared to later versions.

PRP   See PROFIT-RELATED PAY.

psychoanalysis   A form of PSYCHOTHERAPY, invented and developed by SIGMUND FREUD. It places great emphasis on the uncovering and understanding of UNCONSCIOUS MOTIVATION. Any form of psychoanalysis, no matter how far removed it may be from its Freudian origins, would subscribe to this principle. Psychoanalysis is the most arduous and demanding form of psychotherapy, requiring years of (expensive) sessions during which a great amount of powerful emotion will be experienced.

psychodiagnostics   Any technique applied to the interpretation of PERSONAL-ITY, whether PROJECTIVE TECHNIQUE or PSYCHOMETRICS.

psychodynamics   See   DYNAMIC PSYCHOLOGY.

psychographics   Used in MARKETING. [1] To describe the PSYCHOLOGICAL TESTS used as part of MARKET RESEARCH. [2] As a rough and ready way of dividing consumers into broad psychological types like 'conspicuous consumers' (see CON-SPICUOUS CONSUMPTION) or 'high achievers' (see NEED FOR ACHIEVEMENT).

psychological contract   In ORGANIZA-TIONAL PSYCHOLOGY, this refers to an unwritten (and often unspoken) contract, consisting of a set of expectations which the ORGANIZATION and the individual member have of each other. On the degree of fit between these two sets of expectations rest the health and happiness of both.

psychological field   See LIFE SPACE.

psychological price   The retail price of an item that is generally accepted without question by the consumer, though it may be a relatively high one, largely because of its familiarity. Also known as the CHARM PRICE of an item.

psychological segmentation   A form of MARKET SEGMENTATION that tries to analyse the way in which the consumption of particular products relates to the rest of the consumer's life. It adopts the viewpoint of PSYCHOLOGY in its approach to understanding consumer behaviour, and is concerned with such fundamental psychological factors as ATTITUDE change,

LEARNING, MOTIVATION, PERCEPTION and patterns of PERSONALITY. The objective of this form of segmentation is to gain some insight into what makes consumers tick and to arrive at individual profiles which capture the essence of a target consumer. Attempts at constructing consumer profiles usually concentrate on three areas of behaviour: [1] activities (how do people spend their time?); [2] interests (what are people most interested in?); and [3] opinions (how do people view themselves and their world?).

psychological test   This term is generally applied very broadly to include any procedure or technique for assessing any aspect of mental or emotional functioning. It would thus include both PROJEC-TIVE TECHNIQUES and PSYCHOMETRICS.

psychology   Most commonly defined at present as 'the scientific study of mind and behaviour', a definition that accurately describes the route of increasing our psychological *knowledge* (behaviour) as well as a psychological *understanding* of what that behaviour is about and how to make sense of it most intelligently (mind).

psychometrics   Those areas of PSY-CHOLOGY that deal specifically with the measurement of psychological factors. In a management ENVIRONMENT, the term tends to be used as a synonym for PSY-CHOLOGICAL TESTS.

psychosomatic disorders   This term comes from the Greek words *psyche* (mind) and *soma* (body). It relates to psychological disorders in which emotional STRESS produces physiological symptoms. Illnesses such as asthma and stomach ulcers have long been known to be psychosomatic, but it has also been argued that, because of the interrelationship between mind and body, every illness is psychosomatic at least to some extent.

psychotherapy The use of psychological techniques to treat psychological disturbance. The three main forms of psychotherapy are based on the theoretical approaches of BEHAVIOURISM, PSYCHO-ANALYSIS and a broad HUMANISTIC PSYCHOLOGY orientation represented by the work of psychologists like LEWIN and MASLOW.

public relations The systematic attempt by an ORGANIZATION to present itself to the best advantage, both to an external public and to its employees, by a process of persuasive COMMUNICATION. It is used in conjunction with paid ADVERTISING and concentrates usually on the MASS MEDIA. The objective of the exercise is to build up and maintain good relations between the organization, its public and its employees.

public sector The part of a MIXED ECONOMY which is controlled by the state rather than by individuals or private companies. Compare with PRIVATE SECTOR.

public utility An ORGANIZATION that provides an essential public service, like the supply of water or electricity, whether it is part of the PRIVATE SECTOR or the PUBLIC SECTOR.

PWE See PROTESTANT WORK ETHIC.

Pygmalion effect A form of SELF-FULFILLING PROPHECY in a social setting that was first suggested by the American psychologist Robert Rosenthal. Rosenthal led a number of teachers to believe that certain children in their classes had high IQs and were expected to do well in the year ahead. The children did do well – though they were all in fact of average IQ. Hence the name Pygmalion, from the play by George Bernard Shaw (later made into the musical *My Fair Lady*). The concept has been applied to the world of the ORGANIZATION more widely, to describe a MANAGER's expectation of a subordinate.

pyramid hierarchy An ORGANIZATIONAL STRUCTURE having different levels of AUTHORITY with fewer people at each succeeding level, so that a chart of the HIERARCHY would look like a pyramid in shape. See also TALL ORGANIZATION.

Q

QC   See QUALITY CIRCLE.

Q sort   A technique for rating different TRAITS of PERSONALITY, in which an individual is given a large number of statements about himself or herself, or about someone else, which he or she then sorts into piles representing the degree to which the statements are applicable.

qualitative methodology   The use of research methods in BEHAVIOURAL SCIENCE or SOCIAL SCIENCE which are concerned more with the complexity and the richness of the data being collected than with the CONTROL of the research situation, the quantity of data generated, or the sophistication of the statistical analysis of them available to the researcher. The open-ended, UNSTRUCTURED INTERVIEW, which does not use a detailed QUESTIONNAIRE, and PARTICIPANT OBSERVATION are probably the most common methods used. Compare with QUANTITATIVE METHODOLOGY.

quality   The term is now used mainly as a way of measuring or describing how good or bad a product is at performing its function and meeting the needs of its users. It is an important way in which producers can achieve PRODUCT DIFFERENTIATION and maintain the BRAND LOYALTY of their customers. See also LEVITT'S TOTAL PRODUCT CONCEPT and TOTAL QUALITY MANAGEMENT.

quality circle   A technique developed in the 1960s by American and Japanese engineers. Each circle consists of a small local group of employees trying to solve practical problems about the standard of QUALITY of the product they are working on. Membership of the circle is completely voluntary and is seen by MANAGEMENT as a way of improving the PARTICIPATION and MOTIVATION of the workforce, as well as providing the bonus of increased quality and, perhaps as a result, decreased costs. As CONTROL of all the decisions arising from the circle remains with the management, it may be viewed with suspicion by many people on the SHOP FLOOR. The idea of quality circles is based on the work of W. EDWARDS DEMING.

quality control   Any technique, like the QUALITY CIRCLE, that helps to maintain a desired level of QUALITY in the PRODUCTION of a product. Normally, this level will be as high as is feasible, but sometimes CONTROL will be exercised to ensure that quality is not *too* high; for example, in the case of BUILT-IN OBSOLESCENCE. Based on the work of W. EDWARDS DEMING. Compare with TOTAL QUALITY MANAGEMENT.

quality market   Any MARKET in which the QUALITY of a product is generally more important to the customer than is the price.

quality of working life   An approach to work that first became prominent in the 1960s. It is concerned to improve the QUALITY of life for people in the workplace, by emphasizing the importance of good JOB DESIGN in making work more meaningful for workers and giving them more CONTROL over how they do it. This approach has been somewhat less prominent since the 1980s.

quango   An acronym for a 'quasi-autonomous non-governmental organization' in the United Kingdom. This is an ORGANIZATION which is established and funded indirectly by the government to oversee or encourage activity in a particular area of public interest. Examples include the Economic and Social Research Council, or the Scottish Tourist Board.

quantitative methodology   The use of research methods in BEHAVIOURAL SCIENCE or SOCIAL SCIENCE which are concerned more with the precision and generalizability of the data being collected than with their richness of content or complexity; that is, having a narrower but sharper focus than QUALITATIVE METHODOLOGY. The laboratory or field experiment and the structured QUESTIONNAIRE are the most common methods used.

quartile   In STATISTICS, this is one of the three points on a FREQUENCY DISTRIBUTION which divide it into equal quarters; for example, at 25 per cent, 50 per cent and 75 per cent of a list of annual earnings.

question mark   One of the MARKETING situations in the BOSTON MATRIX. It is characterized by high growth but a poor market position. A question mark is a product about which a decision needs to be taken; will it become a STAR or a DOG?

questionnaire   Any set of written questions used in the collecting of information for purposes of comparison. It is widely used in quantitative MARKET RESEARCH and is the basis of all work in SURVEY RESEARCH, where questionnaires tend to have structured items with a narrow range of possible answers. In qualitative research, however, the items will tend to be less structured, or perhaps even open-ended, and allow for a wide variety of responses and possible follow-up by the researcher. See also QUALITATIVE METHODOLOGY and QUANTITATIVE METHODOLOGY.

queueing   In ERGONOMICS, this term is used to describe a way of dealing with SENSORY OVERLOAD, in which all the stimuli but one are 'put on hold' by the brain until that one has been processed.

quick fix   An attempt (often desperate) to deal with a complex MANAGEMENT issue in a business ORGANIZATION by applying a simple-minded, fast-acting 'solution'. Reorganization of the company is a firm favourite, as is the latest management fad from the currently fashionable snake-oil salesman.

quota sampling   In STATISTICS, this is the process of SAMPLING data from each sub-group of a given POPULATION. This is a particular form of STRATIFIED SAMPLING widely used in MARKET RESEARCH, where an interviewer is given a set number or quota of INTERVIEWS to carry out in a given stratum of the population, and stops sampling when the quota has been achieved.

QWL   See QUALITY OF WORKING LIFE.

R

r In STATISTICS, this is the symbol for the most common CORRELATION COEFFICIENT used in BEHAVIOURAL SCIENCE and SOCIAL SCIENCE.

R & D See RESEARCH AND DEVELOPMENT.

racism A negative PREJUDICE against someone of a different race (usually meaning a different skin colour).

radical innovation Often applied to the introduction of products or organizational processes which represent a STEP CHANGE rather than CONTINUOUS IMPROVEMENT for a company. Examples would be major changes in working practices or MARKETING like the introduction of the ASSEMBLY LINE or the supermarket.

RAM An acronym for RANDOM ACCESS MEMORY.

random access memory The immediately available short-term part of a COMPUTER'S MEMORY. Any data stored in this part is lost when the computer is switched off, unless it has been transferred to some form of longer term memory storage.

random sampling In STATISTICS, this is the process of SAMPLING data at random from a POPULATION so that inferences can be made about the population from findings about the sample. The crucial condition is that each individual in the total population should have an equal chance of being chosen for the sample.

rank order Any series of numbers, items or individuals arranged in order of magnitude, either increasing or decreasing (first, second, third, etc.).

rate setting An old-fashioned term for the process of setting PIECEWORK rates of PAY for a job. The process is more often included now under the term WORK MEASUREMENT.

rational-economic A view of human nature which argues that people act only to maximize their self-interest. It is based on the philosophy of HEDONISM and often claims the thought of ADAM SMITH in its support. Any MANAGEMENT STYLE which acted on his view would be described as RATIONAL MANAGEMENT. See also THEORY X.

rational-economic model As applied to MANAGEMENT this MODEL is based on the assumption that the only source of MOTIVATION in the workplace is money.

rationalization [1] In PSYCHOANALYSIS, this term is used to describe an EGO DEFENCE in which a person justifies some action about which he has UNCONSCIOUS guilt feelings because he really knows he shouldn't have acted in that way. [2] In ECONOMICS, the term is used to denote the application of the most efficient methods in the use of resources within an ORGANIZATION. [3] In ORGANIZATIONAL THEORY, the term is supposed to describe the creation of a more effective ORGANIZATIONAL STRUCTURE. In PRACTICE, this often implies one that is cheaper because it has fewer people in it as a result of DELAYERING and DOWNSIZING.

rational management The term is usually used to denote a MANAGEMENT STYLE that emphasizes objective measures of input and output rather than HUMAN RELATIONS. The opposite of PARTICIPATIVE MANAGEMENT.

reaction time   In ERGONOMICS, this term refers to the time elapsed between the presentation of a stimulus and the subject's response to it.

real time   A period of time during which an ONLINE computer is processing the data about a particular situation while that situation is actually in progress, thus allowing for instant updating, as in an airline or hotel reservation SYSTEM.

real wages   [1] Disposable INCOME left after paying TAXATION and so on. [2] The buying POWER of a certain income, as opposed to the actual money received.

recency effect   The finding that, under certain conditions in the process of LEARNING, the last one of a series to be learned is remembered best. See also PRIMACY EFFECT.

recession   A lack of growth or a decline in trading or in the economy generally, though not as seriously as in a DEPRESSION.

reciprocity   In ERGONOMICS, this refers to the principle that a response is produced by a combination of the duration and intensity of a stimulus.

recruitment   The process of identifying possible candidates for a job vacancy. It should start, ideally, with a JOB ANALYSIS, after which a JOB SPECIFICATION should be drawn up. Likely candidates to meet the specification would then be trawled, perhaps by ADVERTISING in the appropriate TRADE PRESS or by HEAD-HUNTING. In principle, this process should be the logical outcome of MANPOWER PLANNING and the first stage of a coherent policy of PERSONNEL MANAGEMENT that continues until RETIREMENT.

redeployment   The process of moving workers from one location to another, often with the objective of finding them alternative EMPLOYMENT.

redundancy   The dismissal of people from their EMPLOYMENT either because their job has ceased to exist or because their SKILLS are no longer required. See also DELAYERING, DOWNSIZING, FIRST IN, FIRST OUT, LAST IN, FIRST OUT and VOLUNTARY REDUNDANCY.

re-engineering   An approach to changing an ORGANIZATION, popularized in the early 1990s by Michael Hammer and James Champy, that focuses on the organization's *processes* rather than its traditional functions. It makes extensive use of INFORMATION TECHNOLOGY to help companies rethink their business from scratch. This invariably requires some DELAYERING and DOWNSIZING, perhaps as a consequence of trying to apply both top-down LEADERSHIP and employee EMPOWERMENT at the same time.

reference group   In SOCIOLOGY, this is the term for a group with which an individual identifies and whose GROUP NORMS she or he follows, whether accepted by it or not and whether physically part of it or not. It is usually compared with MEMBERSHIP GROUP.

referent power   This form of POWER is a function of a given individual rather than his or her position in an ORGANIZATION. It is often thought of as the possession of CHARISMA such that people identify with someone's personal qualities and are happy to accept their leadership because of it.

refreezing   A term introduced by KURT LEWIN to describe the state of an ORGANIZATION following some radical changes, when its members have fully incorporated the required new ways of doing their jobs. It is the final stage in the process of which UNFREEZING is the first stage.

regression [1] A return by an individual to an earlier form of behaviour. In PSYCHOANALYSIS, it is an EGO DEFENCE, where an individual seeks to deal with ANXIETY and avoid UNCONSCIOUS conflicts by reverting to an earlier stage of development where his or her problems were 'solved' by more infantile means. [2] In STATISTICS, the term is used to describe a technique for estimating the relationship between one variable and another. It is applied to FORECASTING, for example, where qualitative ratings on one variable are used to make quantitative predictions on the other.

reinforcement The process of strengthening the likelihood that a given behaviour will occur by providing it with some form of REWARD. This is the basis of all CONDITIONING.

relations analysis One of three techniques suggested by PETER DRUCKER to help a WORK ORGANIZATION decide on its most appropriate ORGANIZATIONAL STRUCTURE. This technique is used to establish what the key relations between MANAGERS and all levels in the ORGANIZATION actually are, as opposed to unquestioned *assumptions* about what they are and unthinking reliance on an ORGANIZATION CHART. The other two Drucker techniques are ACTIVITIES ANALYSIS and DECISION ANALYSIS.

relative deprivation In PSYCHOLOGY, this term is used to describe an individual's feeling of being deprived when she or he compares herself or himself to someone else, regardless of the objective reality or what other people may feel. For example, a managing director might feel deprived with a six-figure salary if it were less than other managing directors got, while an office junior might be delighted with her own salary even though it is one-tenth of the figure.

reliability [1] In STATISTICS, this term describes the internal consistency of a TEST; that is, the extent to which it can be expected to produce the same result on different occasions. [2] The extent to which an instrument, machine or product provides the PERFORMANCE expected of it over its expected lifetime.

relocation The process of settling in a new place, whether for an ORGANIZATION or an individual worker.

reluctant manager A term introduced to MANAGEMENT SCIENCE in the 1980s by two British writers, Richard Scase and Robert Goffee. The term describes a MANAGER suffering from a certain ALIENATION from his job because he sees the REWARD for his efforts as being insufficient to compensate him for the STRESS he feels. This reluctant ATTITUDE to commitment seems to increase as the amount of BUREAUCRACY in an ORGANIZATION increases.

repetitive strain injury The term generally used for a series of injuries to the muscles and skeleton caused by doing repetitive operations on machines for a considerable period of time. It is thought to be particularly prevalent among WORD-PROCESSOR users, and results from the failure of an ORGANIZATION to consider seriously the ERGONOMICS of its workplace.

representation The procedure where someone acts on behalf of an individual or a group of workers in an ORGANIZATION. Usually this refers to the right of a TRADE UNION to represent its members in dealing with MANAGEMENT on issues other than those dealing with PAY and conditions of EMPLOYMENT, which are dealt with by COLLECTIVE BARGAINING.

representativeness heuristic A HEURISTIC in which we pick out something familiar in a new object and then equate it with one that we know; for example, buying something by judging its quality on the basis of its price.

representative sample A sample that is intended to be completely representative of the POPULATION from which it is drawn.

repression In PSYCHOANALYSIS, this term is used to describe a particular kind of EGO DEFENCE, as well as being a crucial concept in Freudian theory. The essence of repression is the holding back from conscious awareness of disturbing feelings and impulses arising from the ID. They are submerged in the UNCONSCIOUS – where they invariably get up to mischief. FREUD considered repression the price we pay for civilization and that psychoanalysis, by making the unconscious conscious, was the only way to come to terms with this dilemma. Contrast with INHIBITION.

resale price maintenance The requirement of a manufacturer or supplier that certain products may not be sold by a retailer below a certain fixed price, thus removing one of the more tiresome effects of COMPETITION on PROFIT. It is now by and large illegal in the United Kingdom and the United States.

research and development The first stage of a PRODUCT LIFE CYCLE, in which science and TECHNOLOGY are applied to the development of new products. The term is also used more generally to describe any systematic activity within an ORGANIZATION aimed at gaining it a competitive edge in the future.

response bias A MENTAL SET to respond in a particular way to certain issues or questions; for example, on a QUESTIONNAIRE.

restraint of trade Any activity which interferes with the operation of a FREE MARKET; for example, price-fixing or preventing a new competitor from entering the MARKET.

restrictive practice This term usually refers to a work practice supported by a TRADE UNION, in the interest of JOB SECURITY for its members, which limits the scope of MANAGEMENT, especially in the allocation of particular kinds of work. The practice may or may not be officially agreed through COLLECTIVE BARGAINING. See also CLOSED SHOP, DEMARCATION DISPUTE and OVERMANNING.

restructuring of industry A term often used to describe the decline of HEAVY INDUSTRY, with its attendant UNEMPLOYMENT, and the increasing importance of the SERVICE SECTOR and of INFORMATION TECHNOLOGY.

résumé A French word which is sometimes used as an American version of a CURRICULUM VITAE.

retail audit A MARKET RESEARCH technique which involves taking a REPRESENTATIVE SAMPLE of retail outlets and studying them to obtain data on DISTRIBUTION, sales, stock and so on.

retailing The selling of goods and services, in relatively small quantities, directly to the consumer through a shop or other retail outlet. Compare with WHOLESALING.

retail price index A figure, calculated monthly, which reflects the cost of a set of basic goods and services used by most of the United Kingdom POPULATION. It is generally used as an indicator of changes in INFLATION and the cost of living, and is often the basis for COLLECTIVE BARGAINING and for government policy-making.

retirement The process of finishing one's full-time work life, traditionally at a designated or generally accepted age. EARLY RETIREMENT has increased greatly in recent years, though later retirement has also been noticed.

retirement on the job A term sometimes used of an employee who experiences such ALIENATION from his job that he does the minimum possible in order to retain it while he waits for RETIREMENT. It may be the end result of PRESENTEEISM.

retroactive inhibition The detrimental effect of later LEARNING on the recall of previous learning. Compare with PROACTIVE INHIBITION.

return on investment One of the more potent forms of FEEDBACK on behaviour, whether by an individual or an ORGANIZATION.

reward Any kind of return (usually positive) as a result of a given behaviour. It is most often used in EMPLOYMENT to refer to monetary gains in return for an individual's PERFORMANCE at work. These gains may be in the form of PAY, FRINGE BENEFITS or PERKS.

reward power A form of POWER which denotes the ability of someone in an ORGANIZATION to reward others, for example, with PROMOTION or better pay or conditions. Usually contrasted with COERCIVE POWER.

right brained A term used to describe people who are visual and intuitive in their thinking rather than verbal. The origin of this rather sweeping generalization is that the major speech centre in the brain is usually found in the *left* hemisphere of the cerebral cortex. It is usually contrasted with LEFT BRAINED.

right first time See ZERO DEFECTS.

rightsizing A little more than just another euphemism for firing people – like DOWNSIZING was in the 1980s – ever since SENIOR MANAGEMENT discovered, in the 1990s, that sometimes you need to hire back some of the people you fired.

ringi system A form of Japanese decision-making where all the members of an ORGANIZATION who will be affected by it participate in reaching a collective decision.

risk [1] The likelihood, or the statistical PROBABILITY, of failure in a business ENTERPRISE; the essence of being an ENTREPRENEUR, and therefore of CAPITALISM. [2] The term is also used of the probability of damage or loss; the essence of insurance.

risk aversive The tendency to avoid taking risky decisions, which is said to be generally true of both individuals and ORGANIZATIONS. However, decision-making is not entirely a rational process and it depends, in part, on how the potential risk is framed.

risk capital CAPITAL invested in an ENTERPRISE with a high RISK of failure, though usually with the possibility of a large financial gain.

risky shift A form of GROUP POLARIZATION where people make riskier decisions under the influence of a group than by themselves. The opposite of CAUTIOUS SHIFT.

robot A machine which can be programmed and controlled by a COMPUTER to function like a person for certain jobs. The term is based on the Czech word for compulsory labour, from a 1920 play by Karel Capek.

robotics The study of ROBOTS, their design, manufacture and applications.

ROI   See RETURN ON INVESTMENT.

role   A term widely used in SOCIAL PSYCHOLOGY to refer to the kind of behaviour expected of a given person in a given situation. The term has been applied generally to the ORGANIZATION and the workplace.

role ambiguity   A situation in which an individual is unclear about the ROLE expected of her or him.

role conflict   A situation in which an individual is expected to play two or more ROLES which are in conflict or in competition with each other.

role differentiation   The processes of the DIVISION OF LABOUR and of SPECIALIZATION within a group. The larger and more complex the group – from the family to the MULTINATIONAL COMPANY – the greater the degree of role differentiation.

role expectation   The expectations other people have about the way a person will play his or her ROLE in a given situation.

role incongruence   This occurs where individuals have high status in some aspects of their job but low status in others, for example, a junior accountant querying the expenses of a senior executive or a personal assistant accruing the POWER of a GATEKEEPER in relation to her boss.

role innovation   The process of changing the goals and objectives of a particular ROLE.

role negotiation   This term is sometimes used to describe a process that may take place during an INTERVIEW with a candidate for a job, where the exact ROLE the individual would play in the ORGANIZATION is subject to negotiation.

role overload   An extreme form of ROLE CONFLICT, where the number of different ROLES expected of an individual are simply too great for her or him to contain. The opposite of ROLE UNDERLOAD.

role playing   [1] Acting the part of another person in a therapeutic or BUSINESS GAME situation. [2] Playing a certain ROLE for the particular effect it will cause.

role relationship   Any relationship between two people which is defined by the ROLE they each play; for example, boss and subordinate.

role reversal   A situation in which people agree to switch their usual ROLE RELATIONSHIPS; for example, army officers serving Christmas dinner to the troops.

role set   The SIGNIFICANT OTHERS who have ROLE RELATIONSHIPS with a given individual. (See Figure 33.)

role structure   The extent to which a ROLE is specified and defined or left open.

role transition   The process of switching from one ROLE to another, a process in which SOCIALIZATION is of great importance.

role underload   A situation in which an individual feels that his or her ROLE is not big enough. The opposite of ROLE OVERLOAD. See also UNDEREMPLOYMENT.

ROMPing   An acronym for Radical Office Mobility Programme, a more advanced and comprehensive form of HOT DESKING.

Rorschach test   The most famous PROJECTIVE TECHNIQUE of all, beloved of cartoonists and comedians. It consists of ten standardized inkblots developed by a Swiss psychiatrist called Hermann Rorschach in the early part of the

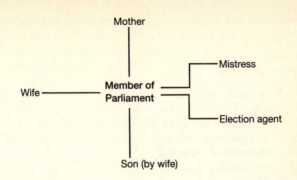

Figure 33 Role set.

twentieth century. The subject's responses to the inkblots are analysed by the tester in the light of certain categories that have also been standardized over the years. No diagnosis of someone's PERSONALITY should ever be made solely on the basis of this (or any other) TEST, but many psychologists regard it as a useful first step.

Rosenthal effect   See PYGMALION EFFECT.

rote learning   LEARNING attempted solely through repetition, without any attempt to find order or meaning in the material. Compare with INSIGHT LEARNING and TRIAL AND ERROR LEARNING.

royalty   A fee paid to an author or composer on each sale of published work for which she or he holds the COPYRIGHT, or to an inventor for the use of an invention for which she or he holds the PATENT.

RPI   See RETAIL PRICE INDEX.

RPM   See RESALE PRICE MAINTENANCE.

RSI   See REPETITIVE STRAIN INJURY.

S

sacred cow   In a business ORGANIZATION, this usually refers to a project that may not be closed down, no matter how inefficient or costly it is, for reasons that are not rational. The reference is to the Hindu veneration of the cow, which is allowed a free run of India while not being used as food for hungry people.

salaried staff   This term is usually applied to STAFF who are WHITE-COLLAR WORKERS and whose PAY is calculated on an annual basis and paid in equal monthly instalments. This is in contrast to the BLUE-COLLAR WORKER, for example, who might be paid on an hourly basis or by the amount of work completed.

salary structure   The arrangement of PAY within an ORGANIZATION such that different grades of employees doing different jobs will receive different rates. These rates are supposed to be based (at least originally) on the processes of JOB ANALYSIS and JOB EVALUATION and each would normally be in the form of a scale with annual increments of pay.

sales promotion   Any attempt to increase the sales of a particular product with a focussed, intensive, short-term campaign of inducements such as gifts, free samples, special offers and so on.

sampling   In STATISTICS, this is the process of analysing a sample drawn from a particular POPULATION when it is too difficult or expensive to deal with each member of that population. The most common ways to obtain a sample are by RANDOM SAMPLING and STRATIFIED SAMPLING, including QUOTA SAMPLING.

sampling error   In STATISTICS, this is the extent to which a sample is not an accurate representation of the POPULATION from which it has been drawn.

sampling frame   The background or catchment area of POPULATION from which a sample is to be taken.

sapiential authority   The idea that the basis for exercising AUTHORITY associated with certain people lies in their perceived wisdom rather than in any formal POWER or STATUS they may hold.

satisficing   A term that originated in ECONOMICS to describe the situation in which an ORGANIZATION was sufficiently satisfied with what it had achieved to stop striving for more, even though it had not reached its ideal or optimal targets. The term is also used more broadly to be almost synonymous with 'compromise' in a situation of CONFLICT, where a solution is reached which satisfies all parties but is less than optimal for any of them. See also SUBOPTIMIZATION.

saving face   Maintaining one's SELF-ESTEEM, or the self-esteem of one's group, in a situation of individual or group CONFLICT, or in any kind of BARGAINING. An essential aspect, for example, of successful INDUSTRIAL RELATIONS.

scab   An alternative term for BLACKLEG, whose origin is likewise unknown.

Scanlon Plan   Named after the American TRADE UNION theorist Joseph Scanlon whose plan, first produced in the late 1930s, was intended to herald a new form of co-operative relationship between MANAGEMENT and unions. One outcome of the plan was a method whereby employees would share in the financial benefits of increased PRODUCTIVITY by receiving, each month, a bonus based on a percentage (usually 50–75 per cent) of savings to the ORGANIZATION in labour costs. The Scanlon Plan is regarded as an important contribution to both the theory and practice of INDUSTRIAL DEMOCRACY.

scapegoating The DISPLACEMENT of frustration and aggression from its real object, which is too threatening, on to individuals or groups who are unlikely to fight back. The origin of the term 'scape-goat' goes back to Biblical times, when the Israelites each year sent a pure white goat out to die in the wilderness on the Day of Atonement, symbolically carrying with it all the sins of the people.

scattergram A graph or diagram in which the individual points are left unconnected in order to show what patterns the data fall into. (See Figure 34.)

scenario writing A technique used in FORECASTING, where expert predictions about the ENVIRONMENT in which an ORGANIZATION operates are used as the basis for exploring several alternative scenarios for its future development. See also BRAINSTORMING and DELPHI METHOD.

scheduling [1] A term used to describe the process of organizing TASKS to be done by a series of machines in order to streamline PRODUCTION. [2] Any way of dividing up time in the course of a working day so that people can synchronize their activities with each other. It is particularly important in cultures of MONOCHRONIC activity.

schema In the PSYCHOLOGY of COGNITION, this term is used to describe a mental MODEL or framework within which new experiences are digested that then allow LEARNING to take place.

Schumacher, Fritz (1911–77) Generally considered to be the father of the 'Small Is Beautiful' movement both in ORGANIZATIONAL THEORY and in thinking about the global ENVIRONMENT. His work also helped Western business theorists to appreciate the Japanese passion for smallness – and with it QUALITY.

scientific management An approach to MANAGEMENT, based on the theories of F.W. TAYLOR, dealing with the MOTIVATION

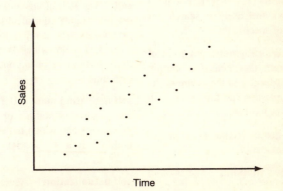

Figure 34 Scattergram (showing high positive CORRELATION in sales of product over time).

to work. It sees it as a MANAGER's duty to find out the best way to do a given job, by a process of WORK MEASUREMENT, then give each worker individual instructions which have to be followed strictly. The individual is thus seen as the extension of his or her machine, and his or her REWARDS are also to be allocated mechanically, with more PAY expected to produce more output regardless of any other factors. Scientific management is thus the antithesis of the HUMAN RELATIONS approach.

screwdriver operation   A factory where only the parts of a product are assembled as opposed to the PRODUCTION of the whole product. Usually applied to a subsidiary of a MULTINATIONAL COMPANY operating in a country with a relatively cheap labour market.

scripts   Based on the theatrical use of the term, these are familiar scenarios of events recognized by the members of an ORGANIZATION. On this interpretation of organizational life different organizations will 'perform' different 'plays' on the basis of the particular SOCIAL NORMS that apply to them.

search engine   An INTERNET service which allows the user to search for information of specific interest.

seasonal unemployment   A form of UNEMPLOYMENT that peaks at certain times of the year due to the nature of the industry in question, as for example in construction or tourism.

secondary group   Another name for a FACE-TO-FACE GROUP.

'second curve' thinking   See SIGMOID CURVE.

secondment   A term used in PERSONNEL practice when moving someone to

another job or ORGANIZATION for a temporary period.

segment of one   The use of computer DATABASES by marketers to generate lists of individuals in their target market segment and send them personalized COMMUNICATIONS based on who they are, where they live, what they do, etc. It is therefore the ultimate in MARKET SEGMENTATION. It is also a return to a time before the advent of MASS PRODUCTION and mass consumption when producer and consumer had a direct relationship with each other.

selection   The process of choosing someone for a particular job, which follows the RECRUITMENT of suitable candidates. The selection process will probably include an INTERVIEW and may also include TESTS of ABILITY, APTITUDE, INTELLIGENCE or PERSONALITY.

selective perception   Literally, the process of seeing what you want to see. The process of perceiving the world as we *need* to perceive it, whatever the relation of that PERCEPTION to objective reality, is the way we satisfy the NEED TO MAKE SENSE.

self   The self, in HUMANISTIC PSYCHOLOGY, is roughly equivalent to the EGO in PSYCHOANALYSIS. It refers to that part of the PERSONALITY which is conscious of its own IDENTITY on a continuous basis over time.

self-activating man   The belief that a person can CONTROL her or his own life to some extent, which is the assumption underlying a PATH–GOAL THEORY of MOTIVATION.

self-actualization   According to the American psychologist ABRAHAM MASLOW this term describes the ongoing striving to fulfil one's creative capacities. This is considered an important sign of psychological health.

self-censorship   A situation in which people do not say what they really think in a group discussion, for the sake of GROUP COHESIVENESS. This is one of the factors contributing to GROUPTHINK.

self-concept   All the elements that make up a person's view of himself or herself, including his or her SELF-IMAGE.

self-esteem   The degree to which a person likes herself; how worthy she deems herself to be. High self-esteem is generally considered to be an important sign of psychological health.

self-fulfilling prophecy   The idea that expectations concerning one's own or other people's behaviour can lead to the expected behaviour actually appearing, such as in the PYGMALION EFFECT.

self-image   The SELF, a person believes himself or herself to be. One's self-image is a composite of many things and may bear little relation to any objective ASSESSMENT of oneself or the assessment of others. It begins very early in life and is probably, to a large extent, physical. This early body image can stay with a person for the rest of his or her life. The judgements of other people are also important in the formation of the self-image, but even though someone's social contacts, and therefore the judgements made of him, may change greatly in later life, he may still think of himself in terms of the earlier judgements.

self-knowledge   Having an accurate awareness of what our SELF is really like. Where such knowledge is painful we will invest an enormous amount of energy in *not* knowing about it. See also EGO DEFENCE.

self-management   Used in TRAINING to describe an approach where trainees are responsible for the content, method and progress of their LEARNING.

seller's market   A MARKET situation in which sellers have more POWER to influence prices and conditions of sale than do buyers, usually because demand exceeds supply. Always contrasted with BUYER'S MARKET.

selling   [1] The process of exchanging goods or services for money. [2] The functions in an ORGANIZATION which are most concerned with this process. These now include ADVERTISING, DISTRIBUTION, MARKETING and QUALITY CONTROL as well as sales and SALES PROMOTION.

semi-autonomous work groups   A term used by SENIOR MANAGEMENT for AUTONOMOUS WORK GROUPS which they wish to CONTROL. Anything less than autonomy for SHOP FLOOR workers means that they have no *real* autonomy over what they do. The concept is therefore a contradiction in terms, like being 'semi-pregnant'.

semiology   A variant of SEMIOTICS.

semiotics   The field of study dealing with the meanings that signs and symbols have for people, both consciously and UNCONSCIOUSLY.

seniority   This term refers to either a higher rank or a greater length of service within a given ORGANIZATION.

senior management   The term applied to MANAGERS who are relatively high in the HIERARCHY of an ORGANIZATION because they are senior in level of responsibility and AUTHORITY, and often in age as well. The precise cut-off point for this category varies from one organization to another. The term implies that someone is part of that group within the organization which makes policy and takes the important decisions.

sensitivity training   A technique for trying to improve interpersonal COMMUNI-CATION and the QUALITY of INTERPERSONAL RELATIONS in FACE-TO-FACE GROUPS. The orientation of this technique is that of HUMANISTIC PSYCHOLOGY and it is based on the methods and experience of GROUP THERAPY. Group leaders try to facilitate open and honest discussion of feelings within the group. The hope is that any newfound sensitivity to one's dealings with other people will carry over to other areas of life, such as WORK GROUPS.

sensory deprivation   A situation in which people are deprived of the usual stimulation their senses encounter in daily life. Apparently when people are isolated from sensory stimulation, as far as possible, in a laboratory, they quickly become bored and then start to halluci-nate. It may be that when we have nothing in our ENVIRONMENT for our brains to work on and make sense of, we feel a need to provide our own sensations and make sense out of nothing. Something similar seems to happen in particularly monotonous and boring jobs. Compare with SENSORY OVERLOAD. See also NEED TO MAKE SENSE.

sensory overload   The opposite prob-lem to SENSORY DEPRIVATION, where there is so *much* stimulation of the senses that the brain cannot process them all and 'shuts down' in self-defence.

serendipity   The experience of finding one thing while looking for another. The term was first coined by the English writer Horace Walpole in 1754 and is based on a sixteenth-century Italian story, *The Three Princes of Serendip*, where the heroes travel the world but never find what they are looking for. However, on their travels they make many other interesting discov-eries, as indeed do researchers in many fields, to say nothing of dictionary users.

serial learning   The process of LEARN-ING material in a particular order or sequence.

server   That part of a computer system which distributes the availability of services to a wider network of users.

service sector   That sector of a MIXED ECONOMY which is concerned not with the conversion of raw materials or the PRODUCTION of goods but with providing a service, such as ADVERTISING, education, health or transport.

servomechanism   A SYSTEM that has CONTROL over another system. FEEDBACK from the system under control enables the servomechanism to regulate its input so that a constant output is maintained. A thermostat is the usual example given of a servomechanism, but HOMEOSTASIS in the body can also be seen in this way.

SES   See SOCIO-ECONOMIC STATUS.

severance pay   A payment made to an employee either because his contract of EMPLOYMENT has ended or because he has to lose his job through no fault of his own; for example, through REDUNDANCY.

sex differences   These refer to all differences in behaviour or ABILITY between males and females. As with sup-posed racial differences, there is no evi-dence that there are any. What looks like a genetic sex difference in aggressive-ness, for instance, is due to a cultural process of LEARNING the SEX ROLE consid-ered appropriate for either males or females. See also SEX-LINKED TRAIT.

sexism   A negative PREJUDICE against someone on the basis of her or his sex.

Usually, though by no means exclusively, by men against women.

sexual harassment   The occurrence of verbal or physical abuse solely on the basis of the sex of the victim. It is very common in the workplace and almost always by men against women. Many countries now have legislation designed to prevent it or to punish it where it occurs.

shadow price   A guess or best estimate of the price of a product in the absence of a MARKET in that product which can actually provide one. See also OPPORTUNITY COST.

shamrock organization   A term introduced by the Irish MANAGEMENT theorist Charles Handy as a description of the FLEXIBLE FIRM. The three leaves of his shamrock are the *professional core*, the *flexible labour force* and the *contractual fringe*.

shareholder value   The idea that the interests of a company's shareholders are the most important (if not the only) objective in doing business. Contrast with the idea of STAKEHOLDER.

shelf-life   The amount of time a product has (e.g. on a supermarket shelf) before it starts to deteriorate. Shelf-life can often be manipulated by the producer, wholesaler or retailer. See, for example, BUILT-IN OBSOLESCENCE.

shift work   A form of SCHEDULING which uses the process of dividing the whole 24-hour day into work periods, often three periods of eight hours each, for example, midnight–8.00 a.m., 8.00 a.m.–4.00 p.m. and 4.00 p.m.–midnight. Shift work is used to obtain maximum use of PLANT in manufacturing, or of the workforce in the SERVICE SECTOR, especially that part of it which includes the

emergency services, where continuous cover is required.

shop floor   A term originally applied to the area of a factory in which PRODUCTION took place. It has been widened in its application to indicate the BLUE-COLLAR WORKERS in an ORGANIZATION as opposed to the WHITE-COLLAR WORKERS, or even the workforce in general as opposed to the MANAGEMENT.

shop steward   A TRADE UNION official elected by fellow workers on the SHOP FLOOR to represent them in their day-to-day dealings with the employers or their MANAGEMENT representatives.

shortlist   A list of the leading candidates for a particular job as the result of a RECRUITMENT process. People on the shortlist will be asked to attend an INTERVIEW, and will perhaps be given some TESTS as well, before the final SELECTION is made.

short termism   The financial equivalent of the organizational QUICK FIX.

short-time working   A situation in which a workplace is forced to work a reduced working week because of a shortage of orders. This is seen as a temporary measure to cut labour costs while retaining the workforce intact, rather than making people redundant (see REDUNDANCY) and then rehiring them when orders pick up.

sick building syndrome   This term was introduced in the late 1980s to describe relatively minor but frequent ailments (like sore throats, headaches or eyestrain) that are attributed to factors in the workplace ENVIRONMENT. It is thought that inadequate lighting and ventilation, combined with a closed, automated physical environment over which workers have no CONTROL, are at the root of the syndrome. It is seen in ERGONOMICS as another instance of workers fitting themselves into an old TECHNOLOGY and suffering from it while NEW TECHNOLOGY is applied only for the benefit of machines.

sickness benefit   See SICK PAY.

sick pay   PAY given to workers who are off work for reasons of illness or injury. As well as statutory provisions there are many occupational schemes and these are sometimes regarded as a FRINGE BENEFIT of a job.

sigmoid curve   This is a way of analysing the relationship between growth and time in the life of a business ORGANIZATION. (See Figure 35.) Before a project or product comes to the end of its useful life it may be advisable to start working on its replacement. Thus, a second 'S' curve will grow out of the first.

signal detection theory   In ERGONOMICS, this theory suggests that the perception (or detection) of a given stimulus (or signal) is related to the sensitivity of the sense receptors (eyes, ears and so on) and the MOTIVATION of the individual to respond.

significant other   A term introduced to SOCIAL SCIENCE in the 1920s by the American sociologist G.H. Mead to denote a person who is particularly important to us, especially in the support of our SELF-IMAGE. This term is usually compared with GENERALIZED OTHER.

SIMO chart   In ERGONOMICS, this is an acronym for a Simultaneous Motion Cycle Chart, used to record and CHART the CO-ORDINATION of workers' limb movements or THERBLIGS. It is one of the techniques of WORK MEASUREMENT invented by FRANK GILBRETH.

simulation   The creation of a controlled replication of a real-life situation for purposes of TRAINING, analysis or policy decision-making. It may be abstract and use sophisticated mathematics (like a MODEL of the world economy) or concrete and use a BUSINESS GAME.

sinecure   Paid EMPLOYMENT with little or no work attached to it; that is, even less than in the case of UNDEREMPLOYMENT.

single loop learning   Central to the concept of ORGANIZATIONAL LEARNING as pioneered, notably, by CHRIS ARGYRIS. It occurs where the effects of FEEDBACK from previous behaviour is used to change present behaviour.

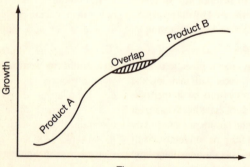

Figure 35 Sigmoid curve.

sitting next to Nellie The traditional form of ON-THE-JOB TRAINING on the British SHOP FLOOR, where the trainee learned the job by observing and emulating the highly experienced 'Nellie'. The American equivalent is called the BUDDY SYSTEM.

16PF test This is a PSYCHOLOGICAL TEST of PERSONALITY, developed by the American psychologist Raymond Cattell, which attempts to measure sixteen major personality factors (hence 16PF). The TEST is sometimes used in OCCUPATIONAL PSYCHOLOGY for the purpose of SELECTION, where the findings are matched against important personality factors that have been identified for various occupations.

skill A learned response, often as the result of specific TRAINING, which affords someone the ABILITY to perform a particular TASK and achieve a particular goal.

skills analysis A part of JOB ANALYSIS.

Skinner, B.F. (1904–90) An American psychologist and the most celebrated exponent of BEHAVIOURISM, not just in the study of PSYCHOLOGY but as a means of running a society. His own technique of CONDITIONING was based on the research of PAVLOV and WATSON. In later years, he expounded the social implications of his views in a number of influential works intended for the general public.

sleep deprivation The lack of a usual amount of sleep over a given period of time. This is an area of particular interest in the study of the effects of SHIFT WORK or jet travel on PERFORMANCE. When people are prevented from sleeping they eventually experience ill effects such as hallucinations and confusions of thought and behaviour. Some scientists engaged in dream research argue that dreaming is the most important aspect of sleeping and

sleep deprivation. Indeed, other than dreaming it is difficult to detect any physiological difference between sleeping and just resting. Note also the similarities to SENSORY DEPRIVATION.

sleeper effect A term used in several different senses in the SOCIAL PSYCHOLOGY of ATTITUDE change. [1] Its most frequent usage is probably in describing a change in an attitude or opinion after a study has been conducted. This may be one reason for inaccuracy in public opinion polls. [2] The term is also used to describe a more favourable response to a COMMUNICATION after some time has elapsed, rather than the expected decline in the effect of the communication. [3] The sleeper effect is also used to describe the dissociation between communication and communicator over time so that people may become less receptive to positive sources and more receptive to negative ones.

Sloan, Alfred P. (1875–1966) An American industrialist who took over a small and ailing motor manufacturer, General Motors, in the early 1920s and turned it into one of the biggest corporations in the world – and at the expense of the Ford Motor Company. He did so mainly by introducing the concept of professional MANAGEMENT to a business world that was still largely run by the personal PROPRIETOR, like HENRY FORD, whose company almost went out of business in competition with GM.

slush fund An informal, unofficial and sometimes dubious source of funds from which an ORGANIZATION can finance a great variety of informal, unofficial and sometimes dubious activities, ranging from STAFF outings to bribing public officials.

small batch production See BATCH PRODUCTION.

SME   An acronym for a Small or Medium-sized Enterprise; usually a company with fewer than 1,000 employees.

Smith, Adam (1723–90)   A Scottish economist and philosopher who based his doctrines of the FREE MARKET on a RATIONAL-ECONOMIC view of human nature. He argued that, as individual self-interest was the driving force whose aggregate effects resulted in social harmony, there should therefore be no state intervention in the MARKET between buyers and sellers. He also proposed SPECIALIZATION and the DIVISION OF LABOUR in manufacturing, though he was concerned about the resulting effects of workers' ALIENATION from their labour.

snowball sample   A form of SAMPLING used in MARKET RESEARCH, where each respondent interviewed is asked to provide the names of additional respondents. The bias in this form of sampling is, of course, that the additional respondents are likely to be of a similar social background to the original respondent.

social accounting   Any aspect of ACCOUNTING with a particular concern for the social aspects of a COST–BENEFIT ANALYSIS.

social audit   See SOCIAL ACCOUNTING.

social class   A rather old-fashioned term for SOCIO-ECONOMIC STATUS. It is considered crude and gauche in some quarters, if not downright subversive.

social cohesion   A similar process to that of GROUP COHESIVENESS, though on a larger scale extending to an entire CULTURE or society.

social comparison   The process of evaluating one's ATTITUDES and behaviour by comparing them with those of other people. In SOCIAL PSYCHOLOGY, there is

an idea that when people are uncertain what to do (or think, or feel) in a given situation they are more likely to take their cue from other people and conform to *their* behaviour.

social contact   See INTERPERSONAL CONTACT.

social control   The CONTROL that a group, CULTURE or society exerts upon the individuals who comprise it. This control stems from the process of SOCIALIZATION and is exhibited as CONFORMITY pressures towards SOCIAL NORMS.

social costs   The data for SOCIAL ACCOUNTING.

Social Darwinism   The application to human society of Charles Darwin's theories of natural selection, where only the fittest members of a species survive because of their successful adaptation to the ENVIRONMENT. In effect, it was in Victorian times (and still is) an attempt to justify the existing order by arguing that the rich and successful have evidently been selected by nature to be rich and successful – the corollary being that the poor are meant to be poor. In practice, it becomes a SELF-FULFILLING PROPHECY.

social deprivation   In SOCIOLOGY, this term is used to describe the situation of an individual or group lacking the material benefits which are generally enjoyed in a society. Compare with RELATIVE DEPRIVATION.

social facilitation   The stimulating effect on someone's behaviour of other people – even the mere presence of other people. The HAWTHORNE EFFECT is an example of social facilitation. Contrast with SOCIAL LOAFING.

social influence   A basic concept of SOCIAL PSYCHOLOGY, which refers to the effects on a person of relations with others, whether individuals, groups or society in general.

social interaction The mutual SOCIAL INFLUENCE that people have on each other's behaviour in a social setting.

socialism An economic SYSTEM, characterized by state ownership of the means of PRODUCTION and DISTRIBUTION, whose major theorist was KARL MARX. It is now very much out of fashion.

socialization The process whereby an individual becomes a social being. (See Figure 36.) Although it is a lifetime process, it is particularly important in childhood, when society is represented by (and through) a child's parents and the rest of her or his family. See also PROFESSIONAL SOCIALIZATION.

social learning This form of learning is based on MODELLING behaviour and is therefore particularly important to ADVERTISING and MARKETING.

social loafing The tendency of people to work less hard on a TASK when part of a group than as individuals, due to a DIFFUSION OF RESPONSIBILITY. Contrast with SOCIAL FACILITATION.

socially acquired needs A term sometimes used in MOTIVATION to describe needs that people might say they have which are not biological (like food or security) but represent aspects of their relationship to themselves and other people, which have been learned (like being accepted or achieving certain goals). See also HIERARCHY OF NEEDS.

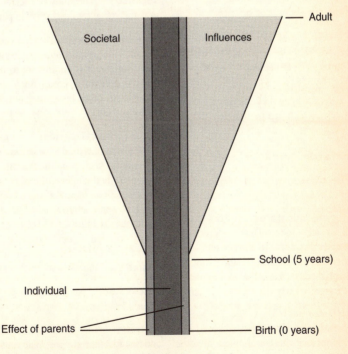

Figure 36 Socialization (as illustrated by the Statt Cone).

social norm Behaviour that is expected of all the members of a society. The NORM of social behaviour is therefore one way of defining social normality.

social psychology The branch of PSYCHOLOGY that deals with social life, the behaviour of people in groups and the behaviour of individuals in social settings.

social science Any field of study concerned with people as social beings. To a greater or lesser extent these are generally considered to include ANTHROPOLOGY, ECONOMICS, history, political science, PSYCHOLOGY and SOCIOLOGY. Compare with BEHAVIOURAL SCIENCE.

social skills A set of SKILLS in dealing with other people which determine someone's effectiveness in a social or group setting. They include INTERPERSONAL SKILLS DEVELOPMENT, INTERPERSONAL RELATIONS and NON-VERBAL COMMUNICATION.

social status Someone's general position in society in relation to, and as determined by, other people.

social support Positive INTERPERSONAL RELATIONS with colleagues, friends or family, which are particularly helpful in dealing with the effects of STRESS.

social system Any set of ROLE RELATIONSHIPS or INTERPERSONAL RELATIONS between people, from a couple to the entire planet.

socio-economic status In SOCIOLOGY, this term refers to the categories produced from the SOCIAL STRATIFICATION of a society by INCOME and occupation. In the United Kingdom, these are six in number and they are widely used in ADVERTISING, MARKET RESEARCH and SURVEY RESEARCH:

A   (upper middle class)
     higher managerial, administrative or professional

B   (middle class)
     intermediate managerial, administrative or professional
C1   (lower middle class)
     supervisory, clerical, junior managerial, administrative or professional
C2   (skilled working class)
     skilled manual workers
D   (working class)
     semi-skilled and unskilled workers
E   (lowest level of subsistence)
     state pensioners, widows, casual and lowest-grade workers.

socio-emotional leader The individual who may emerge in a small group as the person who keeps up the morale and facilitates the INTERPERSONAL RELATIONS of the group. This is usually compared with TASK LEADER.

sociology The study of society in general and social ORGANIZATION in particular.

sociometry A term and a technique invented by the American psychiatrist J.L. Moreno. It is an attempt to measure what people in a group think and feel about each other by setting out the network of their INTERPERSONAL RELATIONS.

socio-technical system In ERGONOMICS, this term is used to describe a SYSTEM combining social and technical factors that underlie the interaction of people and machines in an ORGANIZATION. It emerged from the approach to MANAGEMENT of the Tavistock Institute of HUMAN RELATIONS in London, led by ERIC TRIST. The objective of this approach was to optimize task performance and JOB SATISFACTION jointly.

Sod's Law If something *can* go wrong, it *will*.

software The COMPUTER PROGRAMS, codes and other support materials available for use with particular HARDWARE.

somatizing A term sometimes used in PSYCHOTHERAPY to describe the appearance of physical symptoms as a result of psychological STRESS, as in PSYCHOSOMATIC DISORDERS.

sour grapes reaction The process of convincing yourself that something you can't have is not worth having anyway. In CLINICAL PSYCHOLOGY, this is called RATIONALIZATION; in SOCIAL PSYCHOLOGY, it is regarded as an attempt to resolve COGNITIVE DISSONANCE.

spaced practice Any LEARNING which has a time interval between each PRACTICE, but which does not necessarily distribute the practice to maximum advantage in the time available, as does DISTRIBUTED PRACTICE.

spam Unwanted ELECTRONIC MAIL messages.

span of control The number of subordinates who report directly to a given MANAGER and over whose work he or she exercises AUTHORITY. Generally speaking, the higher a manager is in the HIERARCHY of an ORGANIZATION the smaller the span of control he or she has to deal with.

SPC See STATISTICAL PROCESS CONTROL.

specialist An individual who is an expert in one particular field of study, or in the use of a certain ABILITY or SKILL, or even in the PERFORMANCE of a particular TASK.

specialization In ECONOMICS, this term refers to part of the DIVISION OF LABOUR, in which a given TASK is broken down as far as possible into sub-tasks, each of which then becomes the responsibility of a SPECIALIST worker. Specialization is therefore an important basis for MASS PRODUCTION.

speech processing The capacity of a COMPUTER to recognize and react to the spoken word.

split shift In SHIFT WORK practice, this term refers to a shift which has been divided into two or more periods of time and/or groups of workers.

spontaneous recovery In CONDITIONING, this terms refers to the reappearance of a conditioned response which has been extinguished, after a short rest period.

spreadsheet A technique, which originated in ACCOUNTING, for displaying items in a wide series of columns (i.e. on a spread sheet of paper) so that calculations could be made by row or column as well as by item. The term has now largely been taken over by the COMPUTER world to refer to SOFTWARE packages that produce spreadsheets for VISUAL DISPLAY UNITS, from which rapid electronic calculations can be made.

SPSS An acronym for Statistical Package for Social Science, which is a SOFTWARE package for the statistical analysis of SURVEY RESEARCH data in SOCIAL SCIENCE.

SQC See STATISTICAL QUALITY CONTROL.

stability zones A term introduced in 1970 by the American futurologist Alvin Toffler to describe those relationships, times and places in busy lives, which are otherwise full of STRESS, that provide essential oases of calm and continuity. These can range from a long-term supportive marriage to half an hour's daily meditation.

staff This term is most often used to describe the WHITE-COLLAR WORKERS – usually full-time employees – of an ORGANIZATION, as opposed to BLUE-COLLAR WORKERS. The term often refers to a difference of STATUS in terms of PAY, conditions of EMPLOYMENT and FRINGE BENEFITS.

staff appraisal   The ASSESSMENT of how well a member of STAFF is doing in his or her job. It is usual to include a PERFORMANCE APPRAISAL INTERVIEW as part of this process.

staff association   In terms of INDUSTRIAL RELATIONS, a staff association is equivalent to a COMPANY UNION, as it usually has no powers of COLLECTIVE BARGAINING on PAY and conditions of EMPLOYMENT. It also has the function of organizing social activities for STAFF.

staff inspection   A JOB ANALYSIS of all STAFF positions in an ORGANIZATION as the first step in a process of RATIONALIZATION.

staff management   [1] The MANAGEMENT of STAFF in an ORGANIZATION. [2] MANAGERS who have a SPECIALIST service or advisory support function and are not in the CHAIN OF COMMAND of the organization's HIERARCHY. Compare with LINE MANAGEMENT, and see also LINE AND STAFF CONCEPT.

staff turnover   See LABOUR TURNOVER.

stagflation   In ECONOMICS, this term is used to describe a situation which combines stagnation with INFLATION, where output and consumer demand are static though prices are rising.

stakeholder   Anyone with a specific interest in a company and the way it is run; that is, not just the traditional shareholder interest but that of staff, customers, suppliers and the wider community in which the business operates.

standard deviation   In STATISTICS, this is a measure of the dispersion or variability of the scores in a DISTRIBUTION. It is the square root of the mean of the squares

of each deviation from the MEAN. Or, to put it simply, it is the average distance of each score from the mean.

standard error of the mean   In STATISTICS, this is the STANDARD DEVIATION of the theoretical SAMPLING distribution of the MEAN, or the extent to which the mean obtained differs from the true mean of the POPULATION from which the sample was taken.

standard hour   In WORK STUDY, this term refers to a unit of work rather than time. It is the measure of the PERFORMANCE of a standard operator for a given TASK over one hour.

standardization   [1] The process of PRODUCTION that provides standard machine parts through a wide variety of manufacturing. This is one of the bases of MASS PRODUCTION. [2] The process of setting generally acceptable standards of product QUALITY.

star   One of the MARKETING situations in the BOSTON MATRIX. It is characterized by high growth and a leading market position. A star is a product to invest in.

state intervention   The intervention by government, either directly or indirectly, in the workings of the economy. This is something that all governments do to a greater or lesser extent, whether their primary allegiance is supposed to be to CAPITALISM or SOCIALISM.

state-of-the-art   The very latest product in its field.

statistical process control   The use of statistical techniques to determine the acceptable limits of variation in output on a given process, and to correct the process if the output falls outside these limits.

statistical quality control   The use of statistical techniques to determine the acceptable limits of variation in QUALITY in output on a given process, and to correct the process if the output falls outside these limits.

statistical significance   In STATISTICS, this term refers to the PROBABILITY that the results in question could have occurred by chance alone. The highest probability acceptable to current convention is 5 in 100, or a 0.05 level of significance.

statistics   A form of mathematics used on data gathered in studying behaviour and by which investigators evaluate their findings and make inferences of wider implication than their study sample. See also NON-PARAMETRIC STATISTICS, PARAMETRIC STATISTICS and SAMPLING.

status   [1] The standing of an individual within a given ORGANIZATION. This is based on the amount of respect she or he is accorded by other people, whether it is because of the position in the HIERARCHY or because of personal qualities like CHARISMA. [2] The standing of a document under discussion. How formal or official is it and what is the appropriate way of responding to it?

status symbol   A measure of someone's STATUS and importance (or sometimes self-importance) in an ORGANIZATION. Favourite status symbols are dress (e.g. 'white' collar as opposed to blue) and offices and office furnishings (the size, position and furnishings of an office are often a finely calibrated guide to the occupant's status, both in the HIERARCHY and in the importance attached to his or her function).

steady state   A term used by the Irish writer on ORGANIZATIONAL THEORY, Charles Handy, to characterize the routine day-to-day activities of an ORGANIZATION that keep it going and which account for

about 80 per cent of its work. See also PARETO ANALYSIS.

STEP Analysis   This is sometimes used as an alternative acronym to a PEST ANALYSIS.

step change   This term is sometimes used to denote a change in the life of an ORGANIZATION that is particularly significant and *discontinuous* with what has gone before.

stereotype   In PSYCHOLOGY, this term denotes an oversimplified perception of some aspects of the social world. This often tends to be a basis for PREJUDICE.

store-specific marketing   The ultimate form of GEOGRAPHIC SEGMENTATION, where a MARKETING promotion is targeted at individual retail outlets. For example, in supermarket promotions ELECTRONIC POINT OF SALE information is often obtained from checkout scanners to find out detailed local preferences.

storming   A term sometimes used for the second stage of group formation within an ORGANIZATION where members negotiate and often conflict with each other while they work out what they want from the group both individually and collectively. See also FORMING, NORMING and PERFORMING.

strain   The effect of exceptionally heavy demands being placed on an individual or SYSTEM. Often used interchangeably with STRESS, but where a distinction is made strain tends to be regarded as a preliminary to, or a symptom of, stress.

strategic management   The application of MANAGEMENT principles to the development of CORPORATE STRATEGY.

strategic planning   The basis of a CORPORATE PLAN or other broad-based and

long-term assessment of an ORGANIZA-
TION's future.

stratified sampling   In STATISTICS, this
is a technique frequently used for mass
OPINION POLLING. It involves dividing a
POPULATION into sub-groups or strata
and then taking a RANDOM SAMPLE of
each one.

stress   Physical and psychological tension and STRAIN, usually accumulated
over a period of time, which threatens a
person's ABILITY to go on coping with the
demands of a given situation. If it is not
dealt with it will frequently result in PSY-
CHOSOMATIC DISORDERS.

stress audit   An AUDIT of a business
ORGANIZATION which is designed to identify sources of STRESS perceived by staff.

stress interview   An INTERVIEW that is
deliberately conducted by the interviewer
in a harsh and hostile manner, with the
supposed intention of testing the interviewee's ABILITY to cope with STRESS. It is
more likely to be the sign of a man with
an INFERIORITY COMPLEX testing his
manhood, and thus typical of MACHO
MANAGEMENT.

stressor   Any factor that contributes to
the experience of STRESS.

strike   The ultimate form of INDUSTRIAL
ACTION by employees in dispute with their
employers, where they withhold their
labour until the dispute is settled.

stroking   A term used in TRANSAC-
TIONAL ANALYSIS to describe actions that
demonstrate caring recognition of, and
attention paid to, another person. The
term originates from the analogy of
physically stroking an infant.

Strong–Campbell Interest Inventory
The revised version of the 1927 STRONG
VOCATIONAL INTEREST BLANK, which takes
account of many decades of history in
the world of work and the concomitant
vocational and occupational changes.

Strong Vocational Interest Blank
A QUESTIONNAIRE about a person's interests, which is matched with the reported
interests of people in different vocations
to assess her or his suitability for a particular kind of work. This TEST was first
developed in 1927 and later revised as the
STRONG–CAMPBELL INTEREST INVENTORY
in 1985.

structural change   Deep-seated
changes that affect the very structure of
a society, like the INDUSTRIAL REVOLUTION.

structural unemployment   UNEM-
PLOYMENT that arises from the changing
structure of an industry or society (e.g. in
the pattern of demand) that is long-term
or even permanent, as opposed to SEA-
SONAL UNEMPLOYMENT or unemployment
that is a temporary reflection of prevailing
economic conditions.

structured interview   An INTERVIEW
in which the interviewee is led through
a fixed series of topics based on a set of
prepared questions, often raised in a particular order. This method emphasizes
comparability of respondents at the
expense of flexibility for the interviewer
and scope for amplifying answers by the
interviewee. Compare with UNSTRUC-
TURED INTERVIEW.

subcontracting   The PRACTICE of
making an agreement between the
main contractor responsible for a project
and another ORGANIZATION which will
subcontract to carry out part of the WORK
on it.

subculture   A term borrowed from
ANTHROPOLOGY by SOCIOLOGY to denote
a CULTURE within a culture; that is, one
which shares most of the main features

and values of the parent culture while retaining special characteristics of its own.

sublimation   In PSYCHOANALYSIS, this is an EGO DEFENCE in which unacceptable UNCONSCIOUS impulses are channelled into consciously acceptable forms. For FREUD this was society's main way of handling REPRESSION. It is certainly the most socially acceptable of the ego defences and may be the source of energy of the WORKAHOLIC, for instance.

subliminal advertising   The term 'subliminal' in PSYCHOLOGY refers to sensory stimulation – in this case the presentation of an image – below the 'limen' or threshold above which perception becomes conscious. Subliminal ADVERTISING would therefore mean that the viewer of a film or television message would not be conscious of seeing it – and therefore, it is argued, not conscious of being persuaded. For this reason such advertising is banned in most countries, although its effects are probably not very great, or specific, or controllable by advertisers.

suboptimization   The process of settling for a compromise position which is less than one would ideally need or want. See also SATISFICING.

suggestion scheme   Any scheme which encourages the employees of an ORGANIZATION to suggest ways of improving the organization's operations in, for example, HEALTH AND SAFETY AT WORK, PRODUCTIVITY or QUALITY. A monetary REWARD is usually given for suggestions that are accepted. However, only the Japanese seem to take suggestion schemes seriously, and one way they have formalized them is in the technique of QUALITY CIRCLES.

sunk cost   An expenditure, usually on CAPITAL equipment, which can not be recovered if the project it is intended for is cancelled, but which can be listed as an asset of the ORGANIZATION. Sometimes used to describe any ongoing contracted expenditure, including HUMAN RESOURCES.

superego   Latin for 'over I'. According to FREUD the superego is one of the three main aspects of the PERSONALITY (along with the EGO and ID). Like the id, with which it is always in CONFLICT, the superego is basically UNCONSCIOUS. It is the internalization of restrictions on the impulses of the id, as reflected in the values and standards of behaviour required by society in general and parents in particular. It is the equivalent of a conscience in a SYSTEM of ethics.

supernumerary   Someone who is surplus to requirements for an ORGANIZATION at a given time and place; for example, as a result of OVERMANNING.

superordinate goal   In SOCIAL PSYCHOLOGY, this term is used to denote a goal which is beyond the capacity of any one group by itself to achieve and therefore requires the active co-operation of more than one group. It is regarded as a means of promoting good relations between groups. It is a form of SYNERGY. See also SYNDICATE.

supervisor   Anyone who supervises the work of others, although a supervisor, like a FOREMAN, is usually regarded as being on the first level of LINE MANAGEMENT in the HIERARCHY of an ORGANIZATION. In Western countries supervision usually means having close visual oversight of what people are doing, and this is at the heart of Western assumptions of what MANAGEMENT is about.

Superwoman   A term popularly used of a woman who combines a successful work CAREER with a family life and the rearing of children.

supply chain management   The management of an ORGANIZATION'S INVENTORY from its links with suppliers, through its own internal procedures, and on to its relationship with its customers. All the groups and individuals involved are perceived as being part of the same interdependent chain or network.

supply-side economics   A form of economic policy that emphasizes the importance of supply rather than demand in the workings of the economy. It encourages measures like the removal of RESTRICTIVE PRACTICES, the reduction of the PUBLIC SECTOR in favour of the PRIVATE SECTOR, and the cutting of TAXATION as an INCENTIVE to the ENTREPRENEUR. During the 1980s, this policy was closely associated with the governments of Ronald Reagan in the United States and Margaret Thatcher in the United Kingdom.

survey research   A technique for gathering data from large numbers of people by the use of QUESTIONNAIRES and statistical SAMPLING methods.

survivor guilt   This term was first used by psychologists who noticed that when people escape from some disaster which claimed the lives of friends or family they often exhibited symptoms of guilt at their good fortune. It has been applied in recent years to workers who survived the REDUNDANCY which claimed the jobs of their colleagues.

sweatshop   A small factory where workers are employed, who are not members of a TRADE UNION, for long hours at low PAY in harsh conditions of EMPLOYMENT. See also SUPPLY-SIDE ECONOMICS.

swing shift   A flexible form of SHIFT WORK practice where a shift has no set hours. The workers have a variable number of hours at work, depending on the circumstances, in order to ensure the continuity of PRODUCTION.

SWOT Analysis   A framework for analysing the position of a business ORGANIZATION or a product in the MARKET. The acronym stands for Strengths, Weaknesses, Opportunities and Threats.

symbolic interaction   This term describes a sociological method of approaching the study of SOCIAL PSYCHOLOGY. It emphasizes the part played by language, gestures and other symbols of interaction in our conscious attempts to form ourselves and our world, and it regards our human qualities as the products of that social interaction.

syndicate   A group of individuals or ORGANIZATIONS who combine for some common goal which is to their mutual benefit. See also SUPERORDINATE GOAL.

synectics   A more narrowly focussed form of BRAINSTORMING.

synergy   A situation in which the co-operation of two or more individuals, groups or ORGANIZATIONS produces a combined effect which is greater than could have been produced by the sum of the separate entities; for example, a SUPERORDINATE GOAL achieved by two groups. See also SYNDICATE, and contrast with GROUPTHINK.

system   Any series of interconnected elements forming an organized or organic whole with a common objective. Examples can range from an individual central nervous system to a society's family and kinship arrangements.

System 4　A classification of MANAGE-MENT STYLE by the American psychologist RENSIS LIKERT. There are four styles in all, ranging from the autocratic (System 1) to the democratic (System 4).

systems analysis　The analysis (usually by COMPUTER) of a physical SYSTEM within an ORGANIZATION, like its COMMUNICATION or heating, to see how it might be made more efficient.

systems theory　The attempt to formulate general principles that could be applied to any SYSTEM by a comparative analysis of the structures and functions of as wide a variety of systems as possible.

T

TA See TRANSACTIONAL ANALYSIS.

Taguchi technique This is named after the Japanese MANAGEMENT specialist Genichi Taguchi. It is a technique used in QUALITY CONTROL, which employs statistical methods to determine the best design of a new product in terms of cost efficiency and minimum variability.

takeover The gaining of CONTROL by one business ORGANIZATION over another. A takeover attempt may be unwanted by the target company (a 'hostile' takeover) or it may be welcomed by a company that can no longer compete successfully by itself.

tall organization An ORGANIZATION with a relatively large number of levels in its HIERARCHY. (See Figure 37.) The classic examples are the army and the British Civil Service, with a dozen levels or more. This is usually compared with a FLAT ORGANIZATION. See also PYRAMID HIERARCHY.

task The major element of work that makes up a job. Each task in a JOB DESCRIPTION is intended to contribute to the overall objective of the job.

task analysis The analysis of a TASK into its constituent operations for the purposes of identifying the SKILLS involved and the TRAINING necessary to improve them.

task force A group of people who are brought together for a particular TASK,

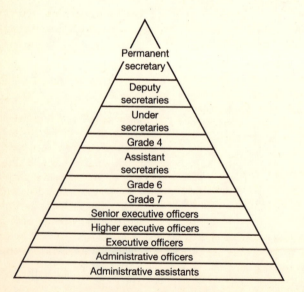

Figure 37 Tall organization (the traditional British Civil Service).

usually involving a special project or unusual problem. The group is normally disbanded when the task has been successfully completed.

task identity The extent to which a TASK is composed of a single, whole and identifiable piece of work.

task leader The individual who may emerge in a small group as the person who tries to keep the attention of the group focussed on its TASK and who tries to ensure that it gets done. This ROLE is usually compared with that of SOCIO-EMOTIONAL LEADER.

task-oriented culture An ORGANIZA-TIONAL CULTURE which emphasizes most the importance of solving problems and completing tasks and is usually associated with working in a large traditional ORGANIZATION. Often compared with PEOPLE-ORIENTED CULTURE.

TAT See THEMATIC APPERCEPTION TEST.

Tavistock approach The approach to MANAGEMENT of the Tavistock Institute for Human Relations in London. See SOCIO-TECHNICAL SYSTEM and ERIC TRIST.

taxation The levying of compulsory charges on certain items by government, as a way of raising revenue for public services, and paid by individuals and ORGANIZATIONS. These charges may be in the form of DIRECT TAXATION or INDIRECT TAXATION.

tax avoidance The legal attempt to reduce the burden of TAXATION on an individual or ORGANIZATION. Compare with TAX EVASION.

tax-deductible Any business expense that can be deducted from INCOME before the calculation of tax due.

tax evasion The illegal attempt to reduce the burden of TAXATION on an individual or ORGANIZATION. Compare with TAX AVOIDANCE.

Taylor, F.W. (1856–1915) An American engineer who invented WORK STUDY and founded the SCIENTIFIC MANAGEMENT approach to the world of work (sometimes known as TAYLORISM) at the beginning of the twentieth century. He placed great emphasis on analysing the constituent operations of a TASK down to the finest details. Taylor also saw the importance of good SELECTION and TRAINING procedures, and argued for better COMMUNICATION between MANAGEMENT and the SHOP FLOOR and better co-operation in general between both sides of industry.

Taylorism An alternative name for the SCIENTIFIC MANAGEMENT approach to the world of work pioneered by F.W. TAYLOR.

teaching company A business ORGANIZATION, usually in the manufacturing field, which provides students with education and TRAINING to degree standard.

teaching machine Any instrument for aiding PROGRAMMED LEARNING.

team briefing The PRACTICE of encouraging COMMUNICATION in an ORGANIZATION via the FACE-TO-FACE GROUP.

team-building A technique that aims to help WORK GROUPS by improving the QUALITY of their members' INTERPERSONAL RELATIONS as well as their SKILL at solving problems and accomplishing their TASK. This is usually done with the aid of an external CONSULTANCY, which will diagnose the way the work group functions, helping members to identify difficulties and suggest improvements.

team roles Literally, the different ROLES played by different members of a team or WORK GROUP. Various elaborate classifications of these roles have been produced, notably by Meredith Belbin in the United Kingdom, who identified nine distinct roles that contributed to the most successful MANAGEMENT teams. He called these, *teamworker, completer, shaper, monitor-evaluator, plant, resource investigator, co-ordinator, implementer* and *specialist*. Teams can be successful in the absence of some of these roles, of course, or there would be no successful eight-person teams! It is the balance of the roles, given the TASK that has to be done, which is important. Generally speaking, people perform those roles best which fit most closely with their basic PERSONALITY characteristics and most people tend to be comfortable with one or two roles.

technocentric   Looking at business and MANAGEMENT issues primarily from a technological point of view.

technocrat   A person who climbs the HIERARCHY of a business ORGANIZATION by virtue of his or her technical expertise.

technological change   Any industrial and social change, leading to changes in the workplace ENVIRONMENT, which can be attributed to the introduction of TECHNOLOGY.

technological determinism   The idea that the kind of TECHNOLOGY an ORGANIZATION uses is the most important factor in trying to understand and explain the behaviour of its members.

technological unemployment   UNEMPLOYMENT that can be attributed directly to the introduction of a particular TECHNOLOGY to the workplace.

technology   The practical application of scientific innovation to industry.

technology transfer   The transfer of a TECHNOLOGY from an area in which it has

been successfully applied to an area in which it has not yet been tried.

technophilia   An irrational attraction to TECHNOLOGY. Compare with TECHNOPHOBIA.

technophobia   An irrational fear of TECHNOLOGY. Compare with TECHNOPHILIA.

technostress   Any evidence of STRESS that is attributed directly to the effects of workplace TECHNOLOGY.

telecommunications   Any form of COMMUNICATION by electronic means.

telecommuting   Another term for TELEWORKING. It has the connotation of being an alternative lifestyle to commuting physically between home and work.

teleconference   A discussion or conference where participants are geographically scattered and linked by means of TELECOMMUNICATION, such as AUDIOCONFERENCING or VIDEOCONFERENCING.

teleworking   The application of TELECOMMUNICATIONS to equip the HOME WORKER and to encourage other people to work from home.

test   Any procedure for the ASSESSMENT of a specific ABILITY, APTITUDE or psychological state. See also PSYCHOLOGICAL TEST.

test marketing   A form of PILOT STUDY on a new product, where it is tried out in a limited area first in order to see whether it would be worth MARKETING more widely.

T-group   A form of SENSITIVITY TRAINING carried out within a group.

Thematic Apperception Test   A PROJECTIVE TECHNIQUE developed in the late 1930s by the American psychologist Henry Murray. It consists of vague and ambiguous drawings (usually of one or two human figures), about each of which the subject has to make up a story. The themes that may emerge from these stories are then used to diagnose areas of emotional CONFLICT or concern in the subject. This technique has been widely used in the SELECTION of SENIOR MANAGEMENT where, for example, the incidence of ACHIEVEMENT imagery might be of particular interest. Companies in ADVERTISING and MARKET RESEARCH sometimes use techniques based on the TAT and other projective techniques to probe beneath the surface reactions of their informants to a particular product.

Theory X In the terminology of DOUGLAS MCGREGOR, this describes the RATIONAL-ECONOMIC view of human nature that people only WORK when they have to and therefore require AUTHORITARIAN MANAGEMENT. McGregor rejected this view in favour of THEORY Y. See also MANAGEMENT STYLE.

Theory Y In the terminology of DOUGLAS MCGREGOR, this describes a view of human nature in which people would like to be creative in their work and take more responsibility for it. They could thus be more responsive to DEMOCRATIC MANAGEMENT and its enabling function than is suggested by the proponents of THEORY X. See also MANAGEMENT STYLE.

Theory Z The term suggested by the American writer on ORGANIZATION THEORY, William Ouchi, for Western adaptations of Japanese MANAGEMENT practices. The Theory Z ORGANIZATION is distinguished by several important features: [1] lifetime EMPLOYMENT, [2] relatively slow PROMOTION, [3] concern for the whole person, [4] informal CONTROL and LEADERSHIP, [5] individual responsibility, [6] consensual decision-making and

[7] less SPECIALIZATION. There is some evidence that Theory Z organizations have less ABSENTEEISM, greater PRODUCTIVITY and better QUALITY output than do others.

therapy See PSYCHOTHERAPY.

therblig A term used in the WORK STUDY area of ERGONOMICS. It is simply its inventor's name spelled backwards (more or less) – GILBRETH. A therblig is one of eighteen fundamental operations in a worker's activities. Therbligs are used in conjunction with a SIMO CHART and each has a symbol that describes the bodily movements involved, like 'hold' or 'select'. (See Figure 38, p156.)

third force A term used in PSYCHOLOGY to describe those psychologists who subscribe to a view of the human condition based neither on BEHAVIOURISM nor on PSYCHOANALYSIS, but broadly on HUMANISTIC PSYCHOLOGY.

360° evaluation A technique used in PERSONNEL MANAGEMENT, where opinions about someone's work are obtained from his or her superiors as well as equal-STATUS colleagues. Compare with 180° EVALUATION.

threshold In ERGONOMICS, this term describes two ways of indicating sensitivity to sensory stimulation. The *absolute threshold* is the minimum amount of stimulation necessary for the subject to detect it. The *differential threshold* is the minimum change in stimulation necessary to produce a JUST-NOTICEABLE DIFFERENCE.

throughput The amount of material that goes through the entire process of PRODUCTION in a given time.

time-and-a-half A form of OVERTIME working in which time worked is paid at one-and-a-half times the normal rate. See also DOUBLE TIME.

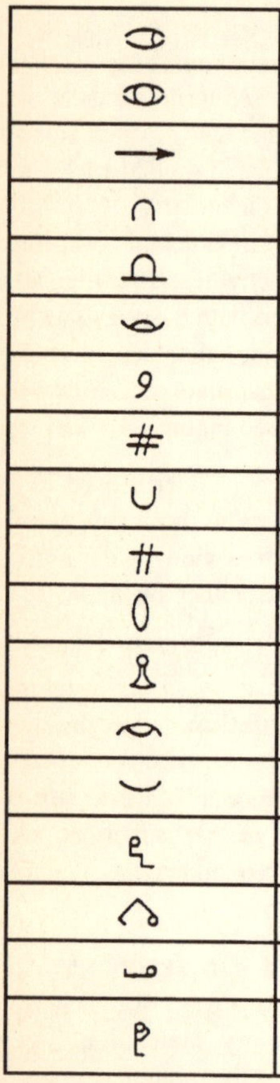

Symbol	Name	Colour coding
⊂⊃	Search	Black
⊂⊙⊃	Find	Grey
→	Select	Light grey
∩	Grasp	Red
⌓	Hold	Gold ochre
⌣	Transport load	Green
9	Position	Blue
#	Assemble	Violet
U	Use	Purple
⧣	Disassemble	Light violet
◯	Inspect	Burnt ochre
⚊	Pre-position	Pale blue
⌢	Release load	Carmine red
⌣	Transport empty	Olive green
ℒ	Rest for overcoming fatigue	Orange
⌂	Unavoidable delay	Yellow
⌐	Avoidable delay	Lemon yellow
ℙ	Plan	Brown

Figure 38 Therbligs.

time-and-motion study See WORK STUDY.

time budget The preparation of a detailed timetable of work activities in order to help improve time MANAGEMENT and efficiency.

time horizon The degree to which the PLANNING or SCHEDULING of an ORGANIZATION or an individual MANAGER extends into the future.

time in lieu A period of time off work, usually taken at the employee's discretion, to make up for time worked over and above normal working hours; that is, an exchange of time for the money that would have been paid for working an OVERTIME rate.

time management   The treatment of time as a resource to be managed like any other. This can only be meaningful to people whose TIME ORIENTATION is that of LINEAR TIME.

time orientation   The experience of working in either CYCLICAL TIME or LINEAR TIME.

time sharing   A situation in which two or more people or ORGANIZATIONS make use of the same workplace and equipment (particularly a COMPUTER) in order to share costs and to maximize use of the resource. One common form of time sharing is where someone uses a desk in the morning and someone else in the afternoon.

time-span of discretion   A term introduced to the WORK STUDY area of ERGONOMICS in the 1960s by the British industrial psychologist Elliot Jaques. It is an attempt at EQUITY in setting salary levels and DIFFERENTIALS following a JOB EVALUATION. What is measured is the length of time during which someone has to exercise discretion – that is, personal judgement and responsibility – in her or his job before requiring decisions from superiors.

TM   See TRADEMARK.

TNA   See TRAINING NEEDS ANALYSIS.

tokenism   An action taken for its symbolic value as opposed to a serious attempt at changing a given situation; for example, appointing a lone woman to an all-male board of directors as an end in itself, namely to show how open-minded and progressive the ORGANIZATION is.

tolerance for ambiguity   The ABILITY to live with a situation that is not clear cut, where different interpretations of what is happening are possible and where the outlook is obscure; in sum, the ability to accept complexity in human affairs without seeking the comfort of simplistic solutions. In PSYCHOLOGY, high tolerance for ambiguity is usually seen as a sign of psychological health and maturity, whether in individuals or ORGANIZATIONS, and as an important PERSONALITY factor in dealing with STRESS.

total hours society   A society in which all major activities, but especially work and shopping, occur at all hours of the day or night.

total quality management   An approach to, and concern for, QUALITY which pervades a business ORGANIZATION from top to bottom. It was originally introduced to Japan in the aftermath of the Second World War by the American engineers W. EDWARDS DEMING and Joseph Juran. It is based on close attention to detail, self-monitoring by workers at each step, and a passionate commitment to quality as part of an organization's IDENTITY, which is internalized by everyone in it. This approach is customer-driven and aims for ZERO DEFECTS, while being imbued with the spirit of KAIZEN or continuous improvement.

TQM   See TOTAL QUALITY MANAGEMENT.

tracking   In ERGONOMICS, this term refers to the SKILL of an individual in making the necessary adjustments of hand and eye to follow a moving object in a visual display.

trade association   A voluntary grouping of ORGANIZATIONS in the same business which combine for mutual benefit; for example, in trying to influence government legislation. See also EMPLOYERS' ASSOCIATION.

trademark   Any form of LOGO and/or wording which a company uses to identify its products or BRANDS and distinguish them from their rivals'. As for a COPYRIGHT or a PATENT, the owner of a trademark that has been officially registered has the MONOPOLY right to use it for a certain period of time.

trade press   Journals, magazines or newspapers that cater for the interests or a particular trade or industry, like the *Pig Breeder's Gazette* or the *Wall Street Journal*.

trade secret   Information or techniques known only to members of a particular trade or PROFESSION, public knowledge of which would detract from their standing and INCOME, such as how a magician saws a lady in half.

training   An area of PERSONNEL MANAGEMENT concerned with making the best use of the HUMAN RESOURCES in an ORGANIZATION by providing them with the appropriate instruction to acquire the necessary SKILLS for their jobs. See also GROUP TRAINING METHODS, MANAGEMENT DEVELOPMENT and TEAM-BUILDING.

training needs analysis   In theory, this should be the first stage in a TRAINING programme; that is, an examination of what training might be required to help improve the working of the ORGANIZATION. There are three components to a TNA: [1] *the organization* (where is training needed?); [2] *the job* (what is training needed for?); and [3] *the person* (who needs training?).

trait   Any enduring characteristic of an individual's PERSONALITY.

trait theory   Any approach to the study of LEADERSHIP which emphasizes the importance of trying to identify distinguishing characteristics or TRAITS of PERSONALITY common to successful leaders.

transactional analysis   A form of GROUP THERAPY in which the interrelationships of the group members are analysed in terms of their transactions with each other in the ROLE of 'parent', 'child' or 'adult' (their EGO states, in TA language). Transactional analysis was developed in the 1960s, its most celebrated exponent being the American psychiatrist Eric Berne.

transactional leadership   A term introduced into the study of LEADERSHIP in the 1960s by the British political scientist J.M. Burns to describe a MANAGER in an ORGANIZATION who is more concerned with the means of achieving the organization's ends or goals than in the nature of these ends. Burns considered this type of leadership essential for the efficient day-to-day running of the organization and the continuing MOTIVATION of the workforce. See also TRANSFORMATIONAL LEADERSHIP, with which it is always contrasted.

transfer of training   The process whereby the LEARNING achieved in one situation is transferred to another situation. This can have positive effects (knowing Spanish helps the learning of Italian) or sometimes negative effects (knowing how to steer a car is detrimental to steering a boat with a tiller). See also LEARNING SET.

transformational leadership   A term introduced into the study of LEADERSHIP in the 1960s by the British political scientist J.M. Burns, to describe a MANAGER in an ORGANIZATION who is more concerned with the nature of the ends or goals of an organization than in the means of achieving them. Burns considered this type of leadership essential in reassessing the organization's goals and values and the direction in which it is going, as well as in the EMPOWERMENT of the workforce to be creative in their jobs. See also TRANSACTIONAL LEADERSHIP, with which it is always contrasted.

transnational company Sometimes preferred now to MULTINATIONAL COMPANY.

travel-to-work area The geographical area over which people are willing to commute daily to work in a given ORGANIZATION.

trial and error learning The step-by-step form of LEARNING, over many trials, characteristic of most animal learning and much human learning, and the basis for CONDITIONING procedures. It is a very laborious process compared to INSIGHT LEARNING. See also ROTE LEARNING.

Trist, Eric A leading British industrial sociologist concerned with GROUP WORKING practices, who developed the concept of the SOCIO-TECHNICAL SYSTEM.

trust–control dilemma The basic problem of DELEGATION, faced, at any level, by a MANAGER in an ORGANIZATION, of how much trust to have in the subordinate to whom the work is delegated and how much CONTROL, if any, of the work to retain.

T-test In STATISTICS, this is a technique for deciding whether the MEANS of two sets of scores are significantly different.

turkey farm That part of an ORGANIZATION in which the most incompetent MANAGERS are placed whenever possible. It is the area least essential to the continuing operation of the organization.

turnover [1] The amount of sales revenue achieved or business transacted during a given period of time. [2] Loss of people from, and appointments to, the workforce during a given period of time. [3] The THROUGHPUT of stock in either manufacturing PRODUCTION or services.

24-hour society See TOTAL HOURS SOCIETY.

two-career family A family in which both partners have full-time CAREERS, and make whatever childcare arrangements may be necessary.

two-factor theory See HERZBERG TWO-FACTOR THEORY.

two-step flow of communication The idea that the MASS MEDIA of COMMUNICATION first influence the OPINION LEADERS in a community, who in turn influence the opinions and ATTITUDES of others.

Type A personality A set of PERSONALITY characteristics that have been linked with a particular susceptibility to heart disease. These characteristics include being impatient, always rushing, trying to do too many things at once, walking, talking and eating fast, being hard-driving at work, having few interests outside work, and hiding feelings. Type A personality is always contrasted with TYPE B PERSONALITY.

Type B personality A set of PERSONALITY characteristics that are the opposite of TYPE A PERSONALITY and therefore considered to be much less susceptible to heart disease. These characteristics include being casual about appointments, being a good listener, never feeling rushed, being slow and deliberate in manner and speech, being easygoing, having many interests outside work, and being able to express feelings. Types A and B are a continuum, and most people would fall towards one end or the other.

Type T The 'T' stands for 'thrill seeker', a type of PERSONALITY identified in American MARKETING, which actively looks for risk in CONSUMER DECISION-MAKING. Type Ts have been estimated at up to 25 per cent of the American population. Contrast with consumers who are RISK AVERSIVE.

typing Shortened form of 'stereotyping'; dealing with people as STEREOTYPES.

U

uncertainty avoidance   Uncertainty in any form is a prime STRESSOR in the workplace which everyone would rather avoid. However, different societies can have different reactions to uncertainty and these have been identified in a wide range of national offices of the same international company. For example, countries high on uncertainty avoidance require activities to be more structured, to have more written rules and to be less likely to take risks than those low on uncertainty avoidance.

unconscious   This is the most important concept in PSYCHOANALYSIS. It refers to the part of the psyche that contains impulses and desires which are too threatening to be allowed into consciousness, from which they have been repressed or inhibited from entering. The effects of this REPRESSION and INHIBITION are expressed in consciousness as disturbed behaviour. While FREUD did not discover the unconscious (and never claimed to have done so), he systematically probed the dynamic mechanisms involved in its relationship with the conscious psyche, and did more than anyone else to expose the great amount of irrationality in human affairs, not least in the world of business.

unconscious ideology   An IDEOLOGY which underlies and guides someone's behaviour but of which she or he is not consciously aware.

unconscious motivation   Any MOTI-VATION of whose origin, or even existence, a person is not consciously aware.

underachiever   Someone who fails to meet the level of ACHIEVEMENT expected

of him or her. This term is sometimes used in the field of education to describe people who don't try hard enough; that is, people whose ABILITY could take them beyond their ambitions. This is usually contrasted with OVERACHIEVER.

underemployment   A situation in which people do not have enough work to do or are not having their SKILLS fully utilized. See also OVERMANNING.

undermanning   A situation in which there are fewer people employed by an ORGANIZATION than are necessary for the efficient PERFORMANCE of its work. Compare with OVERMANNING.

unemployment   The term generally used of people who are able and willing to engage in paid EMPLOYMENT but unable to find any. See also SEASONAL UNEM-PLOYMENT, STRUCTURAL UNEMPLOYMENT and TECHNOLOGICAL UNEMPLOYMENT. The exact definition of unemployment is a matter of some political contention.

unfair dismissal   The verdict of an INDUSTRIAL TRIBUNAL which is sought by an employee who feels he or she has been wrongfully dismissed by his or her employer. The employer has to show that the dismissal was fair and legal. See also CONSTRUCTIVE DISMISSAL.

unfreezing   A term introduced to GROUP DYNAMICS by KURT LEWIN. He saw it as the first in a three-step process of change in the balance of psychological forces at work in an ORGANIZATION (the other two are *moving* and *REFREEZING*). It requires the SENIOR MANAGEMENT of the organization to reduce the level of those forces which have the effect of maintaining the existing behaviour of the workforce.

unique selling point In MARKETING, this term refers to the distinctive feature of a product that gives it a COMPETITIVE ADVANTAGE. See also MARKET NICHE.

unit cost The cost of one unit of PRODUCTION or of a single item. It is found by dividing the total costs by the number of units or items produced.

unity of command In ORGANIZATIONAL THEORY, this is the principle that each member of an ORGANIZATION should report to only one person. See also AUTHORITY and FUNCTIONAL AUTHORITY.

unstructured interview An INTERVIEW which is not guided by a set of fixed questions (or perhaps even topics) from the interviewer, but in which as free and open a discussion as possible is encouraged within the constraints of time and the objective of the interview. This method emphasizes flexibility for the interviewer and scope for expression by the interviewee, at the expense of comparability across respondents. In PRACTICE, most interviews of whatever kind fall somewhere between the completely unstructured interview and the totally STRUCTURED INTERVIEW.

upstream integration See VERTICAL INTEGRATION.

upward communication COMMUNICATION from lower levels of employees up to SENIOR MANAGEMENT in the HIERARCHY of an ORGANIZATION. This is a much more difficult proposition than either DOWNWARD COMMUNICATION or HORIZONTAL COMMUNICATION.

upward management A term sometimes used of the attempt to 'manage' or influence one's boss.

usage segmentation This is a form of MARKET SEGMENTATION which is based on information about volume and frequency of purchase for a given product. It is a popular way of segmenting markets because there is a lot of information readily available about patterns of usage for most goods and services, often supplied automatically by ELECTRONIC POINT OF SALES equipment. Supermarket checkout scanners are probably the most familiar form in which consumers provide this information.

user friendly A product, especially in the COMPUTER world, in which the needs and convenience of the potential user have been fully considered. A (rare) triumph of ERGONOMICS, apparently. See also TOTAL QUALITY MANAGEMENT.

USP See UNIQUE SELLING POINT.

utility [1] In ECONOMICS, the term implies the usefulness or satisfaction to be derived from a product by a potential buyer. [2] Something that performs a useful service, like a PUBLIC UTILITY.

V

validity   As used in PSYCHOMETRICS this refers to how well each item of a TEST measures or predicts what it is supposed to measure or predict.

VALS   An acronym for *Values And Life Styles*. This is an American form of PSY-CHOLOGICAL SEGMENTATION, which classi-fies the adult population into eight categories of consumer, based on their lifestyles and psychological profiles.

value added   See ADDED VALUE.

value for money   A term used, partic-ularly in the PUBLIC SECTOR, to denote the benefit derived from a particular expendi-ture for a particular purpose.

variance   In STATISTICS, this is the square of the STANDARD DEVIATION. It is used to measure the spread of scores in a particular TEST or experiment.

venture capital   See RISK CAPITAL.

vertical communication   A term sometimes applied to DOWNWARD COMMU-NICATION, though more usually to UPWARD COMMUNICATION in an ORGANIZATION.

vertical integration   The process whereby a company extends its business interests into other stages of production of, or sales of, its products. Though some-times a company is able to do this for itself, it is usually accomplished by some form of MERGER with, or TAKEOVER of, another firm concerned with a different stage of the same product; for example, a publisher may take over a bookshop. Compare with HORIZONTAL INTEGRATION.

VFM   See VALUE FOR MONEY.

victimization   The persistently unfair treatment of a worker, by either colleagues or employers. See also SCAPEGOATING.

videoconferencing   A TELECONFERENCE using video, as well as audio, means of COMMUNICATION.

virtual corporation   A company that has only an electronic existence, with no headquarters building or PLANT or any of the other physical manifestations of the traditional corporation.

virtual reality   Three-dimensional images created by a computer system which give the user the experience of reality. It can be used to let people 'walk' through an architect's design of a building, for instance.

visual search   In ERGONOMICS, this term refers to the process of scanning a set of instruments or CONTROLS for relevant information.

vocational guidance   A branch of OCCUPATIONAL PSYCHOLOGY which helps people to choose an occupation or a CAREER which will be of mutual benefit to them and their prospective employers. It makes use of the INTERVIEW technique plus an extensive battery of PSYCHOLOGICAL TESTS, including tests of ABILITY, APTI-TUDE and NEED FOR ACHIEVEMENT.

voluntary reduced time   A situation where employees voluntarily agree to work fewer hours than they have been doing; for example, to save their employer expenses in a time of reduced demand. Like all such agreements the degree of voluntariness may sometimes be open to dispute.

voluntary redundancy   A situation in which an employee requests or agrees to REDUNDANCY, usually in return for favourable terms of compensation.

voluntary work   Unpaid work done by volunteers for a charity or similar ORGANIZATION.

VR   See VIRTUAL REALITY.

Vroom–Yetton model   A CONTINGENCY THEORY OF LEADERSHIP that uses a DECISION TREE to identify the most appropriate LEADERSHIP STYLE for a given situation. It was developed by two American industrial psychologists, Victor Vroom and Philip Yetton.

V-time   See VOLUNTARY REDUCED TIME.

W

wage differentials See DIFFERENTIALS.

wastage See NATURAL WASTAGE.

wasting assets Any form of ASSETS whose economic value decreases as they are used because they cannot practically be renewed or replaced; for example, coalmines or oilfields.

Watson, J.B. (1878–1958) An American psychologist, and later advertising executive, who is generally regarded as the father of BEHAVIOURISM.

web See WORLD WIDE WEB.

welfare function The basic function of PERSONNEL MANAGEMENT which implies responsibility for the well-being of an ORGANIZATION's members, physical, mental and social. At the very least this will include HEALTH AND SAFETY AT WORK but, depending on the policy of the organization, it may also include many other things, like AFFIRMATIVE ACTION, PATERNITY LEAVE, or the provision of a crèche for working mothers of small children.

welfare state A country whose government accepts that it has the primary responsibility for at least the basic welfare of its citizens; their education, health, EMPLOYMENT and RETIREMENT in particular.

whistle-blowing The public exposure of corrupt, illegal or unethical PRACTICES operating in an ORGANIZATION, usually on the part of an individual member, though sometimes by a body responsible for overseeing the organization which lacks the AUTHORITY or POWER to impose penalties for wrongdoing.

white-collar crime Criminal offences associated with businesspeople or WHITE-COLLAR WORKERS, like embezzlement, fraud or insider dealing on the stock market.

white-collar worker Popular term for any member of STAFF who works in an office. The name derives from the practice of (men) wearing a white shirt to work (in the days when men wore only white shirts – with white collars). Usually contrasted with a BLUE-COLLAR WORKER.

white goods A term used to describe consumer goods encased in white painted metal, like refrigerators or washing machines. Contrast with BROWN GOODS.

wholesaling Acting as an intermediary or MIDDLEMAN between the PRODUCTION of goods and their RETAILING to the general public. It usually involves the stocking of relatively large quantities of goods for onward DISTRIBUTION.

widget A NEOLOGISM which is sometimes used in discussions of MARKETING or PRODUCTION to refer to a generalized standard item rather than a specific product.

wildcat strike A local STRIKE that does not have official TRADE UNION backing. It is usually called without warning, or at short notice.

windfall profit An unexpected PROFIT, usually arising from matters not directly connected with the activities of the lucky individual or ORGANIZATION; for example, a bequest, or a change in TAXATION. The original 'windfall' consisted of apples, blown from trees, that had fallen on the ground and were therefore the property of the finder.

word-of-mouth marketing A form of MARKETING for goods or services whose ADVERTISING is based on personal recommendation; for example, finding a plumber or a lawyer.

wordprocessor A MICROCOMPUTER, used only for the wordprocessing functions of typing and editing, which has taken over from the typewriter in the modern ELECTRONIC OFFICE. It consists of a keyboard and a VISUAL DISPLAY UNIT and usually has a printer attached to produce HARD COPY. It works from text stored either in its own memory, on hard drive, or on FLOPPY DISKS.

workaholic Someone who uses work the way an alcoholic uses alcohol, as a way of trying to escape from his or her personal problems.

work design The part of the JOB DESIGN process that is concerned with the actual working operations, as opposed to the PERSONNEL MANAGEMENT aspects.

worker-director A representative of the workforce on the board of directors of an ORGANIZATION. This is sometimes considered the ultimate in INDUSTRIAL DEMOCRACY. It is extremely rare.

workers co-operative An ORGANIZATION that is owned and controlled, and usually operated, by the people who work in it. Each worker is a member of the co-operative and each has a single vote in making decisions. The ultimate form of INDUSTRIAL DEMOCRACY and EMPOWERMENT of workers.

work ethic The PROTESTANT WORK ETHIC as applied to anyone, regardless of religion.

work experience A period of time spent doing unpaid work in a workplace

ENVIRONMENT by young people about to leave school, as preparation for future EMPLOYMENT.

work flow The arrangement of jobs in a particular sequence intended to help an ORGANIZATION run smoothly and productively.

work group A group of people engaged in doing some work together who are also linked by INTERPERSONAL RELATIONS which are important to them.

work–life balance A recent attempt by employees and employers to tackle STRESS in the workplace by consciously looking for a healthy balance between the demands of work life and home life. In practice, this usually means trying to reduce excessive working hours.

work measurement An integral part of the WORK STUDY process in which a variety of (subjective) methods, like WORK SAMPLING, are used to fix a standard time for the acceptable PERFORMANCE of a given TASK by a trained worker.

work organization Any ORGANIZATION which, in the course of trying to fulfil its goals, gives paid EMPLOYMENT (whether full-time or part-time) to one or more workers.

work psychology A term that includes all the material covered by the older INDUSTRIAL PSYCHOLOGY as well as broader issues like UNDEREMPLOYMENT or the GLASS CEILING.

work role See ROLE.

work sampling A technique used in WORK MEASUREMENT and WORK STUDY for obtaining information about a particular job or TASK by the process of SAMPLING (usually RANDOM SAMPLING) from the work activities at various times rather than by continuous observation.

works council   A forum for JOINT CONSULTATION between employees and employers (or their representatives) in an ORGANIZATION.

work simplification   A process used in ORGANIZATION AND METHODS or WORK STUDY where a SYSTEM of work is examined to see if unnecessary expenditure of energy can be removed. Compare with JOB SIMPLIFICATION.

workstation   The physical ENVIRONMENT in which a job is done. It is used most often to refer to the location of a COMPUTER operator or WORDPROCESSOR operator.

work study   A set of techniques, including WORK MEASUREMENT, which analyse a given area of work to see whether PERFORMANCE can be made more efficient and economical. It is based on the SCIENTIFIC MANAGEMENT approach to the study of the ORGANIZATION.

work teams   See TEAM ROLES.

work-to-rule   A form of INDUSTRIAL ACTION, short of a STRIKE, where workers do not withdraw their labour but do withhold any co-operation with their employers, beyond the explicit contractual agreement made for them by their TRADE UNION. The net effect on the ORGANIZATION is usually the same as a GO-SLOW, and they are often used together. One effect of these actions is to expose the degree to which the organization in question depends upon the unwritten co-operation and GOODWILL of its employees, who often, as a matter of course, will ignore the rule book in order get the job done and maintain productivity.

World Wide Web   A computer system which allows the user to tap into the INTERNET. It was created by Tim Berners-Lee, a British computer expert, while working at the atomic research centre CERN (Conseil Européen de Recherches Nucléaires) near Geneva in Switzerland. Berners-Lee found that information kept falling out of the ORGANIZATION's corporate memory and having to be reinvented at a later date, so he created a form of classification using HYPERTEXT that gave the user easy access to all the information the organization possessed. When the web was made generally available in 1992 it vastly expanded the use of the INTERNET.

WP   See WORDPROCESSOR.

WWW   See WORLD WIDE WEB.

Z

zaibatsu   Another term for KEIRETSU.

ZBB   See ZERO-BASED BUDGETING.

Zeigarnik effect   A finding by a GESTALT psychologist named Bluma Zeigarnik that subjects are more likely to remember details of TASKS during which they were interrupted than those they were allowed to complete. The effect has been claimed for many workplace situations where someone is interrupted.

zeitgeist   A German term meaning literally 'spirit of the times'. It is used to denote the prevailing social and political mood of an era, the conventional wisdom, the fads and fashions in everything from hair length to management. A zeitgeist affects the emotional and mental life of everyone who lives through it, and is thought to have similar effects on people of a similar age group, thus providing one basis for generational differences. (See Figure 39.)

zero-based budgeting   The use of BUDGETS which start from a present base of zero and regard all future expenditure as being on new items rather than a continuation of existing ones. In PRACTICE, this means that a budget has to be justified in full for each year of operation. This is a widely used technique of ACCOUNTING that originated in the United States.

zero defects   The objective of a policy of TOTAL QUALITY MANAGEMENT. It is to have every single item produced and delivered to the customer completely perfect, as opposed to working within an acceptable range of QUALITY, and therefore defectiveness.

zero-hours contract   A contract of EMPLOYMENT where the worker has to be available to the employer for a certain period of time even though his or her services may not actually be called upon.

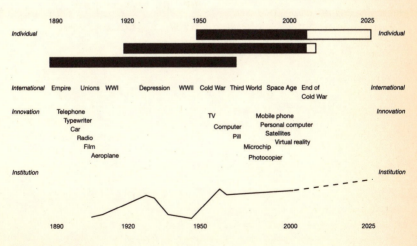

Figure 39 Zeitgeist.

As the worker is only paid for time actually worked, zero hours worked in a given period of time will mean zero PAY. From the employer's point of view this is the ultimate benefit of the FLEXIBLE FIRM. For the employee it is an efficient way to ensure poverty.

zero-sum game   In GAME THEORY, this is a situation where one person's losses are another's gains because there is a finite amount to be won; that is, the gains and losses in the game add up to zero. This situation has been suggested as a MODEL for many people of the DISTRIBUTION of REWARDS in society.

zone of indifference   The range of AUTHORITY which a subordinate is willing to accept from a superior in an ORGANIZATION as his or her right; that is, where the subordinate does not question – is *indifferent* to – the legitimacy of the superior's orders.